GMAT®
Verbal Foundations

GMAT®

Verbal Foundations

Third Edition

The Staff of Kaplan Test Prep

PUBLISHING

New York

© 2013 Kaplan, Inc.

Published by Kaplan Publishing, a division of Kaplan, Inc.
395 Hudson Street, 4th floor
New York, NY 10014

Printed in the United States of America

10 9 8 7 6 5 4 3 2 1

ISBN: 978-1-60978-932-9

CONTENTS

INTRODUCTION

Having an advanced grasp on the English language is essential to scoring well on the GMAT. The GMAT Verbal section has complex question types that test English grammar, style, and usage. The GMAT also has an essay-writing section, called the Analytical Writing Assessment, in which clarity, style, and proper usage are essential to getting a good score.

Improving your grammar and usage doesn't have to be a difficult or tedious process. Allow us to introduce the Foundations Method. This method was devised by the experts at Kaplan to make learning as painless as possible. You'll begin with basic grammar principles and then use the Kaplan system for learning and memorization that draws on real-life situations as practice exercises—a convenient way to learn grammar while going about your everyday life.

HOW TO USE THIS BOOK

The 16 chapters in this book are divided into 3 sections, beginning with fundamentals, so everything else builds upon a firm foundation. The first section covers the fundamentals of grammar, from the most basic parts of sentences to the rules for sentence boundaries and word order. Once you've mastered sentence structure, Section II reviews the fundamentals of clear and effective style, including diction, tone, and concision. The third section reviews the rules for punctuation and other mechanics to make your sentences clear and error-free. Each chapter contains four key components:

1. Detailed Lessons

Each chapter explains in detail a specific grammar or style concept, with lots of relevant examples and memory aids.

2. Plentiful Practice

Repetition is the key to mastery. So be prepared to practice, practice, practice! You'll find everything from simple matching exercises to exercises that ask you to apply the skills you're learning to practical, real-life situations. By "learning from all sides," you're much more likely to retain the information.

3. Summary

Each chapter concludes with a concise review of key points.

4. Chapter Test

At the end of each chapter, you'll take a diagnostic Chapter Test, covering material in that chapter and key concepts from previous chapters. The Chapter Test will help ensure that you master each chapter before you move on to the next.

Cumulative Test

The last section of this book is a test that covers all the concepts you've learned and reviewed throughout the book. It's more great review and focused practice.

THREE BASIC PRINCIPLES

Many people are intimidated by grammar because there are so many rules to remember. But all of those rules are based on just three underlying principles:

Balance   **Consistency**   **Clarity**

Subject-verb agreement is about balance. Pronouns and verb tenses need to be consistent. Correct use of punctuation makes your meaning clear. We'll remind you of these core principles throughout the book. By recalling them, you'll find any rule easier to learn and remember.

With a system as focused as this, great grammar and a high GMAT score are well within your reach. All you have to do is take the first step. Good luck!

Grammar and Sentence Structure

THE PARTS OF SPEECH

Let's begin with a thorough review of the parts of speech—what they are, how they work, and why they matter. Basic? Yes. Essential? You bet.

FORM AND FUNCTION

Words are the building blocks of sentences: we string them together in endless combinations of phrases, clauses, and sentences to express our ideas.

A **phrase** is a related group of words that *does not* contain both a subject and a verb (though it may contain either). A **clause** is a related group of words that *does* contain both a subject and a verb. An **independent clause** expresses a complete thought and can stand alone as a sentence. A **subordinate clause** cannot stand by itself; it depends on another clause to complete its meaning.

Each word serves a particular *function* within a phrase, clause, or sentence. It might describe, name, or connect; it might show the relationship between two ideas or express emotion. A word's function can affect the *form* it will take as well as its placement. So the parts of speech are much more than just another list of things to memorize; they are the foundations of grammar.

Take the word *beauty*, for instance. Its noun form is *beauty,* the thing. If you change its part of speech, you change its form and its function in a sentence:

	Form	Function	Example
Noun	beauty	Names a thing.	I am overwhelmed by your *beauty*.
Verb	beautify	Expresses an action.	Flowers will *beautify* this abandoned lot.
Adjective	beautiful	Describes a noun or pronoun.	You are so *beautiful*.

However, not all words change form when they change part of speech.

Adjective: Hermione is a <u>model</u> student.

Noun: Hermione works as a <u>model</u>.

Verb: Hermione will <u>model</u> her roommate's designs in the student fashion show.

Verb: I am <u>cooking</u> Thanksgiving dinner for the family this year.

Noun: I enjoy <u>cooking</u>.

Adjective: The <u>cooking</u> class has been canceled.

NOUNS

Here we will review the specific function and forms of nouns.

Function

Nouns name a person, place, or thing.

Form

- Nouns can be **singular** (*tree, glass*) or **plural** (*trees, glasses*). Most plurals are formed by adding -*s* or -*es*.

- **Collective** nouns (also called **group** nouns), name a class or a group—a single entity composed of more than one unit (e.g., *team, faculty, series*). They are usually treated as singular.

- **Concrete** nouns name tangible things (things that you can experience directly with your senses: *spider, motorcycle, mountain*). **Abstract** nouns name an idea or quality (things you can't experience with your senses: *love, apathy, peace*).

- **Proper** nouns refer to *specific* people, places, or things, like *Albert Einstein*, the *Milky Way, Middletown Academy*; **common** nouns refer to *general* people, places, or things: *scientist, galaxy, high school*.

MEMORY TIP

To remember what a noun is, try this mnemonic: *Noun* rhymes with *Johnstown*. *John* is a person, *Johnstown* is a place, and *town* is a thing.

PRACTICE 1

In the paragraph below, determine whether each underlined word is or is not a noun.

One of the <u>most</u> well-known fairy tales is "Little Red <u>Riding</u> <u>Hood</u>."
         yes/no   yes/no yes/no

There are hundreds of <u>versions</u> of this story throughout the <u>world</u>.
                    yes/no   yes/no

In the most popular version in <u>America</u>, Little Red Riding Hood is saved
                              yes/no

by a woodsman, who <u>cuts</u> her out of the wolf's <u>belly</u>. In other versions,
                    yes/no   yes/no

<u>Little Red Riding Hood</u> <u>tricks</u> the wolf into letting her out. I find these
          yes/no   yes/no

versions <u>more</u> satisfying, because Little Red Riding Hood saves <u>herself</u>
          yes/no   yes/no

through her own <u>ingenuity</u> rather than being <u>rescued</u> by someone else.
                    yes/no   yes/no

PRONOUNS

Function

Pronouns take the place of, or refer to, one or more nouns (and sometimes they take the place of, or refer to, whole phrases or clauses, which we'll cover later in this chapter).

Form

There are seven main types of pronouns:

Personal pronouns refer to specific people or things: *I love you.*	*Singular:* I, me, you, she, her, he, him, it *Plural:* we, us, you, they, them

(continued on next page)

Possessive pronouns indicate ownership: *This is my house.*	*Singular:* my, mine, your, yours, her, hers, his, its
	Plural: our, ours, your, yours, their, theirs
Reflexive pronouns indicate that the person or thing that performs the action also receives the action: *I hurt myself.*	*Singular:* myself, yourself, himself, herself, itself
	Plural: ourselves, yourselves, themselves
Relative pronouns introduce subordinate clauses that modify a noun or pronoun in the sentence: *Annette is the one who came up with the idea.*	who, whom, whose, what, which
Demonstrative pronouns identify or point to specific nouns: *This is my house.*	this, that, these, those
Indefinite pronouns refer to nonspecific people or things: *Has anybody seen my keys?*	all, another, any, anybody, anyone, anything, both, each, either, everybody, everyone, everything, few, many, neither, nobody, none, no one, nothing, one, several, some, somebody, someone, something
Interrogative pronouns introduce questions: *What is going on here?*	who, whom, whose, what, which

Rachel let me borrow her old wig so that no one will recognize me at the party. Now this is more like it!

The words *this, that, these, those,* and some of the indefinite pronouns can also be adjectives. The test is whether they are alone (and therefore replace a noun) or precede a noun (and therefore modify that noun).

Adjective: This soup is delicious! (*This* modifies *soup.*)
Pronoun: This is delicious! (*This* replaces the noun *soup.*)
Adjective: All dogs go to heaven. (*All* modifies *dogs.*)
Pronoun: Justice for all. (*All* replaces *the people.*)

PRACTICE 2

Find and underline the nine words functioning as pronouns in the paragraph on the following page.

One of the most well-known fairy tales is "Little Red Riding Hood." There are hundreds of versions of this story throughout the world. In the most popular version in America, Little Red Riding Hood is saved by a woodsman, who cuts her out of the wolf's belly. In other versions, Little Red Riding Hood tricks the wolf into letting her out. I find these more satisfying, because Little Red Riding Hood saves herself through her own ingenuity rather than being rescued by someone else.

VERBS

Function

Verbs express an action or state of being.

Form

Verb forms change depending upon the **person(s)** performing the action and the **tense** (when the action takes/took/will take place). We'll review verb forms and tenses in chapters 3 and 4.

In all tenses except the simple present and past, the **verb** consists of several words: the base, which expresses the main action or state of being, and one or more **helping verbs**, which help indicate the tense (as well as voice or mood, which we'll discuss in chapters 3 and 4).

In the following examples, helping verbs are underlined once and base verbs twice:

I am exhausted!

I am having a great time.

You should have been more careful.

We did not know that you were coming.

The evidence does not support your accusations.

We will certify that these documents are real.

Note that *am* is the base verb in the first sentence and a helping verb in the second. Forms of *be*, *do*, and *have* can be either helping verbs or base verbs. Consider the function: Is the verb describing the action of the sentence, or is it helping to indicate the tense—when the action takes place?

PRACTICE 3

Underline the verbs in the following sentences, putting one line under helping verbs and two under base verbs. Only underline verbs that are functioning as verbs.

1. Look before you leap.
2. Don't count your chickens before they hatch.
3. Those who live in glass houses should not throw stones.
4. The early bird catches the worm.
5. You will reap what you sow.
6. Good things come to those who wait.
7. Do unto others as you would have done unto you.
8. Sticks and stones will break my bones, but words will never hurt me.
9. A watched pot never boils.
10. Rome was not built in a day.

ADJECTIVES

Function

Adjectives describe or modify nouns and pronouns. They tell us *which one*, *what kind*, or *how many*.

Talk is <u>cheap</u>. (*Cheap* describes the noun *talk*.)

What an <u>outrageous</u> accusation! (*Outrageous* describes the noun *accusation*.)

There are <u>several</u> problems with this proposal. (*Several* describes the noun *problems*.)

You are so <u>patient</u> with your children. (*Patient* describes the pronoun *you*.)

Form

Adjectives don't take a specific form because just about any kind of word can function as an adjective:

> He is a <u>book</u> aficionado. (What kind of aficionado? *Book*. Here, *book* is not a thing but a modifier of the word *aficionado*.)

> Follow <u>that</u> car! (Which car? *That* one. *That* doesn't replace a noun; it describes one.)

> Please grab the <u>baking</u> powder from the pantry. (What kind of powder? *Baking* powder. *Baking* isn't an action but a description.)

PRACTICE 4

In each sentence that follows, circle which word, if any, is an adjective.

1. Meet me at the farmers' market.
2. Gala apples are in season.
3. I'll buy two dozen of them.
4. Who is that woman?
5. That smarts!
6. Elena is very smart.
7. She's also a very likeable person.
8. I am a musician.
9. Pigs are rather docile animals.
10. I've never seen a more egregious error.

ADVERBS

Function

Adverbs describe or modify verbs, adjectives, and other adverbs. They tell us when, where, how, and why; under what conditions; and to what degree.

Notice the difference between adjectives and adverbs, which are commonly confused:

> **Adjective:** I am very <u>patient</u>. (*Patient* modifies the pronoun *I*.)
> **Adverb:** I am waiting <u>patiently</u>. (*Patiently* tells us how I am *waiting*.)

Here are more examples of adverbs:

Eventually you will learn how to better manage your time. (*Eventually* modifies the verb *learn* and tells us when. *Better* modifies the verb *manage* and tells us how.)

He talks so rapidly that I can hardly understand him. (*Rapidly* modifies the verb *talks* and tells us how. *So* modifies the adverb *rapidly* and also tells us how. *Hardly* modifies the verb *understand* and tells us to what degree.)

Form

Adverbs come in different shapes and sizes: *yesterday, very, clearly, never.* Many adverbs are formed by adding *-ly* to adjectives (e.g., *happy* ⟶ *happily; slow* ⟶ *slowly*).

MEMORY TIP

To remember the difference between adjectives and adverbs, note that adjectives modify nouns or pronouns, while adverbs modify verbs as well as adjectives and other adverbs.

PRACTICE 5

Find and underline the adverbs in the following sentences.

1. Speak softly and carry a big stick.
2. Never say never.
3. Love your children unconditionally.
4. Treat yourself well and be happy.
5. You are what you eat, so choose your foods wisely.
6. Don't be so modest!
7. History often repeats itself.
8. Your spot has already been taken.
9. Just yesterday I finished the second novel in the trilogy.
10. We are desperately trying to get an answer.

PREPOSITIONS

Function

Prepositions express the relationship (often in time or space) between two words in a sentence. Prepositions include the following:

about	before	in	out	underneath
above	behind	inside	outside	unlike
across	below	into	over	until
after	beside	like	past	unto
against	between	near	since	up
along	by	next	through	upon
among	despite	of	throughout	with
around	during	off	to	within
as	for	on	toward	without
at	from	onto	under	

Form

Prepositions always come in **prepositional phrases**, which begin with the preposition and end with a noun or pronoun. Prepositional phrases usually modify the first word (a noun or verb) in the relationship:

Please put the book _on the table_.

_On_ is the preposition; _on the table_ is the prepositional phrase showing the relationship between the verb _put_ (the first word in the relationship) and _table_ (the second). It answers the question _where_, so it functions as an adverb.

We were lost _in the woods_ for hours.

_In_ is the preposition; _in the woods_ is the prepositional phrase. The preposition here shows the relationship between _lost_ and _woods_ and also tells us where. Here are more examples:

During the show, I fell asleep _in my chair_.

Bring your registration form _with you_.

Go _through the tunnel_ and then turn left _at the light_.

PRACTICE 6

Underline the ten prepositional phrases in the following sentences.

In the bottom of the ninth inning, Moses Jones hit a line drive into left field. Ollie Wilkins raced to third, and Javier Mercado scored, sliding into home just before the tag. Behind his glove, pitcher Dennis Delaney spit on the ball. It spun wildly over home plate, but Willie Thomas sent the ball sailing out of the park.

CONJUNCTIONS

Function

Conjunctions join two or more parts of sentences—words, phrases, or clauses—and express the relationship between those parts.

Form

There are four kinds of conjunctions, each with a very specific function.

COORDINATING CONJUNCTIONS

Coordinating conjunctions connect grammatically equivalent elements (words, phrases, or clauses). There are only seven coordinating conjunctions: *and, or, nor, for, but, so, yet*. The grammatically equivalent elements are bracketed in the sample sentences below:

> We are [ready] and [willing] to go.
>
> Hang your coat [in the closet] or [on the door].
>
> [I would like to go], but [I can't].
>
> [Sam is working today], so [he can't go either].

Remember, coordinating conjunctions work with *equivalent* parts; they can connect two words or phrases, or they can connect two independent words, phrases, or clauses. They cannot connect, for example, an independent clause and a dependent clause.

MEMORY TIP

Coordinating conjunctions connect grammatically equivalent elements. You can remember it this way: a *coordinated* outfit has *matching* clothes; a *coordinating conjunction* connects *matching* grammatical elements.

CORRELATIVE CONJUNCTIONS

Correlative conjunctions are used in pairs. They also connect grammatically equivalent elements and include the following:

both…and	neither…nor
not only…but also	whether…or
not…but	as…as
either…or	

You will <u>either</u> wash the dishes <u>or</u> dry them and put them away.

<u>Not only</u> is he handsome, <u>but</u> he's <u>also</u> brilliant.

<u>Whether</u> you like it <u>or</u> not, I'm coming with you!

SUBORDINATING CONJUNCTIONS

Subordinating conjunctions are adverbs that introduce subordinate clauses. They're distinct from "regular" adverbs because they connect subordinate and independent clauses, showing the relationship between the two:

[We'll go outside] [<u>when</u> it stops raining].
[independent clause]　　[subordinate clause]

When connects the two clauses and shows the relationship between them (one action will take place after the other).

Subordinating conjunctions include the following:

after	even though	rather than	until
although	how	since	when
as	if	so that	whenever
as if	if only	than	where
because	in order that	that	wherever
before	now that	though	whether
even if	once	unless	while

In the examples below, the subordinating conjunctions are underlined, and the subordinate clauses are bracketed. Notice that the subordinate clauses cannot stand alone because they do not express a complete thought.

> [Because the proposal is due tomorrow], we need to finish it as soon as possible.

> I'll cancel my meeting [so that we can have lunch together].

> We'll work on the proposal [while we eat].

> After lunch, we can return to my office, [where we'll try to finish it up].

> [After we've submitted the proposal,] we'll go out to celebrate.

Notice that in the second to last example, *after* is simply a preposition, not a subordinating conjunction; *after lunch* is a prepositional phrase, not a subordinate clause. In the last sentence, however, *after* does introduce a subordinate clause, so it functions as a subordinating conjunction.

CONJUNCTIVE ADVERBS

Conjunctive adverbs introduce independent clauses. They're distinct from "regular" adverbs because they connect the clause to the previous sentence or clause and show the relationship between them:

> I mixed the colors over and over; finally, I got the exact shade I was looking for.

Finally introduces the second independent clause and shows its relationship to the first.

The most common conjunctive adverbs are the following:

as a result	moreover
consequently	nevertheless
finally	similarly
furthermore	therefore
however	thus

You cheated; <u>therefore</u>, you are disqualified from the race.

Therefore introduces an independent clause and shows its relationship to the previous clause. Notice how this is different from a subordinating conjunction introducing a subordinate clause:

<u>Because</u> you cheated, you are disqualified from the race.

The independent clause *therefore, you are disqualified from the race* can stand alone, but the dependent (subordinate) clause *because you cheated* cannot. Here are more examples of sentences with conjunctive adverbs:

It may seem as if you have no choice; <u>however</u>, there are actually many options.

Although hybrid cars are more expensive, they are more cost-effective in the long run. <u>Moreover</u>, they are much better for the environment. (Notice the subordinating conjunction *although* introducing the initial subordinating clause.)

You'll need to know these four kinds of conjunctions because they have specific functions; you can't use a conjunctive adverb when you need a coordinating conjunction. Still, the bottom line is this: these words *connect* and show the relationship between words, phrases, or clauses.

Here are the four conjunctions and their functions in a nutshell:

Type	Function	Examples
coordinating	Connects equal parts.	*and, or, for*
correlative	Connects equal parts.	*either…or, not…but*
subordinating	Connects a subordinate clause to an independent clause.	*although, if, because*
adverb	Connects an independent clause to the preceding clause.	*however, thus*

PRACTICE 7

Underline the conjunctions in the following sentences (some have more than one). Underneath each, write which type of conjunction it is: *coord* (coordinating), *corr* (correlative), *sub* (subordinating), or *conj* (conjunctive adverb).

Example: The game is tied, <u>so</u> it'll go into overtime.
coord

1. I'll say yes, <u>even though</u> I should know better than to listen to you.

2. I want to believe you, <u>but</u> I can't.

3. Children are <u>neither</u> as naïve <u>nor</u> as innocent as we like to think.

4. The battle was over, <u>and</u> the general was soundly defeated, <u>yet</u> he still believed the attack was a victory.

5. I will come along for moral support; <u>however</u>, I'm warning you, if you try to get me involved, I will leave.

6. We've had bad experiences the last two times we ate at Café Café; <u>therefore</u>, we've decided to move our weekly brunch to Kate's Kitchen.

INTERJECTIONS

Function

Interjections are sudden, usually emotional words or phrases that can stand alone as sentences.

Form

Interjections can be a single word or a short phrase. They are almost always followed by an exclamation point.

Hey! Look out! Holy cow! Unbelievable!

PRACTICE 8

Write three sentences with interjections.

1. _No way!_
2. _Huh!_
3. _Sweet!_

SUMMARY

When it comes to parts of speech, the key is to look at *what the word is doing* in the sentence.

Part of Speech	Function	Examples	Notes
Noun	Names a person, place, or thing.	book, Ali, infatuation	Nouns can be **singular** or **plural**, **concrete** (tangible) or **abstract** (intangible), **proper** (a specific person, place, or thing) or **common** (general), and **collective** (a group functioning as a unit, such as *team*).

(continued on next page)

Part of Speech	Function	Examples	Notes
Pronoun	Replaces or points to a noun.	me, you, them, that	There are **personal** (*I, me, them*), **possessive** (*mine, ours*), **reflexive** (*yourself, ourselves*), **relative** (*that, which, who*), **demonstrative** (*that, this*) **indefinite** (*anybody, no one*), and **interrogative** (*who, whom, whose, what, which*) pronouns.
Verb	Expresses action or state of being.	believe, juggle, float	**Base verbs** express the main action of the sentence. **Helping verbs** help indicate the tense of the base verb.
Adjective	Modifies a noun or pronoun.	thoughtful, noisy, inquisitive	
Adverb	Modifies a verb, adjective, or another adverb.	hardly, boldly, very, never	
Preposition	Expresses a relationship (often in time or space) between two words.	in, under, over, around, through	
Conjunction	Joins parts of sentences and expresses the relationship between those parts.	and, for, yet; either/ or; because, since; however, therefore	Four types: **coordinating** and **correlative conjunctions** (connect equal parts), **subordinating conjunctions** (introduce subordinate clauses), and **conjunctive adverbs** (introduce independent clauses).
Interjection	Expresses surprise or emotion.	Hey! Ouch! Oh no!	

Practice on Your Own

Choose an article in your favorite newspaper or magazine, a page in the book you're reading, or an email you receive. Spend some time reading it carefully and looking for the eight parts of speech you reviewed in this chapter. Do you see all four types of conjunctions? Do you see helping verbs and base verbs working together?

Practice Answers and Explanations

PRACTICE 1

One of the <u>most</u> well-known fairy tales is "Little Red <u>Riding</u> <u>Hood</u>."
      yes/(no)   yes/(no) (yes)/no

There are hundreds of <u>versions</u> of this story throughout the <u>world</u>.
                        (yes)/no   (yes)/no

In the most popular version in <u>America</u>, Little Red Riding Hood is saved
                                   (yes)/no

by a woodsman, who <u>cuts</u> her out of the wolf's <u>belly</u>. In other versions,
                 yes/(no)   (yes)/no

<u>Little Red Riding Hood</u> <u>tricks</u> the wolf into letting her out. I find these
    (yes)/no   yes/(no)

versions <u>more</u> satisfying, because Little Red Riding Hood saves <u>herself</u>
        yes/(no)   yes/(no)

through her own <u>ingenuity</u> rather than being <u>rescued</u> by someone else.
            (yes)/no   yes/(no)

Hood, versions, world, America, belly, and *ingenuity* are nouns. As a complete phrase, *Little Red Riding Hood* is a noun; that is what the little girl's name is in the story. *America* and *Little Red Riding Hood* are **proper nouns**. All of these nouns are **concrete** except *ingenuity*, which is **abstract**.

Most is an adverb modifying *well-known. Riding* is an adjective describing *Hood.* (As a complete phrase, *Little Red Riding Hood* is a noun; otherwise, *little, red,* and *riding* all describe *hood.*) *Cuts* and *tricks* are both verbs in this paragraph. *More* is an adverb modifying *satisfying. Herself* is a pronoun. *Rescued* is a verb.

PRACTICE 2

<u>One</u> of the most well-known fairy tales is "Little Red Riding Hood." There are hundreds of versions of this story throughout the world. In the most popular version in America, Little Red Riding Hood is saved by a woodsman, <u>who</u> cuts <u>her</u> out of the wolf's belly. In other versions, Little Red Riding Hood tricks the wolf into letting <u>her</u> out. <u>I</u> find <u>these</u> more satisfying, because Little Red Riding Hood saves <u>herself</u> through <u>her</u> own ingenuity rather than being rescued by <u>someone</u> else.

In the second sentence, *this* functions as an adjective because it immediately precedes and points to the noun *story*. In the last sentence, *these* replaces *other versions*, so it functions as a pronoun.

PRACTICE 3

1. <u>Look</u> before you <u>leap</u>.
2. <u>Do</u>n't <u>count</u> your chickens before they <u>hatch</u>.
3. Those who <u>live</u> in glass houses <u>should</u> not <u>throw</u> stones.
4. The early bird <u>catches</u> the worm.
5. You <u>will</u> <u>reap</u> what you <u>sow</u>.
6. Good things <u>come</u> to those who <u>wait</u>.
7. <u>Do</u> unto others as you <u>would have</u> <u>done</u> unto you. (*Do* can be a helping verb, but here it is the main action of the sentence.)
8. Sticks and stones <u>will</u> <u>break</u> my bones, but words <u>will</u> never <u>hurt</u> me.
9. A watched pot never <u>boils</u>. (*Watched* is functioning as an adjective; it describes the kind of pot rather than an action.)
10. Rome <u>was</u> not <u>built</u> in a day.

PRACTICE 4

1. *Farmers'* describes *market*.
2. *Gala* describes *apples*.
3. *Two* modifies *dozen*.
4. *That* modifies *woman*.
5. No adjective. Here, *that* is a relative pronoun replacing an unspecified noun.
6. *Smart* describes *Elena*. (Notice that *smarts* in sentence 5 is a verb.)
7. *Likeable* describes *she*.
8. No adjective. Even though *musician* tells us something about *I*, it is still a noun naming a thing.
9. *Docile* modifies *animals*. Even if you don't know what *docile* means, you should see that it functions as an adjective, telling what kind of animals they are.
10. *Egregious* modifies *error*. If you don't know what *egregious* means, you should still see that it describes *error*.

PRACTICE 5

1. *Softly* modifies the verb *speak.* (*Big* is an adjective modifying *stick.*)

2. The first *never* is an adverb telling us when.

3. *Unconditionally* modifies the verb *love.*

4. *Well* modifies the verb *treat.* (*Happy* is an adjective modifying the unstated subject of the sentence, *you.*)

5. *Wisely* is an adverb modifying the verb *choose.*

6. *So* modifies the adjective *modest.*

7. *Often* modifies the verb *repeats* and tells us when.

8. *Already* modifies the verb *taken.*

9. *Just* modifies the adverb *yesterday,* which modifies the verb *finished.* Both adverbs tell us when.

10. *Desperately* modifies the verb *trying.*

PRACTICE 6

In the bottom of the ninth inning, Moses Jones hit a line drive into left field. Ollie Wilkins raced to third, and Javier Mercado scored, sliding into home just before the tag. Behind his glove, pitcher Dennis Delaney spit on the ball. It spun wildly over home plate, but Willie Thomas sent the ball sailing out of the park.

PRACTICE 7

1. *Even though* is a subordinating conjunction introducing a subordinate clause.

2. *But* is a coordinating conjunction connecting two independent clauses.

3. *Neither... nor* is a correlative conjunction.

4. *And* and *yet* are both coordinating conjunctions connecting independent clauses.

5. *However* is a conjunctive adverb introducing an independent clause. *If* is a subordinating conjunction introducing a subordinate clause.

6. *Therefore* is a conjunctive adverb introducing an independent clause.

PRACTICE 8

Answers will vary. Some possibilities are *Hurry! Yo! What! Uh-oh! Wow! Yikes!*

CHAPTER 1 TEST

Directions: Each underlined word in the paragraphs below corresponds to one of the lettered parts of speech that follow. Write the correct choice under the word, using the most specific choice available. Letters may be used more than once.

Old Mother Hubbard <u>went</u> to the cupboard to fetch her <u>poor</u> doggie a <u>bone</u>.

1. S   2. A   3. J

<u>When</u> she got there, the cupboard was <u>completely</u> <u>bare</u>. "<u>Drat!</u>" said Old

4. F   5. B   6. A   7. H

Mother Hubbard. "<u>This</u> won't <u>do</u>!" "No, it won't," said the dog, who then

8. O   9. S

had Mother Hubbard <u>for</u> dinner.

10. L

<u>Little</u> Miss Muffet sat <u>on</u> a tuffet, eating her <u>curds</u> and whey.

11. A   12. ML   13. J

Along came a spider <u>who</u> sat down <u>beside her</u> and

14. R   15. M

said, "<u>Boo!</u>" "Sorry, Spidey. <u>Your</u> scaring days are over," Miss Muffet replied

16. H   17. Q

<u>calmly</u>   <u>and</u>   <u>dumped</u> her curds and whey on the spider.

18. B   19. D   20. S

(A) adjective
(B) adverb
(C) conjunction
(D) coordinating conjunction
(E) correlative conjunction
(F) subordinating conjunction
(G) conjunctive adverb
(H) interjection
(I) noun
(J) collective noun

(K) proper noun
(L) preposition
(M) prepositional phrase
(N) pronoun
(O) demonstrative pronoun
(P) indefinite pronoun
(Q) possessive pronoun
(R) relative pronoun
(S) verb
(T) helping verb

**ANSWERS AND EXPLANATIONS
BEGIN ON NEXT PAGE**

Answers and Explanations

1. S

Went is a verb expressing action.

2. A

Poor is an adjective describing *doggie*.

3. I

Bone is a noun—a thing.

4. F

When is a subordinating conjunction introducing the subordinate clause *when she got there*.

5. B

Completely is an adverb describing the adjective *bare*.

6. A

Bare is an adjective modifying *cupboard*.

7. H

Drat! is an interjection expressing emotion.

8. O

This is a demonstrative pronoun. It replaces the noun phrase *bare cupboard*.

9. S

Do is the verb expressing the main action of the clause.

10. L

For is a preposition showing the relationship between *Mother Hubbard* and *dinner*.

11. A

Little is an adjective modifying *Miss Muffet*.

12. L

On is a preposition showing the relationship between the verb *sat* and the noun *tuffet*.

13. I

Curds is a noun, a thing.

14. R

Who is a relative pronoun referring to *spider*.

15. M

Beside her is a prepositional phrase showing the spatial relationship between the verb *sat* and *her*.

16. H

Boo! is an interjection.

17. Q

Your is a possessive pronoun.

18. B

Calmly is an adverb modifying the verb *replied*.

19. D

And is a coordinating conjunction connecting the verbs *replied* and *dumped*.

20. S

Dumped is a verb expressing action.

CHAPTER 2

SENTENCE PARTS AND PATTERNS

This chapter will review sentence types and structure. First, a definition:

> A **sentence** is a series of words that (1) contains a **subject** and a **predicate** and (2) expresses a **complete thought**.

Imagine a house in which the front door opens into a closet; to get to the kitchen, you have to go through the attic; and the windows are all in the corners. It might have all the right elements, but they're not in the right place.

Now imagine a house whose kitchen is without a floor. Or a house with a foyer and hallway but no doors. The pieces may be where they belong, but other essential pieces are missing.

To be functional, a house—whatever its size or style—must have certain basic elements joined in a logical way. The same goes for sentences. They may come in different sizes and styles, but they must contain the same basic elements and follow certain patterns.

Just about every rule you read in this book can and will be broken. English grammar is full of exceptions. So when we say that every sentence has a subject and a verb, we mean it—mostly. An interjection like *Wow!*, for example, is a special kind of sentence.

WHAT IT'S ALL ABOUT: THE SUBJECT

The **subject** of a sentence is *who* or *what* the sentence is about. You can usually find the subject by asking who or what carries out the action of the sentence:

<u>I</u> love to paint.	*Who* loves to paint? *I* do.
On Wednesdays and Fridays, <u>Pearl</u> and <u>Jasmine</u> attend karate class.	*Who* attends karate class? *Pearl* and *Jasmine*.
<u>Absolute power</u> corrupts absolutely.	*What* corrupts absolutely? *Absolute power*.
<u>Remaining silent</u> can be just as destructive as telling a lie.	*What* can be just as destructive? *Remaining silent.*

As you can see, the subject usually comes before the verb (what the subject is or does or has done to it). There are three exceptions:

1. When writers invert the order for effect

2. When sentences begin with *there is/are, it is/they are*, or *was/were*

3. Questions

Sorry are <u>we</u> who pretend to be what we are not.	Who or what is sorry? *We* are.
There is <u>no excuse</u> for your behavior.	Who or what is there? *No excuse.*
Do <u>you</u> really believe in UFOs?	Who believes? *You.*

Understood Subjects

Do your homework!

Who or what does the homework? The subject is understood to be *you*. This is an imperative sentence—it gives advice or issues a command:

Please feed the dog.

Try the delicious fried calamari!

PRACTICE 1

Underline the subject in each of the following sentences.

1. A watched pot never boils.

2. Every evening, the sun sets over these hills.

3. There are strange goings-on around here these days.

4. What are you doing?

5. Ever since childhood, Lukas has been very artistic.

6. Choose your friends carefully.

Kinds of Subjects

The **simple** subject is the subject without any modifiers or articles (*a/an, the*). The **complete** subject is the subject with its modifiers and articles

> **Simple:** The old yellow <u>house</u> on Turner Road is being demolished tomorrow.

> **Complete:** <u>The old yellow house on Turner Road</u> is being demolished tomorrow.

The simple subject can be a single word, a phrase (a group of words without a subject and verb), or a clause (a group of words containing both a subject and verb)

> **One word:** There's a <u>rabbit</u> in your hat.
> **Phrase:** The phrase <u>"once in a blue moon"</u> means every two and a half years.
> **Clause:** <u>What you just said</u> was the best thing anyone has ever said to me.

These subjects are still simple even though they contain more than one word.

SINGLE AND COMPOUND SUBJECTS

Subjects can be **single** (one person or thing) or **compound** (two or more people or things):

> **Single subject:** <u>Donovan</u> has entered the contest.
>
> **Compound subject:** <u>Donovan</u>, <u>Ivan</u>, and <u>Melissa</u> have entered the contest.
>
> **Single subject:** <u>Chimpanzees</u> will be placed in the new zoo enclosure.
>
> **Compound subject:** <u>Chimpanzees</u> or <u>gorillas</u> will be placed in the new zoo enclosure.

When a compound subject is joined by *and*, the subject is plural; when it is joined by *or*, it is singular if the last item is singular and plural if the last item is plural.

MEMORY TIP

Don't confuse *singular* with *single*. A single subject is one subject performing the action, but that subject can be plural: *The <u>cats</u> were chased up the tree.*

PRACTICE 2

Underline the complete subject in the sentences below. Is the subject single or compound?

1. Unfortunately, Carlos and Jude did not get along well.   C
2. Thinking of you is my favorite pastime.   S
3. Unlike Lucinda, I do believe in miracles.   S
4. There are many false claims and exaggerated truths during a political campaign.   C
5. No termites or carpenter ants were found by the inspector.   C

Where the Subject Is—and Isn't

Because most subjects come before the verb, we usually find them toward the beginning of a sentence. But sometimes one or more words or phrases precede the subject:

> Honestly, <u>I</u> did not lie to you.
>
> In the middle of the hottest day of the hottest summer on record, <u>Kiku</u> was born.

If you're having trouble identifying the subject, look for the verb. Then, see who or what performs that action. Who didn't lie? *I* didn't. Who was born? *Kiku.*

Sometimes words or phrases—especially those that come between subjects and verbs—impede your search for the subject. Here's a helpful rule: subjects are never in prepositional phrases.

Prepositional phrases—like adverbial and adjectival phrases—are not part of the core sentence. You can eliminate them and still have a completely coherent thought:

Memories, like diamonds, are imperfect.

Both *memories* and *diamonds* are imperfect, but *memories* is the subject. *Diamonds* is part of the prepositional phrase *like diamonds*; we can take that phrase out and still have our core sentence:

<u>Memories</u> are imperfect.

Without *memories,* on the other hand, the sentence wouldn't make sense:

Like diamonds are imperfect.

In the following sentences, we've bracketed and crossed out prepositional phrases to eliminate other candidates for the subject:

Honestly, <u>I</u> did not lie [~~to you~~].

[~~In the middle~~] [~~of the hottest day~~] [~~of the hottest summer~~] [~~on record~~], <u>Kiku</u> was born.

PRACTICE 3

Underline the subject(s) in the following sentences.

1. With my costume on, <u>I</u> won't be recognizable.
2. <u>The boys</u> on the baseball team planned a surprise party for their coach.
3. <u>Raj</u>, terrified of making a mistake, would not raise his hand in class.
4. <u>The gym</u> in the school is in serious disrepair.
5. <u>The color</u> of these walls is quite soothing.

MEET THE PREDICATES

The **predicate** of a sentence is the verb and anything that logically belongs with it—the objects, modifiers, or complements (we'll define these shortly). The predicate usually ends the English sentence. In the sentences below, complete subjects are underlined, and predicates are in brackets:

I [love to paint].

Pearl and Jasmine [attend karate class on Wednesdays and Fridays].

Remaining silent [can be just as destructive as telling a lie].

 MEMORY TIP

The subject is who or what the sentence is about (who or what performs or receives the action). The predicate is the verb and any objects, complements, or modifiers.

Predicates can be single or compound. A compound predicate has the same subject for two or more different verbs:

Single predicate: A good neighbor [helps when asked].

Compound predicate: A good neighbor [helps when asked] and [asks for help].

PRACTICE 4

Put a slash (/) between the subject and predicate in each sentence.

Example: The Willow River/floods every spring.

1. For many years/the Republic of Congo/was a colony of Belgium.
2. Contrary to popular belief/most species of snakes/are not poisonous.
3. The most popular fruit in the world/is the mango.
4. The African continent/is full of rich natural resources, including diamonds and oil.
5. Have/you/heard the news?

Predicates and Sentence Patterns

As you've seen, the basic English sentence pattern is subject-predicate. Predicates come in different shapes and sizes, forming four main sentence patterns:

s-v: subject-verb
s-lv-c: subject–linking verb–complement
s-v-o: subject–verb–direct object
s-v-io-o: subject–verb–indirect object–direct object

LINKING VERBS AND COMPLEMENTS

In some sentences, the base verb is a **linking verb (lv)**—a verb that links a **subject (s)** to its **complement (c)**.

A complement is the part of a predicate that describes or renames the subject. To *complement* means to make perfect or complete; a complement completes the subject. Complements are connected to the subject by a linking verb:

I / am / a painter.
s lv   c

"Once in a blue moon" / means / about once every two and a half years.
     s   lv   c

The complement *a painter* describes the subject *I*. The phrase *about once every two and a half years* defines *once in a blue moon*.

Forms of the verb *to be* (*am, is, are, was, were, being,* and *been*) often serve as helping verbs, but when *to be* is the base verb (as in the first example) it is a linking verb. Descriptive verbs, such as *become, feel, appear, look, seem, taste, sound,* and *smell,* are often linking verbs as well.

To test for a linking verb, remove the verb and insert an equal sign; does it make sense?

I = painter

Once in a blue moon = about once every two and a half years

This *doesn't* work for predicates that do *not* have subject complements:

Absolute power *corrupts* absolutely.	I *understand* your message.
Absolute power ≠ absolutely.	I ≠ your message.

PRACTICE 5

Here are the sentences from Practice 4. Does each follow the **s-lv-c** pattern?

1. For many years, the Republic of Congo was a colony of Belgium. yes
2. Contrary to popular belief, most species of snakes are not poisonous. yes
3. The most popular fruit in the world is the mango.
4. The African continent is full of rich natural resources, including diamonds and oil.
5. Have you heard the news?

RECEIVING THE ACTION: DIRECT OBJECTS

While linking verbs connect a subject and complement, **transitive verbs (tv)** apply their action to a **direct object (o)**: a person or thing in the predicate. There are a number of types of objects; when we simply say *object,* we mean the direct object.

> I / understand / your message.
> s   tv   o

In this sentence, *message* receives the action of the verb; it is what is being understood.

> I / will pick up / some milk on the way home from work.
> s   tv   o   [prepositional phrases]

Like subjects, direct objects are never in prepositional phrases.

PRACTICE 6

Circle the direct objects in the following sentences.

1. For some reason, Peter Pumpkin Eater put his wife in a pumpkin shell.
2. The alarm startled me.
3. The general found shelter for his troops.
4. The bus drops Tyler off at his front door.

WHO IT'S FOR: INDIRECT OBJECTS

The direct object *directly* receives the action of the verb. The **indirect object (io)** receives the direct object:

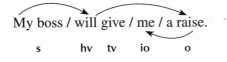

My boss / will give / me / a raise.

     s   hv tv   io   o

A raise is what will be given, so it is the direct object. But who will receive that raise? *Me*—the indirect object.

Here's another example:

    The police / questioned / Anna about the accident.
        s   tv   o   [prepositional phrase]

    The police / asked / Anna / many questions about the accident.
        s   tv   io   o   [prepositional phrase]

In the first sentence, there is no indirect object; Anna directly receives the action of the verb *questioned*. In the second sentence, *questions* is the direct object, and *Anna* is the indirect object.

PRACTICE 7

In the following sentences, put a slash (/) between the subject and predicate, underline the verb, and use arrows to indicate the movement of the action from subject to verb, from verb to direct object, and from direct object to indirect object.

1. Sanford should offer Anne that position.
2. Please give Elliot my best.
3. I am offering you a second chance.
4. Minsun is sending me mixed signals about our relationship.

INTRANSITIVE VERBS

In the most basic sentence pattern, **s-v**, the verb is **intransitive (iv)**; no object receives the action. That doesn't mean nothing follows the verb:

    Geese / fly south in the winter.
       s   iv[adverb]   [prepositional phrase]

Some verbs are only transitive, some only intransitive, and others, like *fly*, can be either. In the sentence before, *fly* is intransitive, but in the following sentence, it's transitive:

> I / fly / a private jet / for a government official.
> s tv   o   [prepositional phrase]

PRACTICE 8

Mark each verb *lv* for linking verb, *tv* for transitive verb, or *iv* for intransitive verb. Circle the direct object, if any.

1. I love chocolate chip cookies.
2. You are my true love.
3. I offer you my unconditional love.
4. I live for love.
5. Only love can save me now.

Pattern Variations

As you've seen, the four basic sentence patterns—**s-v**, **s-lv-c**, **s-v-o**, and **s-v-io-o**—can vary (1) when writers invert order for effect, (2) in *there is/are* constructions, and (3) in questions. Following is an example of a question:

> [Why] did / you / give / Michaela / credit [for my work]?
> [adv] hv   s   v   io   o   [prep phrase]

TYPES OF SENTENCES

Sentence type is determined by the number and type of clauses a sentence contains. Before attacking them, quickly review what a subordinate clause is. A subordinate clause cannot stand alone. It is *subordinate* to an independent clause, without which it doesn't express a complete thought.

As you saw in chapter 1, subordinate clauses usually begin with a **subordinating conjunction** or a **relative pronoun**. In the following examples, each clause is bracketed with a slash between subject and predicate, and the subordinate clause indicator (the conjunction or relative pronoun) is in bold:

[You / act] [**as if** you / don't care].
[independent clause] [subordinate clause]

[[**Whoever /** finds my wallet] / will get a reward].
[[subordinate clause within] independent clause]

Note that in the second example, the subordinate clause is the subject of the sentence.

MEMORY TIP

Subordinate means inferior to or subject to the control of. At work, you are subordinate to your boss. A subordinate clause is inferior to an independent clause.

Type 1: The Simple Sentence

A simple sentence contains one independent clause and no subordinate clauses. The subject and predicate can be single or compound, but the sentence contains only *one* subject-predicate pair:

I / must be true to myself.   Then I / can be true to others.
s   v   s   v

Type 2: The Compound Sentence

A compound sentence contains two or more independent clauses and no subordinate clauses. The two independent clauses are connected by a **coordinating conjunction** or by a semicolon with or without a **conjunctive adverb** (see chapter 1).

[You / must be true to yourself]; otherwise, [you / cannot be true to others].
[independent clause]; conjunctive adverb [independent clause]

Type 3: The Complex Sentence

A complex sentence contains one independent clause with one or more subordinate clauses:

[Before you / can be true to [those you / love]], [you / must be true to yourself].
[subordinate clause [subordinate clause]], [independent clause]

Type 4: The Compound-Complex Sentence

A compound-complex sentence consists of two or more independent clauses and one or more subordinate clauses.

> [I / know that [if I / am not true to myself]], [I / cannot be true to others].
> [independent clause [subordinate clause]], [independent clause]

PRACTICE 9

Identify subject-predicate pairs in each proverb below. Bracket each clause; determine whether it is independent or subordinate and how the clauses relate to each other. Mark each sentence *S* for simple, *C* for compound, *X* for complex, or *CC* for compound-complex.

Example: [The believer is happy]; [the doubter is wise]. —*Hungarian*
　　　　　(s)　　　(p)　　　(s)　　(p)　　=C

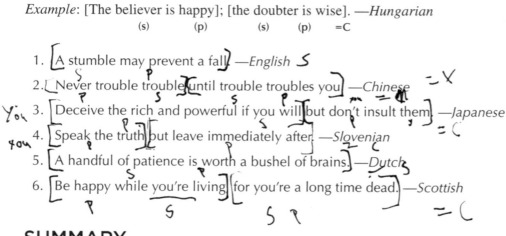

1. [A stumble may prevent a fall] —*English* S
2. [Never trouble trouble until trouble troubles you] —*Chinese*
3. [Deceive the rich and powerful if you will but don't insult them] —*Japanese*
4. [Speak the truth but leave immediately after] —*Slovenian*
5. [A handful of patience is worth a bushel of brains] —*Dutch*
6. [Be happy while you're living for you're a long time dead] —*Scottish*

SUMMARY

A **sentence** is a group of words containing both a **subject** and a **predicate** and expressing a **complete thought**. The subject is who or what the sentence is about. In imperative sentences, the subject is understood to be *you*. Subjects are never in prepositional phrases. The predicate is the verb with its objects, modifiers, and complements.

Both subjects and predicates can be **single** (one singular or plural subject or predicate) or **compound** (two or more singular or plural subjects or predicates).

The basic order for English sentences is subject-predicate, but that order is reversed in questions, *there is/are* statements, and sentences that are inverted for effect. There are four common subject-predicate patterns: **s-v, s-lv-c, s-v-o,** and **s-v-io-o.**

A **clause** is a group of words containing a subject and predicate. Clauses may be **subordinate** or **independent**. There are four types of sentences: **simple** (one independent clause), **compound** (two independent clauses), **complex** (one independent clause and one or more subordinate clauses), and **compound-complex** (two or more independent clauses and one or more subordinate clauses).

PRACTICE ON YOUR OWN

Choose a page in a newspaper, magazine, a memo from work or school, or a book you've been reading. Identify sentence parts and patterns—subjects and predicates, complements and objects. Find all four sentence patterns and all four types of sentences.

Practice Answers and Explanations

PRACTICE 1

1. A watched pot never boils. (The simple subject is *pot*.)

2. Every evening, the sun sets over these hills.

3. There are strange goings-on around here these days.

4. What are you doing?

5. Ever since childhood, Lukas has been very artistic.

6. [You] choose your friends carefully. (The subject is understood to be *you*.)

PRACTICE 2

1. Unfortunately, Carlos and Jude did not get along well. *compound*

2. Thinking of you is my favorite pastime. *single*

3. Unlike Lucinda, I do believe in miracles. *single*

4. There are many false claims and exaggerated truths during a political campaign. *compound*

5. No termites or carpenter ants were found by the inspector. *compound* (Note that the verb is passive; see chapter 4.)

PRACTICE 3

1. *I* is the subject; it is who won't be recognizable.

2. *Boys* is the subject. *Team* is part of the prepositional phrase *on the baseball team.*

3. *Raj* is the subject; he is the one who *would not raise*.

4. The *gym* is in disrepair. *School* is part of a prepositional phrase.

5. *Color* is the subject, so the verb is the singular *is*, not the plural *are*. *Walls* is part of the prepositional phrase *of these walls*.

PRACTICE 4

1. For many years, / the Republic of Congo / was a colony of Belgium. (Note that *for many years* is part of the predicate, not the subject, since it describes how long the country was a colony.)

2. Contrary to popular belief, / most species of snakes / are not poisonous. (Note that *species* is the simple subject, not *snakes*, which is in a prepositional phrase that modifies *species* (What kind of species?). Also note that *contrary to popular belief* is actually part of the predicate, not the subject.)

3. The most popular fruit in the world / is the mango. (Here *fruit* is the simple subject; *world* is in a prepositional phrase that modifies *fruit* (Where is it?).)

4. The African continent / is full of rich natural resources, including diamonds and oil.

5. Have / you / heard the news? (Here, *have* is a helping verb and part of the predicate, but because of the question structure, it is separated from the rest of the predicate.)

PRACTICE 5

1. Yes. *Was* is a linking verb. *A colony of Belgium* describes *the Republic of Congo*.

2. Yes. *Are* is a linking verb. *Not poisonous* describes *species*.

3. Yes. *Is* is a linking verb. *Mango* renames *most popular fruit*.

4. Yes. *Is* is once again a linking verb. *Full of rich natural resources* describes *African continent*.

5. No. *The news* does not describe *you*, and *have heard* is not a linking verb; you cannot replace it with an equal sign and have a coherent sentence.

PRACTICE 6

1. *Wife* directly receives the action of the verb; she is *put*.

2. *Me* directly receives the action of *startled*.

3. *Shelter* directly receives the action; it is what the general *found*.

4. *Tyler* directly receives the action of *drops*.

PRACTICE 7

1. Sanford / should offer Anne that position.

2. [You] / Please give Elliot my best.

3. I / am offering you a second chance.

4. Minsun / is sending me mixed signals about our relationship.

PRACTICE 8

1. tv. *Love* acts on the direct object *chocolate chip cookies*.

2. lv. *Are* links the subject *you* to the complement *true love*.

3. tv. *Offer* acts on the direct object *unconditional love*. *You* is the indirect object.

4. iv. *Live* does not take an object. (*For love* is a prepositional phrase; notice that *love* cannot be an object because it does not receive the action of the verb.)

5. tv. *Save* acts on the direct object *me*.

PRACTICE 9

1. Simple. [A stumble / may prevent a fall.]

2. Complex. [(You) never / trouble trouble] [until trouble / troubles you.]

3. Complex. [(You) / deceive the rich and powerful [if you / will] but don't insult them.] (Note that *deceive . . . but don't insult* is a compound predicate; since both verbs share the same subject, the understood *you*, this is not a compound sentence.)

4. Simple. [(You) / speak the truth but leave immediately after.] (Again, *speak . . . but leave* is a compound predicate. There is only one subject and therefore only one clause here, so this is a simple sentence.)

5. Simple. The subject is *handful*; the linking verb *is*; and the complement *worth a bushel of brains*.

6. Compound-complex. [(You) / be happy [while you / re living], [for you / re a long time dead.]

CHAPTER 2 TEST

Part A: Questions 1–6 refer to the following sentence:

Reading gives me pleasure, but writing gives me peace.

1. <u>Reading</u> is a/an
    - (A) subject.
    - (B) predicate.
    - (C) direct object.
    - (D) indirect object.
    - (E) intransitive verb.

2. [G]ives is a/an
    - (A) linking verb.
    - (B) transitive verb.
    - (C) intransitive verb.
    - (D) helping verb.
    - (E) predicate.

3. [M]e is a/an
    - (A) subject.
    - (B) predicate.
    - (C) direct object.
    - (D) indirect object.
    - (E) complement.

4. [P]leasure is a/an
    - (A) subject.
    - (B) predicate.
    - (C) direct object.
    - (D) indirect object.
    - (E) complement.

5. The sentence pattern is
    - (A) s-v, s-v.
    - (B) s-v-o, s-v-o.
    - (C) s-v-io-o, s-v-io-o.
    - (D) s-lv-c, s-lv-c.
    - (E) s-v-o, s-v-io-o.

6. The sentence type is
    - (A) simple.
    - (B) compound.
    - (C) complex.
    - (D) compound-complex.
    - (E) inverted.

Part B: Questions 7–13 refer to the following sentence:

A professional writer is an amateur who didn't quit. —*Richard Bach*

7. The subject of this sentence is
    - (A) professional.
    - (B) writer.
    - (C) amateur.
    - (D) who.
    - (E) quit.

8. The complete predicate of this sentence is

    (A) a professional writer is an amateur who didn't quit.

    (B) didn't quit.

    (C) who didn't quit.

    (D) an amateur who didn't quit.

    (E) is an amateur who didn't quit.

9. The verb <u>is</u> is a/an

    (A) linking verb.

    (B) helping verb.

    (C) transitive verb.

    (D) intransitive verb.

    (E) predicate.

10. [A]mateur is a/an

    (A) subject.

    (B) predicate.

    (C) direct object.

    (D) indirect object.

    (E) complement.

11. [W]ho didn't quit is a/an

    (A) prepositional phrase.

    (B) independent clause.

    (C) subordinate clause.

    (D) predicate.

    (E) all of the above.

12. The sentence pattern is

    (A) [s-lv-c [s-v]].

    (B) [s-lv-c].

    (C) [s-v-o][s-v].

    (D) [s-v-io-o].

    (E) [s-v [s-lv-c]].

13. The sentence type is

    (A) simple.

    (B) compound.

    (C) complex.

    (D) compound-complex.

    (E) inverted.

Part C: Questions 14–20 refer to the following sentence:

If you wish to be a writer, write!
—*Epictetus*

14. [Y]ou is a/an

    (A) subject.

    (B) predicate.

    (C) direct object.

    (D) indirect object.

    (E) complement.

15. [W]ish is a/an

    (A) linking verb.

    (B) helping verb.

    (C) transitive verb.

    (D) intransitive verb.

    (E) predicate.

16. The direct object of this sentence is

    (A) wish.
    (B) writer.
    (C) you.
    (D) to be a writer.
    (E) no object

17. <u>If you wish to be a writer</u> is a/an

    (A) prepositional phrase.
    (B) independent clause.
    (C) subordinate clause.
    (D) predicate.
    (E) all of the above

18. <u>Write!</u> is a/an

    (A) predicate.
    (B) independent clause.
    (C) imperative statement.
    (D) base verb.
    (E) all of the above

19. The sentence pattern is

    (A) [s-v].
    (B) [s-v-o].
    (C) [s-v-o][s-v].
    (D) [s-v-io-o].
    (E) [s-lv-c][s-v].

20. The sentence type is

    (A) simple.
    (B) compound.
    (C) complex.
    (D) compound-complex.
    (E) inverted.

**ANSWERS AND EXPLANATIONS
BEGIN ON NEXT PAGE**

Answers and Explanations

1. A

The gerund *reading* is the subject of the first independent clause, *Reading gives me pleasure.*

2. B

Gives is a transitive verb, taking the direct object *pleasure.*

3. D

Me is the indirect object of *gives*; *me* receives the *pleasure.*

4. C

Pleasure is the direct object of the verb *gives*; it is what is given.

5. C

There are two independent clauses here joined by the coordinating conjunction *but.* Both clauses follow the s-v-io-o pattern.

6. B

This is a compound sentence—two independent clauses, no subordinate clauses.

7. B

Writer is the subject; the writer *is.*

8. E

The predicate is the verb and any complement, modifiers, and phrases that follow: *is an amateur who didn't quit.*

9. A

Is links the subject (*writer*) to its complement (*an amateur who didn't quit*).

10. E

Amateur describes *writer*; it is the subject complement.

11. C

This clause cannot stand alone; the relative pronoun *who* sets it off as a subordinate clause.

12.   A

The complement includes a subordinate clause *who didn't quit*, so the pattern is [s-lv-c [s-v]].

13.   C

An independent and subordinate clause together create a complex sentence.

14.   A

You is the subject—who or what *wishes*.

15.   C

In this sentence, *wish* is transitive—it takes the object *to be a writer*.

16.   D

The complete object is *to be a writer*—it is what receives the action of *wish*.

17.   C

If is a subordinating conjunction introducing a subordinate clause that cannot stand alone.

18.   E

Write! is an imperative sentence—the understood but unstated subject is *you*. Thus, it is also the predicate and the base verb. It is an independent clause—it can stand alone.

19.   C

The subordinate clause follows the s-v-o pattern (the object is *to be a writer*); the imperative clause is s-v, although the subject (*you*) is unstated.

20.   C

The sentence contains an independent and subordinate clause, so it is complex.

CHAPTER 3

VERB FORMS AND TENSES

Some—perhaps most—of this will be old hat for you. You don't need to be told that the past tense of *do* is *did,* but maybe you need to be reminded of irregular past participle forms or what the subjunctive is. And though you already know many of the rules, it's probably been years since you've seen them written out clearly.

VERBS

As you know, verbs express an **action** or **state of being**. All verbs include a form of the **base verb**, which expresses the main action or state of being. **Helping verbs**, such as *will, would,* and *should,* help express some tenses (when the action occurred).

A **linking verb** connects a subject to its complement (see chapter 2). When *be* is not a helping verb (*When will you be leaving?*), it is usually a linking verb (*I will be free*).

A **transitive verb** takes a direct object (a person or thing that directly receives the action). A transitive verb may have an indirect object as well (a person or thing receiving the direct object). **Intransitive verbs** do not have a complement or a direct object (nothing receives the action of the verb).

BASIC VERB FORMS

English verbs have three basic forms from which the various tenses are fashioned.

Base Form

The base form of a verb is the first-person singular present tense: the form you'd use in a sentence after *I* or *to*:

I *want, think, see, feel, create, carry*

To *want, think, see, feel, create, carry*

The exception is the verb *be*, which uses *be* as its base form, not *am* (I *am*).

Present Participle Form

The present participle is formed by adding *-ing* to the base form:

wanting, thinking, seeing, feeling, creating, carrying

The present participle is used with different helping verbs to form specific tenses:

am thinking   was thinking   had been thinking

Past Participle Form

Irregular verbs take a variety of past participle forms: *thought, seen, felt*. You'll cover these in detail in a moment. For regular verbs, the past participle is formed by adding *-ed* to the base form. If the verb ends in *e*, add *d*; if it ends in *y*, change the *y* to *i* and add *-ed*:

wanted   created   carried   hurried

The past participle is used with different helping verbs to form specific tenses:

have created   had created   should have created

PRACTICE 1

Write the base, present participle, and past participle forms for the verbs listed below. Some may already be in their base form.

Verb	Base	Present Participle	Past Participle
1. fades	Fade	Fading	Faded
2. snores	Snore	Snoring	Snored
3. dry	dry	drying	dried
4. complains	complain	complaining	Complained
5. dances	dance	dancing	danced

TENSES

Simple Tenses

The simple tenses are derived from the base form of the verb. The simple present and past do not use helping verbs.

SIMPLE PRESENT

For regular verbs, all persons and numbers *except* third-person singular use the **base form** of the verb. The third-person singular (*he, she,* and *it*) uses the base form + *s/-es*. (For most verbs ending in *y*, change the *y* to an *i* and add *es*.)

	Singular		Plural	
First person	I	*talk, smile*	we	*talk, smile*
Second person	you	*talk, smile*	you	*talk, smile*
Third person	he, she, it	*talks, smiles*	they	*talk, smile*

Some verbs are irregular. The big present-tense irregulars are *be* and *have. Have's* third-person singular form is *has,* not *haves,* while *be* is irregular all around, as shown in the following table:

	Singular		Plural	
First person	I	*am*	we	*are*
Second person	you	*are*	you	*are*
Third person	he, she, it	*is*	they	*are*

Use the simple present for the following:

1. Habitual actions: Henderson's dog always <u>follows</u> me down the block.

2. Actions occurring at the moment: I <u>think</u> I <u>see</u> someone I <u>know</u> over there.

3. Stating facts or general truths: The first Tuesday in November <u>is</u> election day.
   Absolute power <u>corrupts</u> absolutely.

SIMPLE PAST

For regular verbs, form the past tense by **adding -ed to the verb base**. (Add -*d* if the verb ends in *e*; if the verb ends in *y*, change *y* to *i* and add -*ed*):

      cried   insisted   reviewed   surprised

Use the simple past for actions completed entirely in the past:

      I <u>cried</u> tears of joy when I <u>heard</u> the news.

IRREGULAR PAST TENSE AND PAST PARTICIPLE

Over 100 English verbs are irregular: they take different forms for the past tense and/or past participle. The following pages list the most common irregular verbs and their base, past, and past participle forms. Take a few minutes to review the list. Highlight any verbs whose irregular forms you haven't mastered.

The most irregular verb—*be*—has past and past participle forms that change in person and number:

Person	Present	Past	Past Participle
I	*am*	*was*	*have been*
you	*are*	*were*	*have been*
he, she, it	*is*	*was*	*has been*
we	*are*	*were*	*have been*
they	*are*	*were*	*have been*

Base Form	Simple Past	Past Participle
These past and past participle forms are the same:		
have	had	had
dig	dug	dug
bleed	bled	bled
hear	heard	heard
hold	held	held
light	lit	lit

(continued on next page)

meet	met	met
lay	laid	laid
pay	paid	paid
say	said	said
sell	sold	sold
tell	told	told
shine	shone	shone
shoot	shot	shot
sit	sat	sat
spit	spat	spat
spin	spun	spun
creep	crept	crept
keep	kept	kept
sleep	slept	slept
deal	dealt	dealt
kneel	knelt	knelt
leave	left	left
mean	meant	meant
send	sent	sent
spend	spent	spent
bring	brought	brought
buy	bought	bought
catch	caught	caught
fight	fought	fought
teach	taught	taught
think	thought	thought
feed	fed	fed
flee	fled	fled
find	found	found
grind	ground	ground

Base Form	Simple Past	Past Participle
These have different past and past participle forms:		
begin	began	begun
ring	rang	rung
sing	sang	sung
spring	sprang	sprung
do	did	done
go	went	gone
see	saw	seen
lie	lay	lain
drink	drank	drunk
shrink	shrank	shrunk
sink	sank	sunk
stink	stank	stunk
swear	swore	sworn
tear	tore	torn
wear	wore	worn
blow	blew	blown
draw	drew	drawn
fly	flew	flown
grow	grew	grown
know	knew	known
throw	threw	thrown
drive	drove	driven
strive	strove	striven
choose	chose	chosen
rise	rose	risen
break	broke	broken
speak	spoke	spoken
fall	fell	fallen
shake	shook	shaken
take	took	taken
forget	forgot	forgotten

(continued on next page)

get	got	gotten
give	gave	given
forgive	forgave	forgiven
forsake	forsook	forsaken
hide	hid	hidden
ride	rode	ridden
bite	bit	bitten
write	wrote	written
freeze	froze	frozen
steal	stole	stolen

Base Form	Simple Past	Past Participle
These past participles are the same form as the base:		
come	came	come
overcome	overcame	overcome
run	ran	run

SIMPLE FUTURE

Form the simple future with the helping verb *will* + **base form**:

will debate will be will announce

Use the simple future for the following:

1. Actions that will take place in the future:

   The judges <u>will</u> <u>announce</u> the winner tomorrow.

2. Actions that are predictable given certain circumstances:

   Your property taxes <u>will</u> <u>increase</u> significantly if you move closer to the city.

As you'll see later, the future can also be expressed by the present progressive tense.

PRACTICE 2

In each sentence, put the base form of the verb in the proper form of the simple tense.

Example: Yesterday we ___paid___ (pay) off our mortgage.

1. Next week, I ___will share___ (share) our ideas with the town council.

2. Last month, I ___went___ (go) to the museum six times.

3. Meena always ___buys___ (buy) her produce from an organic farmer.

4. When I was young, I ___lived___ (live) on Main Street and ___rode___ (ride) my bike to school.

Perfect Tenses

The perfect tenses are used to indicate actions that are, have been, or will be completed before another stated time.

MEMORY TIP

One meaning of *perfect* is completed; the perfect tenses describe actions that are, have been, or will be completed.

PRESENT PERFECT

To form the present perfect, add *have* or *has* + **past participle**:

> has asked   have been   has helped

Use the present perfect for the following actions:

1. Actions that began in the past and are still occurring in the present: (Note: This use of the present perfect applies to verbs that describe states of being and is an exception to the general rule, stated above, that perfect tenses indicate completed actions.)

   I have been a volunteer at the hospital for the last 15 years.

2. Actions that began in the past and have been completed at an unspecified time:

   We have explored several alternatives but have not found a viable solution.

PAST PERFECT

This tense is formed with **had** + **past participle**:

      had asked   had been   had suggested

Use the past perfect for actions already completed before another past time or action:

> I <u>had</u> <u>been</u> a hospital volunteer for years before I accepted a paid position.

> Before my eighth birthday, I <u>had</u> already <u>moved</u> ten times.

> He <u>had</u> <u>been</u> <u>digging</u> for over an hour before he asked for a larger shovel.

FUTURE PERFECT

Form this tense by adding **will** + **have** + **past participle**:

      will have decided   will have found   will have forgotten

Use it for actions that will be completed before or by a specific future time:

> By the time the renovations are completed, I <u>will</u> <u>have</u> <u>gone</u> 10 percent over budget.

> Before our vacation is over, we <u>will</u> <u>have</u> <u>seen</u> all seven wonders of the world.

PRACTICE 3

Use the context of the sentences below to determine which tense belongs in each blank.

Example: I <u>have eaten</u> (eat) at Nellie's Diner every Wednesday for over a year now.

1. I ___have missed___(miss) the bus three times already this week.
2. By the time you get back home, you ___will have___ (forget) me. _forgotten_
3. I give up; Cecile's incessant badgering ___has worn___ (wear) me down.
4. I ___had intended___(intend) to say something completely different from what actually came out of my mouth.

Progressive Tenses

The aptly named progressive tenses describe actions *in progress* at a particular time. The six progressive tenses follow. Notice that each tense's name describes its form. For example, the *present progressive* is formed with the *present* tense of *be* and the *progressive* form (the present participle).

PRESENT PROGRESSIVE

To form this tense, use the **present tense of *be* (*am, is, are*) + present participle (*-ing*)**:

is buying   are talking   am thinking

Use the present progressive for the following:

1. Actions currently in progress:

    We <u>are</u> <u>thinking</u> of throwing a surprise party for Ted's birthday.

2. Future actions that will occur at a specific time:

    We <u>are</u> <u>going</u> to win back our title next year.

PAST PROGRESSIVE

The past progressive uses the **past tense of *be* (*was, were*) + present participle (*-ing*)**:

was counting   were looking   were sleeping

Use the past progressive for actions that were in progress in the past:

They <u>were</u> <u>looking</u> for you everywhere!

FUTURE PROGRESSIVE

Form the future progressive by using ***will* + *be* + present participle (*-ing*)**:

will be waiting   will be singing   will be trying

Use the future progressive for actions that will be in progress in the future:

I <u>will</u> <u>be</u> <u>fighting</u> an uphill battle to get this motion approved.

PRESENT PERFECT PROGRESSIVE

The present perfect progressive uses *have/has* + *been* + **present participle**:

>   have been thinking   has been waiting   have been fighting

Use the present perfect progressive to express an action that has been in progress for a length of time:

> We <u>have</u> <u>been</u> <u>thinking</u> about throwing Ted a surprise birthday party.

PAST PERFECT PROGRESSIVE

Form the past perfect progressive with *had* + *been* + **present participle**:

>   had been thinking   had been expecting   had been feeling

Use the past perfect progressive to express an action that had been in progress for a length of time before another past action:

> We <u>had</u> <u>been</u> <u>thinking</u> of throwing Ted a surprise birthday party until he told us how much he hated surprises.

FUTURE PERFECT PROGRESSIVE

For the future perfect progressive, use *will* + *have* + *been* + **present participle**:

>   will have been serving   will have been studying

Use the future perfect progressive to express how long an action will be in progress:

> By the time I finish my degree, I <u>will</u> <u>have</u> <u>been</u> <u>studying</u> ants for two decades.

PRACTICE 4

Use the context to determine the correct form of the verb to insert in the blank.

Example: You <u>have been going</u> (go) on for hours now.

1. I __have been__ (think) about you constantly since the day we met.

2. I __had been__ (think) about you constantly—until I met Horace.

~~was~~
thinking
✗ 3. I ~~~~ ~~~~ (think) about you when you called.

4. I __will be__ (think) about you while you are gone.

Conditional Tenses

The conditional tenses are generally used to express what we *would* do or things that *would* happen. Conditional statements have two parts: a subordinating "if" clause (the condition) and an independent "then" clause (the result):

[If I take one extra course each semester,]   [I should graduate a semester early.]
    [subordinating "if" clause]   [independent "then" clause]

The verb forms in each clause vary depending upon the kind of conditional statement (see the following table).

If your sentence…	Use this in the "if" clause:	Use this in the "then" clause:	Example:
states a conditional fact	simple present	simple present	When the car <u>hits</u> 65 miles per hour, it <u>starts</u> to shimmy.
makes a prediction	simple present	*will, can, may, should,* or *might* + base form of base verb	If I <u>take</u> one extra course each semester, I should <u>graduate</u> a semester early.
speculates about something unlikely to happen	past tense	*could, might,* or *would* + base form of base verb	If I <u>won</u> the lottery, I would <u>quit</u> my job and <u>travel</u> the world.
speculates about something that didn't happen in the past	past perfect	*could have, might have,* or *would have* + past participle	If I <u>had won</u> the lottery, I <u>would have quit</u> my job and <u>traveled</u> the world.
speculates about something that's contrary to fact	*were* (the subjunctive; see next page)	*could, might,* or *would* + base form of base verb	If I <u>were</u> rich, I <u>would quit</u> my job and <u>travel</u> the world.

PRACTICE 5

Circle the correct verb form in each of the sentences below.

1. If I (leave/left) now, I (should get/would have gotten) there on time.

2. If I (could have/had) ten arms, I (could get/could have gotten) a lot more done.

3. If I (was/were) famous, I (would have/will have) no trouble getting a reservation.

4. If I (had gone/went) with you to the party, I (would have been/would be) the only one without a costume.

5. When water (freezes/is frozen), it (will expand/expands).

Subjunctive Mood

Moods are different from tenses in that they are used for certain kinds of statements rather than to indicate when actions take place.

The present subjunctive expresses something wished for, requested, or contrary to fact. The subjunctive **mood** uses the **base form** for all verbs in the present tense except, as usual, *be*, which uses *were* for the subjunctive:

Dentists recommend that you <u>floss</u> your teeth daily.

If I <u>were</u> a little older, I might be a little wiser.

PRACTICE 6

Circle the correct verb form in the parentheses.

1. If only I (was/were) more successful.

2. I ask that you please (refrain/refraining) from applause until the end of the speech.

3. I only wish I (was/were) there for you when you needed me.

4. Connie recommends that Elijah (does/do) some research before he plants his garden.

GETTING YOUR TENSES RIGHT

Knowing which tense to use comes naturally for the most part—unless, of course, English is not your native language. In that case, practice, practice, practice! Here are a few guidelines for those tenses that may tend to get you tangled:

Memorize those irregular forms. If you don't yet know the past tense and past participles of irregular verbs, commit them to memory.

Don't confuse the past tense with the past perfect. The past perfect indicates that an action *has already been completed* by a certain time in the past:

By the time we reached the store, it <u>had</u> closed. (past perfect)

Don't overuse past perfect. Don't use the past perfect to describe two past actions that occurred almost *simultaneously*; use the past tense for both actions:

>**Incorrect:** As soon as the boat <u>had left</u> the dock, Damon <u>began</u> to feel sick.

>**Correct:** As soon as the boat <u>left</u> the dock, Damon <u>began</u> to feel sick.

Don't forget the subjunctive. The subjunctive is slipping out of everyday usage, but it should be used to express what is wished for, requested, or contrary to fact.

PRACTICE ON YOUR OWN

Look through a magazine or newspaper article to identify the tenses covered in this lesson. See if you can find examples of each tense and each conditional construction as well as the subjunctive.

SUMMARY

Basic Verb Forms

Base form: Use the first-person, singular, present-tense form—the form that fills in the blank in the sentence *I* _____. (Exception: The base form of *be* is *be*.)

Present participle: Add *-ing* to the base form.

Past participle: For regular verbs, add *-ed* to the base form.

Main Tenses

Tense	Use for...
Simple present	Habitual actions, actions occurring at the moment, and stating facts or general truths
Simple past	Actions completed entirely in the past
Simple future	Actions that will take place in the future; actions that are predictable given certain circumstances
Present perfect	Actions that began in the past and are still occurring in the present; actions that began in the past and have been completed
Past perfect	Actions already completed at the time of another past action; actions already completed by a specific past time
Future perfect	Actions that will be completed before or by a specific future time
Present progressive	Actions currently in progress; future actions that will occur at a specific time

Tense	Use for...
Past progressive	Actions that were in progress in the past
Future progressive	Actions that will be in progress in the future
Present perfect progressive	Actions that have been in progress for a length of time
Past perfect progressive	Actions that had been in progress for a length of time
Future perfect progressive	Actions that will be in progress for a length of time leading up to a specific future time

Conditional and Subjunctive

Conditional statements have two parts: the "if" clause and the "then" clause. The tenses you use depend upon the kind of conditional statement you're making.

The **subjunctive** expresses things that are wished for, requested, or contrary to fact. Because you don't often use the subjunctive in speech, it may sound awkward or incorrect.

Practice Answers and Explanations

PRACTICE 1

1. fade, fading, faded

2. snore, snoring, snored

3. dry, drying, dried

4. complain, complaining, complained

5. dance, dancing, danced

PRACTICE 2

1. *will share.* The action will take place in the future, so use the simple future.

2. *went.* The action was completed entirely in the past, so use the simple past.

3. *buys.* This is a habitual action, so use the simple present.

4. *lived, rode.* Both actions were completed entirely in the past, so the verbs should be in the simple past.

PRACTICE 3

1. *have missed.* The context suggests that this action occurred in the past and may still be occurring.

2. *will have forgotten.* The action will be completed by a specific time.

3. *has worn.* The action began in the past and has been completed at some unspecified time.

4. *had intended.* The action had already been completed by the time of another past action (saying something).

PRACTICE 4

1. *have been thinking.* The present perfect progressive expresses actions that have been in progress for a length of time.

2. *had been thinking.* The past perfect progressive is used for actions that had been in progress for a length of time until another past action.

3. *was thinking.* The past progressive indicates that actions were in progress in the past (*when you called*).

4. *will be thinking.* The future progressive expresses actions that will be in progress in the future.

PRACTICE 5

1. *leave, should get.* This sentence makes a prediction, so it needs the simple tense in the "if" clause and *should* + base form in the "then" clause.

2. *had, could get.* This sentence speculates about something unlikely to happen, so it requires the past tense in the "if" clause and *could* + base form in the "then" clause.

3. *were, would have.* This sentence speculates about something that's contrary to fact, so the "if" verb should be *were* and the "then" verb *would* + base form.

4. *had gone, would have been.* This sentence speculates about something that didn't happen in the past, so the "if" verb should be in the past perfect and the "then" verb *would* + *have* + past participle.

5. *freezes, expands.* This sentence states a conditional fact, so both verbs should be in the simple present.

PRACTICE 6

1. *were.* The present tense subjunctive of *be* is *were.*

2. *refrain.* This verb expresses a request, so it is subjunctive.

3. *were.* This verb expresses a wish, so it is subjunctive.

4. *do.* This verb uses the subjunctive to express recommendation or request.

CHAPTER 3 TEST

Choose the verb or verbs that correctly complete each sentence.

1. The dream I had last night is one I _____ for many years now.

    (A) have
    (B) have had
    (C) am having
    (D) have been having
    (E) had

2. Cheyenne _____ she would never lie to me again.

    (A) swears
    (B) swored
    (C) sworn
    (D) did swear
    (E) swore

3. By the time the troops _____, the city _____ deserted.

    (A) arrived, had been
    (B) arrived, was
    (C) had arrived, had been
    (D) arrive, is
    (E) did arrive, was

4. The boat _____ less than a quarter mile off shore.

    (A) sank
    (B) sunk
    (C) sinked
    (D) sanked
    (E) been sinking

5. LuAnne _____ five classes this semester.

    (A) took
    (B) did take
    (C) takes
    (D) is taking
    (E) will have taken

6. If you _____ the truth, you wouldn't be in this position now.

    (A) know
    (B) knew
    (C) had known
    (D) did know
    (E) known

7. We _____ there on time.

    (A) had been
    (B) was
    (C) were
    (D) having been
    (E) were being

8. Today more people _____ by email than ever before.

    (A) communicates
    (B) have communicated
    (C) communicate
    (D) are communicating
    (E) have been communicating

9. The foreperson has asked that Tyson _____ an anger management class.

    (A) would attend
    (B) will attend
    (C) does attend
    (D) attends
    (E) attend

10. The number of families living in poverty _____ by another 5 percent by the time Maya leaves office.

    (A) will have dropped
    (B) will drop
    (C) will be dropping
    (D) dropped
    (E) is dropping

11. I _____ devastated if you go.

    (A) am
    (B) will be
    (C) have been
    (D) will have been
    (E) were

12. Studies show that most voters _____ their leaders based on personality rather than issues.

    (A) will choose
    (B) have chosen
    (C) are choosing
    (D) choose
    (E) chose

13. If you have numbness in your arms, it _____ a sign of carpal tunnel syndrome.

    (A) is
    (B) were
    (C) might be
    (D) could have been
    (E) was

14. Immediately after he uttered the words, Rashaad _____ what he said.

    (A) regretted
    (B) did regret
    (C) had regretted
    (D) would have regretted
    (E) was regretting

15. We have been _____.

    (A) forsaked
    (B) forsaken
    (C) forsook
    (D) forsoken
    (E) forsake

16. It took me 20 years, but I have finally _____ my fear of heights.

    (A) overcame
    (B) overcomed
    (C) overcoming
    (D) overcomes
    (E) overcome

17. Contrary to what they previously believed, scientists _____ that spinal cord cells *can* regenerate.

    (A) discovered
    (B) did discover
    (C) have discovered
    (D) discover
    (E) had discovered

18. Complaints about customer service _____ steadily since Juliana took over.

    (A) have been declining
    (B) declined
    (C) are declining
    (D) were declining
    (E) had declined

19. Rudy _____ getting rid of his television, but he is not sure he can live without it.

    (A) considered
    (B) is considering
    (C) was considering
    (D) had considered
    (E) considers

20. At least once a week, Jelena _____ her house top to bottom.

    (A) is cleaning
    (B) has cleaned
    (C) will clean
    (D) will be cleaning
    (E) cleans

**ANSWERS AND EXPLANATIONS
BEGIN ON NEXT PAGE**

Answers and Explanations

1. B

The present perfect is used for actions that began in the past and are still occurring.

2. E

The irregular past tense form of *swear* is *swore*.

3. A

The second action was completed by the time of the first, so it is in the past perfect.

4. A

Sank is the simple past form of *sink*.

5. D

The present progressive expresses actions that are currently in progress (*this semester*).

6. C

The past perfect is used for actions already completed by a specific past time.

7. C

The simple past expresses that an action has been completed entirely in the past.

8. C

The simple present expresses facts or current general truths (*today*). Note that while choice (D) is not grammatically incorrect, choice (C) is more concise, and the focus of this sentence is not on an action in progress at the present moment.

9. E

This sentence expresses a request and requires the subjunctive.

10. A

The future perfect expresses actions that will be completed by a specific future time.

11. B

The simple future expresses actions that will take place in the future and actions that are predictable given certain circumstances (*if you go*).

12. D

The simple present tense is used for stating general facts or truths as well as habitual actions.

13. C

This conditional statement makes a prediction and needs the present tense *might* + base in the "then" clause.

14. A

These actions both occurred at essentially the same time in the past, so both should be in the simple past.

15. B

The irregular past participle form of *forsake* is *forsaken*.

16. E

The irregular past tense form of *overcome* is *overcome*.

17. C

The present perfect expresses actions that began in the past and have been completed.

18. A

The present perfect progressive expresses actions that have been in progress for some time (*since Juliana took over*).

19. B

The present progressive is for actions currently in progress.

20. E

The simple present expresses habitual actions.

CHAPTER 4

HELPING VERBS, INFINITIVES, AND OTHER TRICKY MATTERS

Helping verbs can indicate the tense of the base verb; only two tenses (the simple past and simple present) don't require them. Helping verbs also have specific meanings—so it's important to use the right one.

HELPING VERBS

There are two kinds of helping verbs. The first are forms of **have**, **do**, and **be** that indicate different tenses. The second, called **modals**, do not change.

	Modals:
Have: have, has, had	can, could
Do: do, does, did	may, might
Be: be, am, is, are, was, were, being, been	must, ought, need
	shall, should
	will, would

Some of these are always helping verbs—*must* and *should*, for example. (Even in a sentence like *I must*, the action verb is unstated but understood from the context: *I must* go or *I must* try.) But some helping verbs also function as base verbs. *Have* can be a transitive verb meaning *to possess* (I *have* a dog); *been* can be a linking verb indicating a state of being (I have *been* lonely).

Forms to Use with Helping Verbs

Idiomatically, only certain verb forms can follow a helping verb, and some helping verbs must work in specific combinations. Even if they're old hat to you, these rules are worth a thorough review:

- Use the **base form** after modal helping verbs:

    I must <u>talk</u> to you right away.

- Use the **base form** after forms of *do*:

    Judges <u>do</u> not <u>make</u> laws; they interpret them.

- Use the **present participle** after forms of *be*:

    I had <u>been</u> <u>expecting</u> such a reply.

Notice that this is true only when *be* is a helping verb, not when it's a linking verb:

> **Helping verb:** They have <u>been</u> thwarting our efforts to pass this measure. (*Have* and *been* are helping verbs; *thwarting* is the base verb.)

> **Linking verb:** Our efforts to pass this measure have <u>been</u> thwarted. (*Have* is a helping verb, *been* is the base verb linking the subject [*efforts*] to the complement [*thwarted*].)

Remember, a word's *function* determines its part of speech. *Thwarted* could be the past tense verb or the adjective.

- Use the **past participle** after forms of *have*:

    I <u>had</u> <u>given</u> up on finding them.

- *Be* should be preceded by a modal, unless it is used as an imperative:

    This <u>could</u> <u>be</u> very interesting.
    <u>Be</u> good for grandma. (imperative)

- *Been* must be preceded by *have, has,* or *had*:

    I <u>had</u> <u>been</u> expecting such a reply.

PRACTICE 1

How would you correct the following verb errors?

1. I would have ~~help~~ *helped* you if you had ask.
2. I *have* been waiting for hours!
3. The air conditioner does not ~~working~~ *work* anymore.
4. The package should ~~arrived~~ *arrive* today.
5. Their predictions are always been correct.
   have

What Helping Verbs Mean

As the following chart shows, the modal helping verbs suggest very specific meanings.

Helping Verb	Meaning	Examples
will/would, shall	intention, obligation	We *shall* do our best. I *would* like to come along.
can/could	ability	I *can* say the alphabet backwards. We *could* help you paint that room.
may/might, can/ could	permission	*May* I join you? You *can* join us if you'd like.
may/might	possibility	I *may* join you later. The bill *might* pass by a slim margin.
should	recommendation, obligation	You *should* join us! You *should* do your homework.
should	expectation	We *should* win by a large margin.
must, have (to), ought (to), need (to)	necessity	You *must* join us. We *have to* win.

Note that some have more than one meaning. *He may come* can mean he has permission to come or that it's possible he will come. *I can come* means I am able to come.

PRACTICE 2

Insert the helping verb that conveys the correct meaning for the context.

1. Helene said we ___will___ [*may or can*] attend the meeting if we want.
2. We ___Shall___ do our best to make you comfortable during your stay.
3. Applications ___Should___ be received by January 1.
4. I think Col. Jenkins ___will___ [*may or might*] openly challenge you at the meeting tonight.

INFINITIVES AND GERUNDS

Which is correct: *I like to cook* or *I like cooking*?

Both are correct. Idiomatically, the verb *like* can be followed by either an **infinitive (*to* + base form)** or a **gerund (base form + -*ing*)**. But not all verbs are so flexible.

Gerunds

A gerund is a base verb form + -*ing* that functions as a noun. Don't confuse it with a present participle, which may be part of the verb or may function as an adjective:

> **Gerund** (noun; direct object): I love <u>cooking</u>.
>
> Part of the **verb** (present participle): I <u>am</u> <u>cooking</u>.
>
> **Adjective** (present participle): I've signed up for a <u>cooking</u> class.

Gerunds can be subjects, complements, or objects (direct objects, indirect objects, or objects of a preposition):

> **Subject:** <u>Painting</u> is my passion.
>
> **Complement:** My passion is <u>painting</u>.

PRACTICE 3

Determine whether the underlined words are gerunds or part of the verb. For each gerund, identify whether it is a subject, complement, or object.

1. <u>Helping</u> others is my main goal. *[handwritten: Gerund, Subject]*
2. I love <u>helping</u> others. *[handwritten: Part of verb — Gerund]*
3. My goal is <u>helping</u> others. *[handwritten: Gerund complement]*
4. Lulu has been <u>helping</u> me all day. *[handwritten: Part of verb]*

Use a gerund in the following situations:

- After a preposition:

   I am sorry *for* <u>asking</u> such a silly question.

- After certain verbs, including these:

admit	deny	imagine	quit
appreciate	discuss	keep	recall
avoid	dislike	miss	resist
can't help	enjoy	postpone	risk
consider	escape	practice	suggest
delay	finish	put off	tolerate

   Please *keep* <u>working</u> while I take this call.

Infinitives

Unlike gerunds, which share a form with present participles, infinitives have a form unto themselves: *to* + **base form**. Infinitives are often part of a verb phrase:

   I plan <u>to submit</u> my letter of resignation tomorrow.

MEMORY TIP

A **gerund** is a verb form ending in -*ing* functioning as a noun. An **infinitive** is the base form of a verb preceded by *to*.

To can also be a preposition, of course, as in *to the moon*. If it is followed by a verb, it is part of an infinitive; if it is followed by a noun or pronoun, it is a preposition.

   Infinitive: to bar an action, to screen applicants

   Preposition: to the bar, to the screen

Use an infinitive in the following situations:

- After certain verbs, including these:

agree	decide	need	refuse
ask	expect	offer	venture
beg	fail	plan	want
choose	hope	pretend	wish
claim	manage	promise	

  I *want* <u>to go</u> to the movies.

- After the following verbs, when they are directly followed by a noun or pronoun:

advise	convince	order	urge
allow	encourage	persuade	want
ask	expect	remind	warn
cause	force	require	
command	need	tell	

  I *warned* <u>you</u> not <u>to touch</u> that snake!

MEMORY TIP

If you're a native English speaker, you've heard these idioms all your life and know *"I have asked Wilma coming to the meeting,"* is wrong. If English is your second language, memorize these guidelines and then *read, read, read* to develop your understanding.

PRACTICE 4

In each sentence below, a verb in base form follows a blank. Indicate whether the gerund (*G*) or infinitive (*I*) correctly completes the sentence.

1. The commission hopes __I__ (stabilize) the wolf population within two years.

2. I have been thinking of __G__ (buy) a new car.

3. Nothing you say can convince me __I__ (change) my mind.

4. Lately, I've gotten into the habit of ___6___ (talk) out loud to myself.

5. We will not tolerate ___6___ (cheat) of any kind.

6. I miss ___6___ (talk) to you every day.

7. We will manage ___5___ (clean) up this mess somehow.

TROUBLESOME VERBS

Pop quiz: Which of the following sentences is correct?

    a. I will <u>lie</u> down for a nap.   **b.** I will <u>lay</u> down for a nap.

The correct answer is **a.** Even people with PhDs have trouble with this one! In fact, three sets of English verbs tend to give *everyone* trouble:

    lie/lay   **rise/raise**   **sit/set**

The words in each pair mean similar things, but not exactly the same thing. That's because one verb in each set takes an object—the action is performed on someone or something—and the other verb doesn't (the subject performs the action on itself):

No Object (Intransitive)	Takes an Object (Transitive)
lie: to rest or recline	**lay:** to put or place (something) down
I will lie down.	*Lay your body down.*
rise: to go up	**raise:** to move (something) up
[You] Rise and shine!	*Raise your hand.*
sit: to rest, to be seated	**set:** to put or place (something)
Please, Henrietta, sit down.	*Set your bags down.*

Note: The verb *set* can also mean to go down: *The sun <u>sets</u> in the west.* When *set* has this meaning, it does not take an object.

These troublesome verbs are also irregular in their past tense and past participle forms. The following chart gives their present participle, past, and past participle forms (see chapter 3).

Present	Present Participle (with *am*, *is*, *are*)	Past	Past Participle (with *have*, *has*, *had*)
lie	lying	lay	lain
lay	laying	laid	laid
rise	rising	rose	risen
raise	raising	raised	raised
sit	sitting	sat	sat
set	setting	set	set

PRACTICE 5

Choose the verb that will correctly complete each sentence. If the verb is transitive, circle the direct object.

1. It's been a long day; I'm going to (lay/lie) down for a while.
2. Please (raise/rise) for the National Anthem.
3. That's Glen, (setting/sitting) over there in the corner.
4. The stakes have (raised/risen); the project is more important now than ever.
5. After you (sit/set) your things down, come in the kitchen for some coffee.

CONSISTENCY

Remember the three core principles that underlie the rules for grammar and style: **balance**, **clarity**, and **consistency**. Consistency in verb tense, mood, and voice is essential for correctness and clarity.

Consistent Tense

A common grammar mistake, especially in narrative writing, is an unnecessary shift in verb tense. We do this in speech all the time: when describing a past event, we may get involved in the story and switch to the present tense (and back again):

> The storm intensified, and soon it starts raining so hard I can't see more than a few feet in front of me. I had to stop, praying that no one will hit me from behind.

You know that the action took place in the past—it starts in the past tense, and the context makes the present tense wrong. But the shifts between tenses are still disconcerting.

You may wish to tell the story in the present; it's a convention writers often use to make the story feel more immediate. But the verb tenses should be consistent:

Past: The storm <u>intensified</u>, and soon it <u>started</u> raining so hard I <u>couldn't</u> see more than a few feet in front of me. I <u>had</u> to stop, praying that no one <u>would</u> hit me from behind.

Present: The storm <u>intensifies</u>, and soon it <u>starts</u> raining so hard I <u>can't</u> see more than a few feet in front of me. I <u>have</u> to stop, praying that no one <u>will</u> hit me from behind.

Remember that consistency is a matter of avoiding *unnecessary* shifts. The shift is *necessary* if it indicates that the actions occurred at two different times:

Here we <u>are</u>—Telford, the town where I <u>was</u> born.

PRACTICE 6

Correct any unnecessary shifts in tense in the following paragraph.

I'd always wanted to go to the Grand Canyon, so I was thrilled when my dad announced we ~~will be~~ going there for our family vacation. Then he ~~tells~~ us we're going to drive instead of fly—a four-day journey with three kids crammed into a small car. I ~~tell~~ him he's off his rocker. That's when he told us we weren't going in *our* car—we're renting a Winnebago, and we're going to stay at campsites along the way. That was the kind of vacation I ~~have~~ always dreamed of. I am sure it wasn't easy for my parents to plan that trip, but I will always remember it as the best vacation of my life.

Consistent Mood

Grammatical **mood** refers to the kind of statement you are making. Moods are not tenses; they indicate the nature of the statement—whether it is a fact, wish, or command. You already know the **subjunctive**, the least common of the three moods in English (see chapter 3), and the **imperative** (see chapter 2). The mood in which most sentences are written is the **indicative**.

INDICATIVE

The indicative mood indicates or expresses facts, opinions, and questions. Conjugate verbs normally—that is, use the tense that will accurately express when the action occurs.

George Washington <u>was</u> the first president of the United States.

What <u>did</u> you <u>say</u>?

IMPERATIVE

The imperative is used for commands or expressions of advice. The imperative takes the base form of the verb and often omits the subject (usually an understood *you*):

Always <u>proofread</u> your résumé before sending it.

Hurry up!

SUBJUNCTIVE

Use the subjunctive for things wished for, requested, or contrary to fact:

We ask that Kyle <u>keep</u> his dog in a cage while we visit with the baby.

If I <u>were</u> you, I'd accept Josh's offer.

Shifting Mood

An unnecessary mood shift, like an unnecessary tense shift, can be disconcerting or confusing. The following paragraph shifts from the indicative to the imperative midway through. To be consistent, it should be entirely in the imperative or the indicative mood:

Shifting: Applicants must fill out all forms completely. All forms should be typed or filled out in black or blue ink. Staple and clearly label each supporting document. Submit your application no later than January 12.

Indicative: Applicants must fill out all forms completely. All forms should be typed or filled out in black or blue ink. Each supporting document must be stapled and clearly labeled. Applications must be received no later than January 12.

Imperative: Fill out all forms completely. Type your application or fill it out using black or blue ink. Staple and clearly label each supporting document. Submit your application no later than January 12.

Again, remember that sometimes a shift is necessary:

As Mary Heaton Vorse wrote, "The art of writing is the art of applying the seat of the pants to the seat of the chair." So, if you want to be a writer, sit down and write!

Imp! Replace smoke detector batteries twice a year.

PRACTICE 7

Rewrite the following paragraph to make it consistent in mood.

> Smoke detector batteries should be replaced twice a year. A good time to do this is at daylight saving time each spring and fall. Also, make sure your carbon monoxide detector is functioning properly.

Ind. Also, you should make sure your carbon monoxide detector is functioning properly.

Consistent Voice

There are two voices: **active** and **passive**. Active sentences have a clear agent of action: the subject. Passive sentences remove or displace the agent of action—they demote it to a prepositional clause or lose it entirely:

> **Active:** <u>Someone</u> stole my purse.

> **Passive:** <u>My</u> <u>purse</u> has been stolen [by someone].

The active voice is more direct and more engaging than the passive, and in general it is preferred. But the passive is correct (1) when you want to minimize the significance of the agent of action, (2) when you want to emphasize the receiver of the action, or (3) when the agent is unknown.

Unnecessary shifts between the active and passive voices make for awkward and potentially confusing writing:

> **Shifting:** James Joyce absorbed the details and ethos of Dublin, and these are what is portrayed in his short stories.

This sentence shifts to the passive for no reason—the same subject performed both actions (see chapter 9).

> **Consistent:** James Joyce absorbed the details and ethos of Dublin and portrayed them in his short stories.

PRACTICE 8

Rewrite the following paragraph to make it consistently in the active voice.

> Mark your calendar: it's time for our five-year reunion! Included in the cost of $40 per couple is dinner. Music for the evening will be provided by a live band, so please plan to dance. If you wish to be included in the class directory, please fill out the attached form. It should be returned no later than April 15.

Dinner is included in the cost

The live band

will provide

music

Return it no later than April 15th

SUMMARY

There are two kinds of **helping verbs**: forms of *have, do,* and *be* and the modals—*can/could, will/would, shall/should, may/might,* and *must/ought/need*. Specific verb forms must precede or follow certain helping verbs.

Helping Verb	Should be preceded by...	Should be followed by...
be	modal	present participle
been	have, has, had	—
do	—	base
have	—	past participle
modal	—	base

Helping verbs also have specific meanings:

Helping Verb	Meaning
will/would, shall	Intention
can/could	Ability
may/might, can/could	Permission
may/might	Possibility
should	Recommendation
should	Expectation
must, have/had (to)	Necessity

A **gerund** is a verb form ending in *-ing* that acts as a noun. An **infinitive** consists of *to* + **base verb.**

- Always use gerunds after prepositions.

- Always use gerunds after certain verbs, including *admit, enjoy,* and *resist.*

- Always use infinitives after certain verbs, including *agree, need,* and *want.*

- Always use infinitives after certain verbs, including *advise* and *tell,* when the verb is followed by a noun or pronoun.

The verbs *lie/lay*, *sit/set*, and *rise/raise* are often confused because they have similar meanings. Remember that *lie, sit,* and *rise* do not take objects. *Lay, set,* and *raise,* on the other hand, have different meanings because an object receives the action.

Avoid unnecessary shifts in verb tense, mood, or voice. The three moods (or types of statements) are the **indicative** (for facts, opinions, and questions), the **imperative** (for commands or advice), and the **subjunctive** (for things that are wished for or contrary to fact). The two voices are the **active** and the **passive**.

Practice Answers and Explanations

PRACTICE 1

1. *Help* needs to be in the past participle form, *helped*, since it follows *have.* Likewise, *ask* needs to be *asked*, again the past participle form.

2. *Have* needs to be inserted before *been*: *I have been waiting.*

3. *Working* needs to be changed to *work*; the base form follows forms of *do.*

4. *Arrived* needs to be changed to the base form *arrive* since it follows a modal. Or you could insert *have—should have arrived*—because *arrived* is the past participle and the past participle should follow the helping verb *have.*

5. *Are* needs to be changed to *have* since it precedes *been.*

PRACTICE 2

1. *may* or *can*. The context suggests permission, so either of these verbs will do.

2. *will* or *shall*. The context suggests intention, so either of these verbs will work.

3. *must*. The context suggests necessity.

4. *may* or *might*. The context suggests possibility, so either of these verbs will work.

PRACTICE 3

1. *Helping* is a gerund and the subject of the sentence. (The complete subject is *helping others*.)

2. Here *helping* is also a gerund and the direct object of *love.*

3. Again, *helping* is a gerund; this time it is part of the complement.

4. Here *helping* is part of the verb of the sentence and is a present participle.

PRACTICE 4

1. *to stabilize*. An infinitive should follow the verb *hope*.

2. *buying*. A gerund should always follow a preposition.

3. *to change*. An infinitive should follow the verb *convince* when *convince* is followed by a noun or pronoun (in this case, *me*).

4. *talking*. A gerund should always follow a preposition.

5. *cheating*. A gerund should follow the verb *tolerate*.

6. *talking*. A gerund should follow the verb *miss*.

7. *to clean*. An infinitive should follow the verb *manage*.

PRACTICE 5

1. *lie*

2. *rise*

3. *sitting*

4. *risen*

5. *set*. The direct object is *things*.

PRACTICE 6

I'd always wanted to go to the Grand Canyon, so I was thrilled when my dad announced we <u>would</u> be going there for our family vacation. Then he <u>told</u> us we <u>were</u> going to drive instead of fly—a four-day journey with three kids crammed into a small car. I <u>told</u> him he <u>was</u> off his rocker. That <u>was</u> when he told us we weren't going in *our* car—we <u>were</u> renting a Winnebago, and we <u>were</u> going to stay at campsites along the way. That was the kind of vacation I <u>had</u> always dreamed of. I am sure it wasn't easy for my parents to plan that trip, but I will always remember it as the best vacation of my life.

(Remember, some tense shifts are correct.)

PRACTICE 7

<u>Imperative</u>: Replace smoke detector batteries twice a year. A good time to do this is at daylight saving time each spring and fall. Also, make sure your carbon monoxide detector is functioning properly.

<u>Indicative</u>: Smoke detector batteries should be replaced twice a year. A good time to do this is at daylight saving time each spring and fall. Also, carbon monoxide detectors should be checked to ensure they are functioning properly.

PRACTICE 8

Mark your calendar: it's time for our five-year reunion! Dinner is included in the cost of $40 per couple. A live band will provide music for the evening, so please plan to dance. If you wish to be included in the class directory, please fill out the attached form and return it no later than April 15.

CHAPTER 4 TEST

Part A: For questions 1–13, choose the verb or verb phrase that correctly completes the sentence.

1. Ever since she was four, Hailey _____ great at sports.

    (A) is
    (B) has been
    (C) is been
    (D) has be
    (E) have been

2. No one _____ the extent to which Shakespeare has influenced the Western world.

    (A) predicted
    (B) could have predict
    (C) could have predicted
    (D) could predict
    (E) could have predicting

3. Some _____ say such claims about the influence of Shakespeare are grossly exaggerated.

    (A) must
    (B) have
    (C) could
    (D) may
    (E) should

4. But here's something you might want _____: many common sayings in use today were first introduced by Shakespeare.

    (A) to consider
    (B) considering
    (C) considered
    (D) consider
    (E) have considered

5. Sally's college degree can be credited with _____ her career.

    (A) jumpstart
    (B) jumpstarted
    (C) having jumpstart
    (D) to jumpstart
    (E) jumpstarting

6. In her doubtful financial situation, Sally _____ able to complete her degree if it weren't for her brother's help.

    (A) could not be
    (B) might not have been
    (C) might not being
    (D) should not have been
    (E) would not have been

7. If you have never tried homemade ice cream, you _____; it's often creamier and more flavorful than store-bought ice cream.

    (A) could
    (B) would
    (C) should
    (D) might
    (E) must

8. From the beginning, Caroline decided she wanted her teaching style _____ to the students.

    (A) appealing
    (B) to appeal
    (C) appeal
    (D) appealed
    (E) appeals

9. Over the years, the test scores of many of Caroline's students have _____ in math and science.

    (A) rised
    (B) rose
    (C) rosed
    (D) risen
    (E) raised

10. Some say that with the emergence of competing technologies, the sun _____ on the factory's long-dominant position in the market.

    (A) is setting
    (B) is sitting
    (C) sat
    (D) sit
    (E) setted

11. Who knows what _____ ahead for the factory and its employees?

    (A) lay
    (B) lie
    (C) lays
    (D) lain
    (E) lies

12. The factory owners have certainly _____ their plans with the future in mind—most analysts contend that the coming years look bright.

    (A) lain
    (B) laid
    (C) lied
    (D) lay
    (E) layed

13. However, it would be wise for management to address concerns investors have _____ about the factory's outdated machinery.

   (A) rose
   (B) risen
   (C) raised
   (D) rosed
   (E) rosen

Part B: For questions 14–20, choose the answer that will make the sentence consistent in tense, mood, and/or voice.

14. When it started over 20 years ago, the neighborhood's annual block party was only for adults—there _____ any children.

   (A) aren't
   (B) haven't been
   (C) will not be
   (D) weren't
   (E) were not being

15. Now the block party not only includes teenagers, but children and babies _____.

   (A) are seen by neighbors as well
   (B) are also part of the party
   (C) are allowed to attend
   (D) are found throughout the party
   (E) can be seen throughout the night

16. Over the years, many new celebrities have often shocked and sometimes _____ the public.

   (A) offending
   (B) having offended
   (C) offends
   (D) offended
   (E) will offend

17. But _____; older generations have always been appalled by the tastes of the teen generation.

   (A) admit it
   (B) listen
   (C) don't be surprised
   (D) face the facts
   (E) this shouldn't be surprising

18. Remember how offended so many parents were by Elvis—yet _____?

   (A) how adored he was by the younger generation
   (B) how the younger generation loved him
   (C) how he was so popular with teenagers
   (D) how much teens adored him
   (E) how successful he was

19. Of course, television programming has changed dramatically over the years. _____

    (A) Take a look and see for yourself.
    (B) Check it out.
    (C) You can watch it and see for yourself.
    (D) Find out for yourself.
    (E) Watch it and see.

20. If you grew up with PBS in the 1970s, _____.

    (A) a channel that is very different today is what you will see
    (B) you will see a channel that's very different today
    (C) many changes over the years will be found
    (D) many differences will be clear
    (E) a very different channel will be seen

Answers and Explanations

1. B

The present perfect *has been* is needed here to indicate that the action began in the past and is still occurring in the present.

2. C

The helping verb *could* means *ability* and is therefore needed here. In addition, the past participle (*predicted*) must follow the helping verb *have*.

3. D

The helping verb *may* means *possibility*. This is the only helping verb that fits in the context of the sentence.

4. A

An infinitive should follow the verb *want*.

5. E

A gerund should always follow a preposition (in this case, *with*).

6. B

The context suggests possibility, so *might* is the correct helping verb (not *could, should,* or *would*). The helping verb *have* must be followed by the past participle (*been*).

7. C

The helping verb *should* is needed, as the context of the sentence suggests recommendation.

8. B

The verb *want* should be followed by an infinitive.

9. D

There is no object, so the verb should be *rise*, not *raise*. *Rise* means to go up; *raise* means to move something up. The past participle of *rise* is *risen*.

10. A

To be consistent and logical in tense, the verb should be in the present progressive form. Because the subject is *sun, set* means *to go down*.

11. E

There is no object, so the intransitive verb *lie* is the correct verb. Its third-person singular present tense form is *lies*.

12. B

There is an object here (*plans*), so the sentence needs the verb *lay*, meaning to put or place something. The past participle of *lay* is *laid*.

13. C

The verb *raise* is needed here for the object *concerns*; *raise* means to move *something* up, while *rise* means to go up. *Raise* should also be in the past participle form *raised*.

14. D

To be consistent in tense and fit the context of the sentence, the verb should be in the simple past tense, *were*. Since it is negated, *were* is combined with *not* to form the contraction *weren't*.

15. B

To be consistent in voice, the second clause should also be active. Only (B) uses the active voice.

16. D

To be consistent in tense, the verb needs to be in its past participle form.

17. E

To be consistent in mood, the opening clause should be in the indicative mood. All other choices are in the imperative.

18. A

To be consistent in voice, both clauses should be passive. All other choices use the active voice.

19. C

To be consistent in mood, the second sentence should also be in the indicative mood. All other choices are in the imperative.

20. B

To be consistent in voice, the second clause should be in the active voice. All other choices use the passive voice.

CHAPTER 5

SUBJECT-VERB AGREEMENT

Remember the three principles: **balance**, **clarity**, and **consistency**. Subject-verb agreement is all about balance. Subjects and verbs **agree** (that is, are **equal**) in number and person. If the subject is the first-person singular *I*, the verb must be the first-person singular: *am*. Simple enough, right?

But there are reasons to devote a chapter to subject-verb agreement. For one thing, it isn't always easy to find the subject. For another, certain subjects (like indefinite pronouns and collective nouns) confuse the best of us.

BASIC SUBJECT-VERB AGREEMENT

Fortunately, subject-verb agreement is an issue only in the present tense, including the present perfect tense (with the usual exception, *be*).

	Singular		Plural	
First person	I	*pretend*	we	*pretend*
Second person	you	*pretend*	you	*pretend*
Third person	he, she, it	*pretends*	they	*pretend*

All use the **base** form *except* the third person singular, which adds *-s* (or *-es*) to the base form.

The verb *be* is irregular in form and must agree in both the present and past tenses:

	Singular		Plural	
First person	I	*am, was*	we	*are, were*
Second person	you	*are, were*	you	*are, were*
Third person	he, she, it	*is, was*	they	*are, were*

MEMORY TIP

Only the third-person singular (*he, she, it*) takes the -*s* ending. All other subjects use the base form (except with the verb *be*).

PRACTICE 1

Circle the correct verb in each pair in parentheses below.

1. Devon (is/are) babysitting for the Smiths this afternoon.
2. If we (concedes/concede), that (do/does) not mean we (agree/agrees) with your position.
3. So then Julia (tell/tells) Wanda, and Wanda (tell/tells) Annette—and the next thing you (know/knows), the whole town (know/knows) about my problem.

IDENTIFYING THE SUBJECT

You learned to find the subject in chapter 2. Here we offer more detail about "interrupters," inverted sentences, and other things that can befuddle that process.

Remember that the subject can be **single** (one subject) or **compound** (two or more subjects) and each subject can be either singular or plural. Sometimes, especially in imperatives, the subject is unstated (usually an understood *you*). Each clause in a sentence contains a subject and a verb.

[After <u>Ted</u> / **changes** the oil,] [<u>I</u> / **will** rotate the tires.]

Agreement with Single and Compound Subjects

For a single subject, the rule is simple: match the verb to the subject, whether it's singular or plural:

> The <u>oil</u> **needs** to be changed. (third-person singular subject and verb)

> The <u>tires</u> **need** to be rotated. (third-person plural subject and verb)

Compound subjects are a bit more complicated. There are two rules:

1. If the subjects (whether singular or plural) are joined by *and*, the verb is plural:

    > The <u>president</u> and <u>his cabinet members</u> **are** on vacation this week.

    There are two exceptions:

    - If the parts refer to the same person or thing, or work as a single unit, then the verb should be singular:

    <u>Spaghetti and meatballs</u> **is** the special this evening.

    - If the compound subject is preceded by *each* or *every* (thus referring to each subject individually), then the verb should be singular:

    Every <u>freshman</u> and <u>transfer student</u> **is** required to take Student Life.

2. If the subjects are joined by *or* or *nor*, the verb should agree with the subject that's closest to the verb:

    > Neither the <u>president</u> nor <u>his cabinet members</u> **are** in Washington this week.

    > Neither the <u>president</u> nor the <u>first lady</u> **is** in Washington this week.

PRACTICE 2

Underline the subject(s) and circle the correct verb in each of the following sentences.

1. Neither <u>Bob</u> nor <u>Rob</u> (admit/**admits**) to starting the rumor.

2. <u>Republicans and Democrats</u> alike (**share**/shares) a belief in the separation of church and state.

3. Either <u>Santa</u> or his <u>elves</u> (**check**/checks) the list twice.

4. Either Mrs. Claus or Santa (check/checks) the list twice.

5. The scouts and their leader (was/were) lost in the woods for hours.

6. Every problem and setback (is/are) an opportunity.

Eliminating Interrupters

The basic order for sentences is *subject-verb*, but that doesn't mean the verb immediately follows the subject. Many "interrupters" can come between subject and verb, including **prepositional phrases** and **modifiers** of all sorts:

> Carlos, in fact, will be the best man at my wedding. (prepositional phrase)

> Carlos, who is my favorite cousin, will be the best man at my wedding. (clause modifying *Carlos*)

In each example, the subject *Carlos* is separated from the verb by an underlined phrase or clause. The subject of a sentence will not be in one of these interrupters. You can eliminate them to make sure your subject and verb agree:

> *The Scream*, [to the surprise] [of millions], **was** stolen in broad daylight from a museum in Norway.

> *The Scream*, [which is [by far] the most famous painting] [by Edward Munch], **was** stolen in broad daylight from a museum in Norway.

PRACTICE 3

Cross out interrupters, underline the subject(s), and circle the correct verb.

1. A house without a good foundation (is/are) sure to crumble.

2. My sister Meena, the only one of us who doesn't love animals, (have/has) fallen in love with a farmer.

3. A true democracy, it turns out, (is/are) a true challenge.

4. All good things, the saying goes, (come/comes) to an end.

5. The concert, featuring the Oak City Banjo Kings, (begin/begins) at 7:00.

Inverted Sentences

The typical subject-verb sentence pattern may be reversed (1) in questions, (2) in *there is/are* statements, and (3) for effect:

There <u>is</u> no doubt in our minds.

Long <u>are</u> the dog days of summer.

If you're unsure of the subject, locate the verb. Note that the helping verb may be separated from the main verb, as in the example below. Once you've identified the verb(s), determine who or what performs that action (eliminate prepositional phrases and other interrupters):

Where **has/have** the cartons of milk **gone**?

What *has/have gone*? The cartons. The verb should be the plural *have*.

PRACTICE 4

Underline the subject and circle the correct verb.

1. How many times (have/has) I asked you to stop?
2. There (is/are) strength in numbers.
3. Wise (is/are) the quiet tongue and open heart.
4. When (do/does) the admissions office close?
5. In the supply closet, there (is/are) probably dozens of boxes of envelopes.

TRICKY SUBJECTS

Let's say you've identified the subject of a clause: *someone* or *who*. Now what? Here are the rules for titles or phrases, indefinite or relative pronouns, or collective nouns.

Collective Nouns

A **collective** or **group** noun identifies a single entity that is composed of more than one unit: *class, team, faculty, majority, family, series, committee, audience, crowd.* Collective nouns are singular when they act as one unit:

The <u>committee</u> **meets** Friday at noon.

A <u>majority</u> **is** needed to pass the bill.

But if the context of the sentence emphasizes the individual members of the group, collective nouns are plural:

>The <u>faculty</u> **meet** with their students at assigned times throughout the week.

>A <u>majority</u> of students **feel** unsafe when they walk alone on school grounds.

Titles, Phrases, and Singular Plurals

If the subject is a title, a specified phrase, or a gerund phrase, it is singular:

>**Title:** <u>*Cats*</u> **is** my favorite musical.

>**Specified phrase:** "<u>Once upon a time</u>" **is** the standard introduction to a fairy tale.

>**Gerund phrase:** <u>Delivering pizzas</u> **is** not a glamorous job, but it pays my bills.

Some words are plural in form but function as singular entities. These include names of academic subjects or bodies of knowledge, such as *mathematics*, *statistics*, *economics*, and *physics*, as well as a handful of other words, including *athletics*, *measles*, *mumps*, and *news*. Foreign words and medical terms may also appear to be plural because they end in *-s* (e.g., *diagnosis*; the plural is *diagnoses*). Consult a dictionary if you are unsure.

>Physics **is** my favorite subject.   No <u>news</u> **is** good news.

However, when one of these words describes individual items rather than a collective entity, the verb should be plural:

>These <u>statistics</u> **show** a strong correlation between goal setting and achievement.

PRACTICE 5

Circle the correct verb in each sentence below.

1. The audience (is/are) in for a real surprise in the second act.
2. Many classes (is/are) overcrowded this semester.
3. *In the Lake of the Woods* (is/are) my favorite novel.
4. Economics (is/are) much more interesting than I'd imagined.

5. *Psychosis* (is/are) a widely misunderstood term.

6. The news (is/are) drawn from many different sources, which explains why accounts can vary so widely.

7. Treating patients (takes/take) up most of my day.

Indefinite Pronouns

As you saw in chapter 1, **indefinite pronouns** are pronouns that don't refer to or replace a specific person, place, or thing. The following indefinite pronouns should always be treated as third-person singular subjects:

anybody	everybody	no one
anyone	everyone	nothing
anything	everything	somebody
each	neither	someone
either	nobody	something

Has <u>anyone</u> seen my cat?

"<u>Nothing</u> **is** more real than nothing." —*Samuel Beckett*

If <u>somebody</u> **has** something to say, now is the time to say it.

MEMORY TIP

Most of the singular indefinite pronouns are **-body/-one/-thing** words. Remember that **one** is a single item, so all of these -body/-one/-thing words are singular.

The indefinite pronouns *both*, *few*, *many*, and *several* are always plural:

<u>Many</u> of us **agree** with the proposal.

<u>Several</u> of the pipes **have** burst from the cold.

Remember, though, sometimes *many* acts as an adjective:

Many <u>a day</u> **has** gone by since you promised you'd return.

Finally, a handful of indefinite pronouns—*all*, *any*, *none*, and *some*—can be either singular or plural, depending upon their **antecedent**: the noun or pronoun they refer to or replace. Often, that antecedent is in a prepositional phrase following the pronoun:

> <u>None</u> of the money **is** left. (*None* refers to *money*.)
>
> <u>None</u> of the jewels **are** real. (*None* refers to *jewels*.)

Note: The word *plenty* isn't usually an indefinite pronoun, but it can function like one and take a singular or plural verb depending upon what it refers to:

> There **are** <u>plenty</u> of napkins on the table.
>
> There **is** <u>plenty</u> of gas in the car.

PRACTICE 6

Circle the correct verb in each sentence below.

1. I have a feeling something good (is/are) about to happen.
2. Unfortunately, nothing (have/has) changed since you were last here.
3. Each of the band members (has/have) a solo in this song.
4. Everything (seem/seems) under control now.
5. If anyone (find/finds) out, we're in big trouble.
6. None of his excuses (is/are) legitimate, but all of them (is/are) creative.
7. All of the cookies (has/have) been eaten, but there (is/are) still plenty of cake.
8. I don't think any of these stamps (is/are) valuable.

Relative Pronouns

The **relative pronouns** *who*, *that*, and *which* often introduce subordinate clauses (see chapters 1 and 2), which means they are often the subject of those clauses. To determine whether the verb should be singular or plural, identify the pronoun's antecedent. In the examples below, the relative pronouns are <u>underlined</u>, the verbs are in **bold**, and the antecedents are *italicized*:

> This is a *story* <u>that</u> **gets** wilder every time he tells it.
>
> These are *stories* <u>that</u> **get** wilder every time he tells them.

PRACTICE 7

Underline the antecedent for each relative pronoun in the sentences below. Then circle the correct verb.

1. Freud's case studies, which often (read/reads) more like novels than medical tracts, are fascinating.

2. The film sparked a lively discussion that (was/were) continued in the hallway after class.

3. Frankenstein, which most critics agree (is/are) the first science-fiction novel, was written by Mary Shelley, who (was/were) just 19 years old when it was published.

4. His taste in music is one of the things about him that (drive/drives) me crazy.

5. His taste in music is one thing about him that (drive/drives) me crazy.

SUMMARY

Subject-verb agreement means that subjects and verbs are the same in number (singular or plural) and person (first, second, or third). The third-person singular (*he, she, it*) adds -s or -es to the base form: *I eat, he eats*. Except for the verb *be*, subject-verb agreement is an issue only for present tense verbs.

To correctly identify the subject, eliminate interrupters such as prepositional phrases and modifying clauses.

Here are the ten rules regarding subject-verb agreement:

1. When you have a single subject, the verb must match that subject (singular or plural).

2. When you have a compound subject (two or more subjects) connected by *and*, the verb must be plural.

3. When you have a compound subject connected by *or* or *nor*, the verb must match the closest subject. If the subject closest to the verb is plural, the verb should be plural; if the subject closest to the verb is singular, the verb should be singular.

4. For *there is/are* sentences, determine first what *is*—for this is the true subject. Then check for subject-verb agreement.

5. For questions and other inverted sentences, identify the verb (remember, helping verbs will often be separated from main verbs in these constructions). Then determine who or what performs that action—this is the subject. Now check for subject-verb agreement.

6. When the subject is a collective noun (e.g., *team*), it should be followed by a singular verb—unless the collective noun is plural (*teams*) or the context of the sentence emphasizes each individual in the group.

7. When the subject is a title, a specified word or phrase, or a gerund phrase, treat it as a single unit and follow it with a singular verb.

8. A handful of plural words are actually singular most of the time (e.g., *economics* and *news*). Follow these words with a singular verb unless they describe individual entities.

9. Most indefinite pronouns are singular subjects (remember the *one/body/thing* word groups). Some indefinite pronouns are plural subjects (e.g., *both, few, many, several*). The indefinite pronouns *all, any, none*, and *some* can be singular or plural depending upon their antecedents. Determine what noun or pronoun they are referring to.

10. The relative pronouns *who, that*, and *which* can be singular or plural, depending upon their antecedent. Identify the antecedent to determine correct subject-verb agreement.

Subject-verb agreement is all about **balance**; sentences need harmony between subjects and verbs. When they are the same in person and number, you will be correct and clear.

PRACTICE ON YOUR OWN

Write your own sample sentences for each of the subject-verb agreement rules in the Chapter Summary.

Practice Answers and Explanations

PRACTICE 1

1. *is. Devon* is a third-person singular subject.

2. *concede, does, agree.* Only *that* is a third-person singular subject, so it is the only one that takes the -*s* form.

3. *tells, tells; know, knows. Julia, Wanda*, and *town* are third-person singular subjects and take the -*s* form. *You* is the second-person singular and takes the base form.

PRACTICE 2

1. Subjects: <u>Bob</u> and <u>Rob</u>. Correct verb: *admits*. The verb needs to be singular because the compound subject is joined by *nor*, and the closest subject is third-person singular.

2. Subjects: <u>Republicans</u> and <u>Democrats</u>. Correct verb: *share*. The compound subject is joined by *and* and thus requires a plural verb.

3. Subjects: <u>Santa</u> and his <u>elves</u>. Correct verb: *check*. The compound subject is joined by *or*, so the verb must agree with the closest subject, *elves*, which is plural.

4. Subjects: <u>Mrs. Claus</u> and <u>Santa</u>. Correct verb: *checks*. The compound subject is joined by *or*, so the verb must agree with the closest subject, *Santa*, which is the third-person singular.

5. Subjects: <u>scouts</u> and their <u>leader</u>. Correct verb: *were*. The compound subject is joined by *and*, so the verb must be plural.

6. Subjects: <u>problem</u> and <u>setback</u>. Correct verb: *is*. The compound subject is joined by *and*, but it is preceded by *every*, so the verb should be third-person singular.

PRACTICE 3

1. A <u>house</u> ~~without a good foundation~~ (**is**) sure to crumble.

2. <u>My sister Meena</u>, ~~the only one of us who doesn't love animals~~, (**has**) fallen in love with a farmer.

3. <u>A true democracy</u>, ~~it turns out~~, (**is**) a true challenge.

4. <u>All good things</u>, ~~the saying goes~~, (**come**) to an end.

5. The <u>concert</u>, ~~featuring the Oak City Banjo Kings~~, (**begins**) at 7:00.

PRACTICE 4

1. How many times (**have**) <u>I</u> asked you to stop?

2. There (**is**) <u>strength</u> in numbers.

3. Wise (**are**) the <u>quiet tongue</u> and <u>open heart</u>.

4. When (**does**) the <u>admissions office</u> close?

5. In the supply closet, there (**are**) probably <u>dozens</u> of boxes of envelopes.

PRACTICE 5

1. *is.* *Audience* is a singular collective noun.

2. *are.* *Classes* is a plural collective noun.

3. *is.* *In the Lake of the Woods* is a singular title.

4. *is.* *Economics* here refers to the academic discipline and is singular.

5. *is.* *Psychosis* is a medical term and is singular.

6. *is.* Even though *news* looks like a plural noun, it refers to a body of information and is singular.

7. *takes.* The gerund phrase *treating patients* should be treated as a singular subject.

PRACTICE 6

1. *is.* *Something* is a singular indefinite pronoun.

2. *has.* *Nothing* is a singular indefinite pronoun.

3. *has.* *Each* is a singular indefinite pronoun. (Note that *each* is the subject, not *band members*, which is part of a prepositional phrase.)

4. *seems.* *Everything* is a singular indefinite pronoun.

5. *finds.* *Anyone* is a singular indefinite pronoun.

6. *are, are.* Both *none* and *all* refer to the plural noun *excuses.*

7. *have, is.* *All* refers to *cookies*; *plenty* refers to *cake.*

8. *are.* *Any* refers to the plural noun *stamps.*

PRACTICE 7

1. Freud's <u>case studies</u>, which often (**read**) more like novels than medical tracts, are fascinating.

2. The film sparked a lively <u>discussion</u> that (**was**) continued in the hallway after class.

3. <u>*Frankenstein*</u>, which most critics agree (**is**) the first science-fiction novel, was written by <u>Mary Shelley</u>, who (**was**) just 19 years old when it was published.

4. His taste in music is one of the <u>things</u> about him that (**drive**) me crazy.

5. His taste in music is the one <u>thing</u> about him that (**drives**) me crazy.

CHAPTER 5 TEST

Choose the letter that identifies the subject-verb agreement error in each sentence below. If there is no error, choose (E).

1. A jury consist of 12 randomly selected men and women whose duty it is to
   (A)   (B)   (C)
   decide the fate of the defendant. No error
   (D)   (E)

2. I promise that neither fame nor fortune are going to change the way I feel
   (A)   (B)   (C)   (D)
   about you. No error
            (E)

3. I can't believe that no one have taken you up on your offer. No error
   (A)   (B)   (C)   (D)   (E)

4. I know that patience is a virtue, but I seem to have so little of it. No error
   (A)   (B)   (C)   (D)   (E)

5. Did you know that Les Demoiselles d'Avignon, one of Picasso's most famous
   (A)   (B)
   works, hang in the Museum of Modern Art in New York City? No error
   (C)   (D)   (E)

6. I am not a morning person, so it is my bad luck that statistics, one of my
   (A)   (B)   (C)
   most difficult classes, meets at 8:00 A.M. No error
                          (D)   (E)

7. Can you tell me who else besides you have seen these results? No error
   (A)   (B)   (C) (D)   (E)

8. Kathy confesses that the New York Times has become her favorite newspaper
          (A)   (B)   (C)
   and she reads it religiously. No error
           (D)   (E)

9. I believe either Carlos or his children is going to pick up the cake and bring
     (A)   (B)   (C)
   it to the party, so we don't have to worry about it. No error
                               (D)   (E)

10. I was surprised to hear that the Senate has repealed the amendment we had
      (A)   (B)   (C)   (D)
    fought so hard for. No error
                        (E)

11. These dreams of mine that keeps me awake always have the same ending:
    (A)   (B)   (C)

    I am falling into a dark, bottomless pit. No error
    (D)   (E)

12. We have discovered a wonderful new restaurant that feature fresh
    (A)   (B)

    seafood—and we are happy to say it is only a few blocks away. No error
    (C)   (D)   (E)

13. I want to believe you, but there aren't any question in my mind about what
    (A)   (B)   (C)

    happened. No error
    (D)   (E)

14. I am concerned about these statistics, which suggests our customer base has
    (A)   (B)   (C)

    shrunk considerably since we switched suppliers. No error
                                (D)   (E)

15. I have checked with Denise, and she do not know what happened to the
    (A)   (B)

    printer that was supposed to go in your office. No error
                (C)   (D)   (E)

16. As Rebecca smiles and places the wrapped gift on the table, Thayer slip the
               (A)   (B)   (C)

    letter from Anna into his pocket before Rebecca sees it. No error
                                                     (D)   (E)

17. I have asked all of the teachers, and none of them has seen the painting that
    (A)   (B) (C)

    was stolen from the lounge. No error
    (D)   (E)

18. Leading the list of household dangers to children is cleaners that contain
    (A)   (B)   (C)   (D)

    poisonous chemicals. No error
                         (E)

19. Everyone in the class is looking forward to spring, when the days will be
                           (A) (B)   (C)

    longer and recess will once again be outdoors. No error
                       (D)   (E)

20. Are Joline or Aiden coming to help, or do we have to do all the work
    (A)   (B)   (C)   (D)

    ourselves? No error
               (E)

**ANSWERS AND EXPLANATIONS
BEGIN ON NEXT PAGE**

Answers and Explanations

1. A

Jury is a singular collective noun, so it requires the third-person singular verb *consists*.

2. B

The compound subjects *fame* and *fortune* are connected by *neither…nor*, so the verb should be the singular *is*.

3. C

The indefinite pronoun *no one* is singular, so the verb should be the third-person singular *has*.

4. E

No error.

5. D

The subject of the verb *hang* is *Les Demoiselles d'Avignon*, a title that should be treated as a singular subject. Thus, the verb should be the third-person singular *hangs*.

6. E

Statistics here is both the academic discipline and the title of a class, both of which should be treated as singular. *Classes* is part of a prepositional phrase.

7. C

The subject of the verb *have seen* is *who*, which should be treated as a singular subject. Thus, the verb should be *has*.

8. E

Note that the *New York Times* is a title that requires a singular verb.

9. B

The compound subjects *Carlos* and *his children* are connected by *or*, so the verb must agree with the closest subject, *children*. Thus, the verb should be the plural *are*.

10. E

Senate is a collective noun and requires a singular verb.

11. A

The subject is the plural *dreams*, not *mine*, which is part of a prepositional phrase. Thus, the verb should also be plural: *keep*.

12. B

The relative pronoun *that* refers to the antecedent *restaurant*, which is singular and requires the third-person singular verb *features*.

13. C

The subject of the verb *aren't* is the singular *question*, so the verb should be the singular *isn't*.

14. B

In this case, *statistics* refers not to the academic discipline but to individual numbers. Thus, the verb should be the plural *suggest*.

15. B

The subject *she* requires the third-person singular *does*.

16. C

The subject *Thayer* requires the third-person singular *slips*.

17. B

Here the subject *none* refers to the antecedent *teachers*, so the verb should be the plural *have*.

18. C

In this inverted sentence, *cleaners* are *leading the list*, so the verb must be plural.

19. E

Everyone is one of the indefinite pronouns that requires a singular verb.

20. A

The compound subject *Joline* and *Aiden* is connected by *or*, so the verb should be the singular *is*.

CHAPTER 6

PRONOUN AGREEMENT, REFERENCE, AND CASE

Pronouns replace nouns, other pronouns, phrases, or clauses. Without pronouns, we'd have to keep repeating those antecedents.

> **Without pronouns:** Kendall says Kendall's mom fixed Kendall's mom's flat tire before Kendall got there to help.

> **With pronouns:** Kendall says his mom fixed her flat tire before he got there to help.

But as handy as pronouns are, they can be problematic. This chapter is devoted to three key pronoun issues: agreement, unclear reference, and pronoun case.

Pronouns must **agree** with the words they replace. It must be **clear** to which words they refer. Pronouns must also be in the proper **case**.

KINDS OF PRONOUNS

Pronouns come in six types: personal, possessive, reflexive, relative, demonstrative, indefinite, and interrogative (see chapter 1). Possessive pronouns function as adjectives.

> **Adjective:** <u>My</u> dog is a fantastic swimmer. (*My* modifies *dog*.)

> **Pronoun:** That dog is <u>mine</u>.

> **Adjective:** <u>Several</u> children have the chicken pox. (*Several* modifies *children*.)

> **Pronoun:** There are <u>several</u> left.

PRONOUN AGREEMENT

Pronouns must agree in number, person, and gender with their antecedents. An **antecedent** is what a pronoun replaces or refers to. A third-person, singular, male antecedent (for example, *Joe*) needs a third-person, singular, male pronoun (*he, his, him, himself*):

Joe parked <u>his</u> car on the curb.

PRACTICE 1

Circle the antecedent for each underlined pronoun below.

Example: I love <u>my</u> dog.

1. Mia was the first vegetarian in <u>her</u> family.
2. I thought I'd left my keys here, but now I can't find <u>them</u>.
3. Pass me the folder <u>that</u> has a big coffee stain on the cover.
4. Are <u>all</u> of the children asleep?
5. I think <u>these</u> are the most interesting photographs.

PRACTICE 2

Circle the correct pronoun in parentheses in each sentence below.

1. Ice skaters practice (its/their) routines for hours each day.
2. As Americans, (I/we) celebrate July 4th as the birth of (my/our) nation.
3. I am impressed by LuAnne's ability to control (her/my) temper.
4. The male peacock displays (their/its) feathers to attract a mate.
5. The photos in this album are losing (their/its) color.

Compound Antecedents

Like subjects, antecedents can be single or compound:

Single: I love <u>my</u> dog.

Compound: Toby and **I** love <u>our</u> dog.

The rules for agreement with compound antecedents are as follows:

1. If a compound antecedent is connected by *and*, the pronoun should be plural. (Notice the plural verbs.)

    L.J. **and** Elliot have finished <u>their</u> homework.

    The house **and** garage both have cracks in <u>their</u> foundations.

2. If a compound antecedent is connected by *or* or *nor*, and both are singular, the pronoun should be singular. (Notice the singular verbs.)

    Neither L.J. **nor** Elliot has finished <u>his</u> homework.

    Neither the house **nor** the garage has a crack in <u>its</u> foundation.

If one antecedent is female and the other male, the sentence must be rewritten:

> **Incorrect:** Neither Elliot **nor** Magdalena has finished <u>his</u> homework.
>
> **Incorrect:** Neither Elliot **nor** Magdalena have finished <u>their</u> homework.
>
> **Correct:** Both Elliot **and** Magdalena still have to do <u>their</u> homework.
>
> **Correct:** Neither Elliot **nor** Magdalena has finished the assignment.

3. If a compound antecedent is connected by *or* or *nor*, the pronoun must agree with the nearest antecedent.

    Neither Elliot **nor** his sisters have finished <u>their</u> homework.

    Neither Sam **nor** Elliot has finished <u>his</u> homework.

PRACTICE 3

Choose the correct word in the following sentences.

1. The penguins and the walrus have had (its/**their**) breakfasts.
2. Neither the walrus nor the penguins have had (its/**their**) breakfast.
3. Neither the penguin nor the walrus has had (**its**/their) breakfast.
4. Has Maria or Arnold fed (his/her/their/**the**) animals yet?
5. Have Maria and Arnold fed (his/her/**their**) animals yet?

Collective and Other Singular Nouns

As you learned in chapter 5, collective nouns (e.g., *class*, *committee*, *crowd*) are singular unless the context emphasizes the individual members of the group. Titles, phrases, and "singular plurals" (e.g., *economics* and *news*) are also singular antecedents:

The **class** expressed <u>its</u> approval with loud applause.

The **class** put <u>their</u> signatures on the petition.

Delivering pizza is not a glamorous job, but <u>it</u> pays the bills.

Physics is my favorite subject, but <u>it</u> is also my most challenging.

PRACTICE 4

Circle the correct choice in each sentence below.

1. The committee will announce (its/their) selection tomorrow.
2. I admit the news is bad, but (it/they) could be worse.
3. The team (has its/have their) final playoff game Thursday.
4. I don't feel comfortable with these statistics because I don't trust (its/their) source.
5. *The Three Musketeers* was a popular book long before (it was/they were) made into a film.

Indefinite Pronouns

The following indefinite pronouns require a singular verb and a singular pronoun:

anybody	everybody	each	nobody	somebody
anyone	everyone	either	no one	someone
anything	everything	neither	nothing	something

Unless you know that everyone referred to is of the same gender, you cannot pick one gender-specific pronoun or the other. Revise the sentence one of three ways:

1. Use two pronouns: Does everyone have <u>his or her</u> password?
2. Rewrite the sentence so that the antecedent is plural: Do all of the students have <u>their</u> passwords?
3. Rewrite the sentence to eliminate the pronoun: Does every student have a password?

Generic Nouns

A **generic** noun refers to one or more members of a group *in general*:

> A <u>student</u> must work hard to earn good grades.

> A <u>customer</u> expects to be treated with respect.

Like collective nouns, singular generic nouns require a singular pronoun. Since in most cases, the group includes males and females, the pronoun must agree with both genders; revise as you would for a singular indefinite pronoun:

> **Incorrect:** A student must work hard if <u>he</u> wants to earn good grades.

> **Incorrect:** A student must work hard if <u>they</u> want to earn good grades.

> **Correct:** A student must work hard if <u>he or she</u> wants to earn good grades.

> **Correct:** Students must work hard if <u>they</u> want to earn good grades.

> **Correct:** A student must work hard to earn good grades.

MEMORY TIP

For singular indefinite antecedents and generic nouns, either use *two* third-person singular pronouns or revise the sentence to include a plural antecedent or to eliminate the pronoun altogether.

PRACTICE 5

Correct any pronoun-antecedent agreement errors in the following sentences.

1. I don't know anybody who hasn't had a crush on one of his teachers.
2. A scientist must be guided by her observations, not her emotions.
3. Someone has left their keys on the table.
4. To be great, an artist must listen to his heart and not his critics.
5. Each of the sculptures have their own unique charm.

UNCLEAR REFERENCE

How quickly can you find the problem in this sentence?

> Tyler and Leon are going to his house after school.

Ambiguous Reference

Whose house are they going to? The sentence is unclear because the pronoun *his* could refer to either *Tyler* or *Leon*. This is an **ambiguous** reference—a pronoun that has two or more possible antecedents. In most cases, the best fix is either to rewrite the sentence to avoid the need for a pronoun or to repeat the antecedent:

> Tyler and Leon are going to <u>Tyler's</u> house after school.

Vague Antecedents

Sometimes a writer thinks there is a clear antecedent when actually none exists. That's the problem in the following sentence:

> **Incorrect:** After Dylan finished vacuuming, he put <u>it</u> away.

You might have assumed that *it* refers to a vacuum, but the word *vacuum* isn't anywhere in the sentence. The verb is being used as an antecedent, and this is a mistake.

> **Correct:** After Dylan finished vacuuming, he put <u>the vacuum</u> away.

This next sentence may seem clearer, but it makes the same kind of mistake:

> **Incorrect:** Jules walks to work because <u>it</u> only takes her 15 minutes.
> **Correct:** Jules walks to work because <u>the trip</u> only takes her 15 minutes.

Here's another common vague antecedent problem:

> <u>They</u> predict that it's going to be a very cold winter.

> Yesterday <u>they</u> shut down the turnpike because of a serious accident.

Who are *they*? In both sentences, the *they* referred to is unspecified. Of course, these sentences might be correct if *they* refers clearly to an antecedent in a prior sentence. But this structure, often used because the agent is unknown or unimportant, should be avoided. Don't leave it to your reader to decide whether *they* refers to the National Weather Service or Channel 4 in the first sentence or the police, vigilantes, or emergency workers in the second. Make your sentences clear.

PRACTICE 6

Correct vague pronoun references in the following sentences.

1. The Cobras versus Stingrays match should be no contest because they're playing at the top of their game.

2. Shonda ran into Isabelle, and she gave her your number.

3. Sami put some thick logs into the fireplace, and it burned brightly for hours.

4. I got the application, and it took me over an hour.

5. As Bernice was putting the last toothpick on top of her model Eiffel Tower, it broke.

Overly Broad Reference

Another common pronoun error is to use *this, that, which,* or *it* to refer to a whole idea or sentence rather than a specific antecedent:

> The characters wrestle with matters of race, religion, and free will, and <u>that's</u> what makes the novel so powerful.

Here, *that* refers to the whole first clause, which expresses a broad idea. Pronouns are most effective and clear when they replace a *specific* antecedent. This sentence should be revised:

> The characters wrestle with matters of race, religion, and free will, and <u>their struggle</u> is what makes the novel so powerful.

RELATIVE PRONOUNS

- Use *who, whom, whose* (and some authorities permit *that*) to refer to people.

- Use *which* and *that* to refer to animals or things. (Exception: If you are referring to a pet or other beloved creature, you can use *who.*)

- Use *which* for clauses that are *not* essential to the meaning of the sentence: *I'm going to the laundromat, which is my favorite place for people watching.*

- Use *that* for clauses that *are* essential to the meaning of the sentence: *I will only go to a laundromat that offers free soap.*

PRACTICE 7

Revise the following sentences to correct overly broad or indefinite pronoun references or errors.

1. They have raised tuition by 2 percent for next year.

2. Residents of the embattled town have survived two hurricanes and a tornado, which has brought everyone together as a community.

3. On the phone, they said to bring three forms of ID.

4. I'm making this sweater for my dog Glenda, which loves to play in the snow.

5. I'm going to the same dermatologist that treated Rashaad's eczema.

PRONOUN CASE

Personal pronouns come in three **cases**: **subjective**, **objective**, and **possessive**. Most of us know when to use the possessive, but many confuse the subjective and objective cases.

Subjective Case	Objective Case
I	me
you	you
he, she, it	him, her, it
we	us
you (plural)	you (plural)
they	them
who	whom

Use the **subjective case** when the pronoun is the **subject** or **subject complement** of its clause. Otherwise, use the **objective case**:

> I hope they don't ask me too many questions.
> [subject] [subject]   [indirect object]

> It was I who called the police.
> [subject complement]

> For me, the most difficult part of the day is just getting out of bed.
> [object of preposition]

MEMORY TIP

Use the subjective case when a pronoun is the subject or complement. Otherwise, use the objective case.

Simple enough, right? But we develop bad habits, so what sounds right is actually wrong:

> Between you and (I/me), Lotta should keep her opinions to herself.

Between is a preposition, and both pronouns are its objects, so they should be in the objective case: *between you and* me.

Comparative Statements

Pronouns used in comparisons are notoriously challenging:

> You like chocolate more than me.

> You like chocolate more than I.

Both are correct—but they convey very different meanings. In the first sentence, *me* is an object and the sentence means you like chocolate *more than you like me*. In the second, because *I* is a subject, the sentence means that you like chocolate *more than I do*.

As in the second example, the verb of the subjective pronoun is often omitted in comparisons, which is why it's so easy to make a mistake. Look carefully at the context to determine the intended meaning. If putting *I do* or *I am* at the end of the sentence makes sense, then you probably need the subjective case.

Modifiers

When a pronoun is in a modifying phrase or clause, determine whether it is modifying or renaming a subject or an object:

> Though many students were involved in the fight, the principal only called two people to the office: Darlene and me.

> Only two people, Darlene and I, were called to the principal's office, though many students were involved in the dispute.

In the first sentence, the phrase *Darlene and me* refers to *people*, a direct object; the pronoun should be in the objective case. In the second, the phrase relates to the subject of the sentence, *only two people*, and is in the subjective case.

PRACTICE 8

For each sentence below, determine whether the pronouns are functioning as subjects or objects. Then choose the correct pronoun from the choices.

1. Zach is not coming, for (I/me) asked him to wait until tomorrow.

2. This present is not for you but for (I/me).

3. Come and meet my cousin Charles, (who/whom) works as a clown in the circus.

4. You have your interview earlier than (I/me).

5. I assure you, only two people know your secret—Marcus and (I/me).

We versus Us

Occasionally, we put the pronouns *we* or *us* in front of nouns to emphasize our membership in that group or category: *we Americans* or *us snowboarders*. But which pronoun should we use? Again, it depends upon whether the antecedent is a subject in its clause:

> Does Uncle Sam think we **taxpayers** have money growing on trees?

> Uncle Sam needs to give us **taxpayers** a break.

In the first sentence, *taxpayers* is a subject—*taxpayers have*—so the pronoun must be the subjective. In the second, *taxpayers* is an indirect object, therefore objective. To help you determine which case to use, simply eliminate the noun:

> Uncle Sam needs to give (we/us) a break.

Who versus Whom

Use *who* (or *whoever*) for subjects and *whom* (or *whomever*) for objects. In the following sentences, *who* functions as a subject:

> The award will be given to the student <u>who</u> earns the highest overall GPA.
>
> Do you know <u>who</u> has the keys to the shed?

In these sentences, the pronoun *whom* is an object:

> To <u>whom</u> should I address this letter? (object of preposition)
>
> <u>Whom</u> are you going to ask to the prom? (direct object)
>
> At tomorrow's meeting, we will decide <u>whom</u> to hire. (direct object)

To see more easily which case to use, replace the pronoun with *he* or *him* (you may need to invert word order in questions and other inverted sentences):

> <u>He</u> has the keys to the shed = use *who*.
>
> I am going to ask <u>him</u> to the prom = use *whom*.

PRACTICE 9

Circle the correct pronoun.

1. The reason (we/us) clowns are not smiling is that we've been fired.
2. Can you give (we/us) clowns another chance?
3. The flu shot will be given to (whoever/whomever) is most at risk.
4. (Who/whom) did you buy this necklace for?
5. We will select the candidate (who/whom) is most qualified.
6. The panel will decide (who/whom) to charge for this offense.

CONSISTENCY

Pronouns should be consistent in person, number, and gender.

> **Inconsistent:** If <u>you</u> are thinking of buying a new car, <u>one</u> should carefully consider the safety ratings of the cars <u>they're</u> considering.
>
> **Consistent:** If <u>you</u> are thinking of buying a new car, <u>you</u> should carefully consider the safety ratings of the cars <u>you're</u> considering.

SUMMARY

Pronouns must **agree** with their antecedents in **number** (singular or plural), **person** (first, second, or third), and **gender** (male or female). Rules for pronoun-antecedent agreement are similar to those for subject-verb agreement:

- Compound antecedents (whether singular or plural) connected by *and* take a plural pronoun.

- Compound antecedents that are singular and connected by *or* or *nor* use a singular pronoun—unless one antecedent is male and one female. In that case, the sentence must be rewritten.

- If a singular antecedent and plural antecedent are connected by *or* or *nor*, the pronoun must agree with the closest antecedent.

- If the antecedent is a collective noun, title, specified word or phrase, or "singular plural," use a singular pronoun unless the context emphasizes the individuals in the group.

- If the antecedent is a singular indefinite pronoun such as *anybody*, use a singular pronoun—but *he* or *she* alone will not do, unless it is clear that everyone is of the same gender.

- Generic nouns refer to one or more members of a group in general and are singular. Use two pronouns to include both genders, rewrite the sentence to make it plural, or revise it to eliminate the pronoun.

Unclear pronoun reference is a common problem.

- **Ambiguous** reference means there are two or more possible antecedents; rewrite the sentence or repeat the correct antecedent to make the sentence clear.
- **Vague antecedent** means the antecedent is not present—often it is the unspecified *they*, which should be replaced by a specific noun. To be grammatically correct, the antecedent needs to be clear.
- **Overly broad reference** means a pronoun refers to a whole phrase, clause, or sentence when it should have a specific antecedent.

Who (and according to some authorities *that*) refers to people (and beloved creatures), *which* and *that* to animals and things. Use *who* or *which* for clauses that are not essential to the meaning of the sentence; use *that* for clauses that *are* essential.

Pronouns have three **cases**: **subjective**, **objective**, and **possessive**. Use the subjective case (*I, you, he/she/it, we, they, who*) when the pronoun is the subject or subject complement of its clause and use the possessive to show ownership. Otherwise, use the objective case (*me, you, him/her/it, us, them, whom*). In **comparisons** and in **modifying clauses and phrases**, be sure the pronoun case accurately reflects your intended meaning. Determine whether the clause or phrase modifies a subject or object in its clause, then use the appropriate case.

PRACTICE ON YOUR OWN

Practice identifying different types of pronouns in material that you read for school, work, or leisure. Locate the antecedent for each pronoun and determine whether the correct pronoun has been used. If not, rewrite the sentence correctly. Likewise, if a pronoun has an unclear reference, practice rewriting the sentence to fix the issue. Apply the same kind of analysis to your own writing so that you will build the habit of using pronouns correctly.

Practice Answers and Explanations

PRACTICE 1

1. *Mia*

2. *keys*

3. *folder*

4. *children*

5. *photographs*

PRACTICE 2

1. *their.* The antecedent is *ice skaters*, so the pronoun is third-person plural.

2. *we, our.* The antecedent is *Americans*, so the pronoun is first-person plural.

3. *her.* The antecedent is *LuAnne*, so the pronoun must be third-person singular and feminine.

4. *its.* The antecedent is *male peacock*, so the pronoun is third-person singular.

5. *their.* The antecedent is *photos*, so the pronoun is third-person plural.

PRACTICE 3

1. *their*. The compound antecedents *penguins* and *walrus* are connected by *and*, so the pronoun is plural.

2. *their*. The same antecedents are connected by *or*, so the pronoun agrees with the closest antecedent.

3. *its*. This time the closest antecedent is the singular *walrus*, so the pronoun should be singular.

4. *the*. None of the pronouns work. *Maria* and *Arnold* are different genders, so neither *his* nor *her* is correct. *Their* is also incorrect because *or* calls for a singular pronoun. Only *the* is correct.

5. *their*. This time the antecedents are connected by *and*, so the plural pronoun is correct.

PRACTICE 4

1. *its*. *Committee* is a singular collective noun.

2. *it*. *News* is a singular collective noun.

3. *has its*. *Team* is a singular collective noun.

4. *their*. The word *these* indicates that *statistics* is plural in this context, so the pronoun must be plural.

5. *it was*. The title *The Three Musketeers* is singular.

PRACTICE 5

Here are two possible revisions for each sentence.

1. a. I don't know anybody who hasn't had a crush on one of his or her teachers.

   b. I think all students have had a crush on one of their teachers.

2. a. Scientists must be guided by their observations, not their emotions.

   b. A scientist must be guided by observation, not emotion.

3. a. Someone has left his or her keys on the table.

   b. Somebody's keys have been left on the table.

4. a. To be great, an artist must listen to his or her heart and not his or her critics. (4b is a better, less clumsy option.)

   b. To be great, artists must listen to their hearts and not their critics.

5. a. Each of the sculptures has its own unique charm.

    b. All of the sculptures have their own unique charm.

PRACTICE 6

1. The Cobras versus Stingrays match should be no contest because <u>the Cobras</u> (or *the Stingrays*) are playing at the top of their game.

2. Shonda ran into Isabelle, and <u>Shonda</u> (or *Isabelle*) gave her your number.

3. Sami put some thick logs into the fireplace, and <u>the fire</u> burned brightly for hours.

4. I got the application, and <u>filling it out</u> took me over an hour.

5. As Bernice was putting the last toothpick on top of her model Eiffel Tower, <u>the tower</u> (or *the toothpick*) broke.

PRACTICE 7

Answers will vary slightly.

1. <u>The school officials</u> have raised tuition by 2 percent for next year. (The indefinite *they* must be replaced by a specific noun.)

2. Residents of the embattled town have survived two hurricanes and a tornado; <u>the hardship</u> has brought everyone together as a community. (The pronoun *which* refers to an overly broad antecedent.)

3. On the phone, <u>the representative</u> said to bring three forms of ID. (The indefinite *they* should be replaced by a specific noun.)

4. I'm making this sweater for my dog Glenda, <u>who</u> loves to play in the snow. (The pronoun *which* could be *who*, as the dog is named and referred to as a person. *Which* could also be correct, however, because the clause is unnecessary to the meaning of the sentence.)

5. I'm going to the same dermatologist <u>who</u> treated Rashaad's eczema. (While some authorities accept *that*, it's preferable to use *who* to refer to a person.)

PRACTICE 8

1. *I*. Here *for* is not a preposition but a coordinating conjunction, and *I* functions as a subject.

2. *me*. Here *for* is a preposition, so the pronoun is in the objective case.

3. *who*. In this subordinate clause, *who* is a subject.

4. *I*. The subjective case is required because putting *I do* at the end of the sentence would make sense.

5. *I*. The modifier *Marcus and I* refers to the subject *two people* (the verb: *know*).

PRACTICE 9

1. *we*. The noun *clowns* is a subject.

2. *us*. Here the noun *clowns* is an indirect object.

3. *whoever*. The pronoun is the subject of the clause *whoever is most at risk*. This entire clause is the object of the preposition *to*.

4. *Whom*. The pronoun is the object of the preposition *for*.

5. *who*. The pronoun introduces the subordinate clause *who is the most qualified*, so it is the subject of the verb *is*.

6. *whom*. Remember, use *whom* before an infinitive.

CHAPTER 6 TEST

Choose the best version of the underlined portion of each sentence below. If the sentence is correct as written, choose (A).

1. The belief that time is linear, <u>that is</u> a Western notion, contrasts with the Native American belief that time is circular.

   (A) that is
   (B) which is
   (C) which are
   (D) that are
   (E) being

2. When you go to a fancy restaurant, <u>one</u> should always place the napkin on your lap.

   (A) one
   (B) people
   (C) he
   (D) she
   (E) you

3. Neither the hydrangea nor the rose bushes have any flowers on <u>it</u> yet.

   (A) it
   (B) itself
   (C) them
   (D) themselves
   (E) they

4. This isn't about <u>you and me</u>; it's about our daughter.

   (A) you and me
   (B) you and I
   (C) yourself and myself
   (D) yourself and I
   (E) we

5. This is the house <u>which</u> I was telling you about.

   (A) which
   (B) whichever
   (C) who
   (D) whoever
   (E) that

6. <u>A soldier must be loyal to his</u> country.

   (A) A soldier must be loyal to his
   (B) A soldier must be loyal to her
   (C) A soldier must be loyal to one's
   (D) A soldier must be loyal to its
   (E) Soldiers must be loyal to their

7. I was going to go grocery shopping, but it closed early.

   (A) it
   (B) they
   (C) the store
   (D) shopping
   (E) that

8. The founders of the club—Tazjeer and I—are the only permanent members.

   (A) Tazjeer and I
   (B) Tazjeer and me
   (C) Tazjeer and myself
   (D) Tazjeer himself and me
   (E) us

9. They recommend that you floss your teeth every day.

   (A) They recommend that you floss
   (B) They recommend flossing
   (C) Dentists recommend that you flosses
   (D) Dentists recommend that you floss
   (E) Dentists recommend that we floss

10. Us tenants have about had it with our superintendent.

    (A) Us tenants
    (B) We tenants
    (C) Us tenants ourselves
    (D) We ourselves
    (E) Our tenants

11. Someone has parked their car illegally in front of the fire hydrant.

    (A) their car
    (B) his car
    (C) her car
    (D) his or her car
    (E) its car

12. You can give that extra notebook to who wants it.

    (A) who wants
    (B) who want
    (C) whoever want
    (D) whoever wants
    (E) whomever wants

13. Neither Lisa nor Jennifer has seen the movie.

    (A) has seen
    (B) have seen
    (C) has saw
    (D) have saw
    (E) did see

14. Either that dog lost his collar, or it doesn't have an owner.

    (A) his collar, or it
    (B) its collar, or it
    (C) his collar, or she
    (D) her collar, or he
    (E) its collar, or he

15. Imani has always liked sports <u>more than me; I've</u> never been much of an athlete.

    (A) more than me; I've
    (B) more than myself; I've
    (C) more than I; I've
    (D) more than I; I was
    (E) more than I; while I've

16. Zoe and Elizabeth are coming over <u>after she finishes</u> work.

    (A) after she finishes
    (B) after they finishes
    (C) after Zoe finishes
    (D) after Zoe and Elizabeth finishes
    (E) after Zoe finishing

17. The committee <u>will have their final meeting</u> of the year tomorrow.

    (A) will have their final meeting
    (B) has their final meeting
    (C) will have his or her final meeting
    (D) will have its final meeting
    (E) will has its final meeting

18. I am tired, hungry, and bored, <u>which makes</u> me very grumpy indeed.

    (A) which makes
    (B) which make
    (C) that makes
    (D) a combination that makes
    (E) making

19. Neither the magazine nor the books <u>has its</u> original copyright information printed inside the cover.

    (A) has its
    (B) have its
    (C) have their
    (D) has their
    (E) have the

20. My mom, <u>whom has</u> a degree in early childhood education, will start teaching next fall.

    (A) whom has
    (B) who has
    (C) who have
    (D) whom have
    (E) which has

Answers and Explanations

1. B

The clause is not essential, so it should be introduced by *which*, not *that*. The subject is singular, so the verb must be *is*, eliminating (C) and (D).

2. E

To be consistent, all pronouns should be in the second person.

3. C

When two antecedents are connected by *nor*, the pronoun must agree with the closest. *Rose bushes* is plural, so the correct pronoun is *them*.

4. A

The pronouns are objects of the preposition *about*, so they should be objective.

5. E

The second clause is essential to the meaning of the sentence; without it, we wouldn't know which house is being referred to. So the clause should be introduced by *that*.

6. E

A generic noun needs to include both genders. Only (E) does so by revising the antecedent to make it plural.

7. C

The pronoun *it* refers to *the store*, a word that is not stated in the original sentence.

8. A

This modifier refers to *founders*, which is the subject, so the pronoun must be subjective.

9. D

The pronoun *they* doesn't refer to a specific antecedent; replace it with *dentists*. The verb is subjunctive because it expresses a recommendation.

10. B

Tenants is a subject, so the pronoun must be subjective. *We* makes a correct sentence.

11. D

Someone is a singular indefinite pronoun and must include both singular third-person pronouns.

12. D

The underlined words are a clause, which needs a subject and verb—thus, the subjective pronoun *whoever* fits the context.

13. A

The two singular antecedents are connected by *nor*, so the antecedent and verb must be singular.

14. B

The pronouns must be consistent; only (B) uses the same third-person singular pronoun.

15. C

It's clear from the context that the comparison is between how much Imani and the speaker like sports. The subjective *I* is needed. In the second clause, the correct verb form is *have never been*.

16. C

The pronoun *she* is ambiguous because it could refer to either *Zoe* or *Elizabeth*. Only (C) identifies a specific singular antecedent.

17. D

Committee is a singular collective noun, so it requires a singular pronoun. The verb *have* must be in its base form following *will*, so (E) is incorrect.

18. D

Which makes an overly broad reference to the whole clause *I am tired, hungry, and bored*. What *makes me very grumpy* is *a combination* of the three.

19. C

With a compound antecedent, the pronoun and verb must agree with the closest referent—*books*.

20. B

The clause *who has . . . education* modifies the subject of the sentence, *my mom*. So the pronoun must be subjective and the verb must be singular.

CHAPTER 7

MODIFIERS AND THEIR PLACEMENT

Without adjectives and adverbs, the world would lack great words like *rambunctious* and *vile*. It would have no color or comparison, no *now* or *later*. It would lack temperature or degree: no *sweltering* or *frigid*, no *totally* or *almost*.

English is rich with modifiers—words, phrases, and clauses that describe or restate. After a brief review of these parts of speech (see chapter 1), this chapter moves on to comparisons and modifier placement.

ADJECTIVES

Adjectives modify nouns and pronouns. They tell us which one, what kind, or how many or how someone or something looks, smells, tastes, or feels:

> The shopkeeper was helpful and friendly.

> I'd like to try that burgundy loafer on the wire rack, please, in size 8.

Because they describe people, places, and things, adjectives can function as subject complements:

> They said the apartment was charming and cozy; it turned out to be tiny and dank.

ADVERBS

Many adverbs are formed by adding *-ly* to an adjective. Adverbs modify verbs, adjectives, and other adverbs, telling us where, when, how, and to what extent:

We drifted <u>slowly</u> <u>away</u>.

I will <u>never</u> eat <u>here</u> <u>again</u>!

Though often similar in form, adjectives and adverbs are not interchangeable:

Incorrect: The car in front of me was going so <u>slow</u> that I was late for work.

Correct: The car in front of me was going so <u>slowly</u> that I was late for work.

Say What You Mean

Using adjectives and adverbs properly isn't just a matter of being grammatically correct. Using one instead of the other can drastically change your meaning:

Ilka found the test <u>easy</u>.   Ilka found the test <u>easily</u>.

In the first sentence, *easy* is an adjective modifying the noun *test*: Ilka found it to be easy. In the second sentence, *easily* is an adverb modifying the verb *found*: Ilka had no trouble finding the test.

Good and Bad, Well and Badly

The most commonly confused adjective and adverb pairs are *good*/*well* and *bad*/*badly*. *Good* and *bad* are adjectives; *well* and *badly* are adverbs.

Justine took the <u>bad</u> news very <u>well</u>. (*Bad* modifies *news*; *well* modifies *took*.)

Justine took the <u>good</u> news quite <u>badly</u>. (*Good* modifies *news*; *badly* modifies *took*.)

MEMORY TIP

To remember that *well* and *badly* are adverbs, note that both words have an *l*, and *-ly* is a common adverb ending.

The exception: *Well*, when referring to health or condition, is an adjective. When someone asks about your health, the correct response is "I'm *well*," not "I'm *good*." In all other cases, use *well* only to modify verbs, adverbs, and adjectives:

Adjective: The patients are <u>well</u>.

Adverb: The students did <u>well</u>.

Adverb: A <u>well</u>-known author will speak.

Adverb: <u>Well</u> said, Jacob!

PRACTICE 1

Determine which word in the parentheses correctly completes the sentence.

1. How (bad/badly) was he hurt?
2. Please be (careful/carefully)!
3. It's not a (good/well) situation, but we'll get through it.
4. The phone rang so (loud/loudly), it startled us all.
5. You look (good/well) in that dress.

COMPARISONS

Most adjectives and adverbs come in three forms: **positive**, **comparative**, and **superlative**. The positive is used to modify; the comparative and superlative forms are used in comparisons:

For one- and two-syllable adjectives and some one-syllable adverbs, the comparative is formed by adding -er, the superlative by adding -est. For longer adjectives and most adverbs (including all of those that end in -ly), use more and less for the comparative and most and least for the superlative.

Positive	Comparative	Superlative
nice	nicer	nicest
sweet	sweeter	sweetest
less	lesser	least
challenging	more challenging	most challenging
desirable	less desirable	least desirable
likely	more likely	most likely

Two sets of words have irregular comparative and superlative forms:

good/well	better	best
bad/badly	worse	worst

Incorrect: excitingest, worser

Correct: most exciting, worst

PRACTICE 2

Write the comparative and superlative forms of the adjectives and adverbs below.

1. scary   _____
2. beloved   _____
3. surprisingly   _____
4. friendly   _____
5. clearly   _____

Comparative versus Superlative

The comparative is used to compare **two** things; the superlative compares **three or more**:

Incorrect: Zach and Juliana both play chess, but Juliana plays <u>best</u>.

Correct: Zach and Juliana both play chess, but Juliana plays <u>better</u>.

Double Comparisons and Double Negatives

The comparative and superlative take only *one* form: **either** the suffix (*-er* or *-est*) **or** *more/less, most/least*. Do not use both forms together:

Incorrect: This is the <u>most fanciest</u> hotel room I have ever seen.

Correct: This is the <u>fanciest</u> hotel room I have ever seen.

Similarly, only one negative is necessary to express a negative meaning. (In fact, two negatives make a positive—they cancel each other out.) Therefore, do not use double negatives unless you intend a positive meaning:

Negative: I was <u>unhappy</u> with the contract.

Positive: I was <u>not</u> <u>unhappy</u> with the contract.

The adverbs *hardly*, *barely*, and *scarcely* are inherently negative, so don't pair them with a negative like *not*, *never*, or *none*:

Incorrect: I ca<u>n't</u> <u>hardly</u> see a thing through this fog.

Correct: I can <u>hardly</u> see a thing through this fog.

PRACTICE 3

Correct any modifier errors in the following sentences.

1. I am the most luckiest person in the world

2. Who is the greatest genius: Einstein or da Vinci?

3. This is much more worse than I thought.

4. I couldn't barely hear her.

5. Monaco, Nauru, and Tuvalu are all tiny countries, but Monaco (at just 1.95 square miles!) is by far the smaller of the three.

MODIFIER PLACEMENT

Whether a single word or a lengthy phrase, modifiers should be as close as possible to the word(s) they modify. A **misplaced modifier** may appear to modify a different word or phrase than the one the writer intended—often with humorous effect:

Misplaced: <u>Lost deep in a daydream</u>, Ed's boss startled him when she walked into his office.

Correct: <u>Lost deep in a daydream</u>, **Ed** was startled when his boss walked in.

Ed was lost in a daydream, but the modifying phrase in the first sentence seems to modify *Ed's boss*. The possessive *Ed's* is an adjective, not a noun, so it can't be the word modified.

MEMORY TIP

Modifiers should be as close as possible to the word(s) they modify.

Misplaced modifiers can create an **ambiguous** sentence (one with two possible meanings):

> **Ambiguous:** The volunteers who help us out <u>occasionally</u> want permanent, paid positions.

> **Clear:** The volunteers who <u>occasionally</u> help us out want permanent, paid positions.

> <u>Occasionally</u>, the volunteers who help us out want permanent, paid positions.

PRACTICE 4

How would you correct any misplaced modifiers in the following sentences?

1. After they robbed the jewelry store, the police caught the thieves.
2. Covered in mud from head to toe, Eunice screamed when she saw her filthy children.
3. Your meal comes with a free drink or dessert on Sunday.
4. In painstaking detail, the deposition required Zelda to describe her accident.
5. The painting depicted a knight on an armor-covered horse throwing a lance.
6. As a baby, my mother said I loved peas, but now I can't stand them.

Dangling Modifiers

A **dangling modifier** is an adjective (word, phrase, or clause) that lacks a clear referent: the word or words it modifies are never specifically stated:

> **Dangling:** <u>Lurching violently in the waves</u>, the captain was afraid of capsizing.

Who or what was *lurching...in the waves*? Presumably the captain's boat—but *boat* is not mentioned in the sentence. To correct the problem, the person or thing being modified (in this case, *boat*) must be added. (Sometimes a more substantial revision may be required; see below.)

> **Correct:** <u>With the boat lurching violently in the waves</u>, the captain was afraid of capsizing.

Dangling modifiers often begin with a present participle or gerund, but they come in all shapes and sizes:

Dangling: After seeing the flooded basement, the house was taken off the market.

Correct: After <u>the inspector saw</u> the flooded basement, the house was taken off the market.

Dangling: At four years old, my family moved to Nevada.

Correct: <u>When I was</u> four years old, my family moved to Nevada.

MEMORY TIP

Just as pronouns need a clear and specific antecedent, modifiers need a clear and specific referent.

PRACTICE 5

How would you correct any dangling modifiers in the following sentences?

1. Growing up an only child, my parents gave me all of their attention.
2. While preparing dinner, a mouse ran across the counter and disappeared behind the oven.
3. Sleeping peacefully on the beach, the sudden storm took us by surprise.
4. In selecting an outfit for her interview, a conservative look was the first priority.
5. Sandwiched between a woman shouting into her cell phone and a man snoring as loud as thunder, it was impossible to get any work done on the train.

Limiting Modifiers

Limiting modifiers include such adverbs as *almost, even, just, nearly,* and *only*. These modifiers belong in front of the word they limit:

Wrong place: The workers have finished <u>nearly</u> remodeling the kitchen.

Right place: The workers have <u>nearly</u> finished remodeling the kitchen.

Interrupter Modifiers

As you saw in chapter 2, the usual sentence pattern is *subject-verb-object*. As a rule, avoid putting lengthy modifiers between subjects and verbs or between helping and main verbs—and don't put *any* adverbs between verbs and their objects:

Interrupted: Captain Jones, after 14 years at sea, finally returned home.

Correct: After 14 years at sea, Captain Jones finally returned home.

Interrupted: Juanita threw down angrily the letter.

Correct: Juanita angrily threw down the letter.

However, *who*, *that*, and *which* clauses, if not excessively long, are acceptable between subject and verb:

Acceptable: My son, who is obsessed with trains, hopes to be an engineer.

Too long: My son, who has been obsessed with trains since he was two, hopes to be an engineer.

Corrected: Obsessed with trains since he was two, my son hopes to be an engineer.

Split Infinitives

Today, the occasional split infinitive is acceptable if it is not awkward. In the right context, it is actually better to split the infinitive:

Awkward: I want you to <u>very carefully</u> think about my offer.

Better: I want you to think <u>very carefully</u> about my offer. (Does not split the infinitive *to think*.)

Awkward: I would like <u>actually</u> to hear the rest of the story, so please be quiet!

Better: I would like to <u>actually</u> hear the rest of the story, so please be quiet! (Splits the infinitive *to hear*.)

PRACTICE 6

Correct any modifier errors in the following sentences.

1. Be sure to thoroughly chew your food before you swallow it.
2. Are you ready yet? Already it's time to go.
3. Renee Yeager, author of several self-help books and creator of a series of children's workbooks, will be the keynote speaker at the conference.
4. I will only help if you promise to never tell anyone what I told you.
5. The control group will receive each week a placebo, while the experimental group will be given small doses of the new drug.

SUMMARY

The adjectives *good* and *bad* are often confused with the adverbs *well* and *badly*. *Well* functions as an adjective only when it refers to health.

The **comparative** compares two items, and the **superlative** compares three or more. The comparative is formed by adding *-er* to the end of the word or using *more/less* in front of the word; the superlative is formed by adding *-est* to the end of the word or using *most/least* in front of the word.

Two common modifier errors are **double comparisons** and **double negatives**. Use only one comparative or superlative form and only one negative (unless you intend a positive meaning).

Modifiers should be placed **as close as possible** to the word(s) they modify. Correct **dangling modifiers** by clearly stating the person or thing being described. **Limiting modifiers,** such as *almost* and *only,* should immediately precede the word(s) they modify. Avoid placing **lengthy modifiers** between subject and verb, between helping verb and main verb, or between verb and object. The occasional **split infinitive** is acceptable if the resulting sentence is not awkward.

PRACTICE ON YOUR OWN

Practice identifying adjectives and adverbs. Look for modifying phrases and clauses as well as single adjectives and adverbs. Identify the referent—who or what is modified. Find instances when infinitives are split and pay attention to the placement of modifiers. Find examples of modifier errors and decide how to fix them.

Practice Answers and Explanations

PRACTICE 1

1. *badly*. The modifier describes the verb *was hurt*, so it should be an adverb.
2. *careful*. The unstated subject is *you*, and *be* is a linking verb, so an adjective is required in the subject complement position to modify *you*.
3. *good*. The modifier describes the noun *situation*, so it should be an adjective.
4. *loudly*. The modifier describes the verb *rang*, so it should be an adverb.
5. *good*. The subject complement should be an adjective.

PRACTICE 2

1. scarier, scariest
2. more/less beloved, most/least beloved
3. more/less surprisingly, most/least surprisingly
4. friendlier, friendliest
5. more/less clearly, most/least clearly

PRACTICE 3

1. I am the <u>luckiest</u> person in the world. (*Most* must be deleted.)
2. Who is the <u>greater</u> genius: Einstein or da Vinci? (The comparative is required.)
3. This is much <u>worse</u> than I thought. (*More* must be deleted.)
4. I <u>could</u> barely hear her. (*Couldn't* must be changed to *could*.)
5. Monaco, Nauru, and Tuvalu are all tiny countries, but Monaco (at just 1.95 square miles!) is by far the <u>smallest</u> of the three. (The superlative is required.)

PRACTICE 4

Answers may vary slightly.

1. After the thieves robbed the jewelry store, the police caught them. (The clause *after they robbed the jewelry store* appears to modify *police* because of its placement, and it is ambiguous because *they* could refer to either *police* or *thieves. They* should be changed to *the thieves* to eliminate the ambiguity.)
2. Eunice screamed when she saw her filthy children covered in mud from head to toe. (The modifying phrase *covered in mud from head to toe* appears to modify *Eunice* in the original; it needs to be moved to the end of the sentence to clearly modify *children*.)
3. On Sunday, your meal comes with a free drink or dessert. (The modifier *on Sunday* needs to be moved to eliminate ambiguity. Does the free drink/dessert come when you purchase a meal on Sundays, or do you have to return on Sunday to get that free drink/dessert you earned during the week?)
4. The deposition required Zelda to recount the story of her accident in painstaking detail. (The modifier *in painstaking detail* appears to describe *deposition* in the original and needs to be moved to the end of the sentence.)

5. The painting depicted a knight riding an armor-covered horse and throwing a lance. (The modifier *throwing a lance* appears to modify *horse* in the original.)

6. My mother said that as a baby I loved peas [*or* I loved peas as a baby], but now I can't stand them. (The modifier *as a baby* needs to be moved so it doesn't modify *my mother*.)

PRACTICE 5

Answers may vary, as there is more than one way to revise each sentence.

1. Because <u>I</u> was an only child, my parents gave me all of their attention. (The referent *I* needs to be added so we know who was *growing up an only child*.)

2. While <u>I</u> was preparing dinner, a mouse ran across the counter and disappeared behind the oven. (A clear referent needs to be added to the modifier *while preparing dinner*; otherwise, the sentence states that the *mouse* was cooking!)

3. As <u>we</u> slept peacefully on the beach, the sudden storm took us by surprise. (The referent *we* needs to be added so we know who was *sleeping peacefully on the beach*.)

4. In selecting an outfit for her interview, <u>Susan</u>'s first priority was a conservative look. (A clear referent needs to be added to the sentence—who was selecting an outfit? *Susan* [or any other name you choose].)

5. Sandwiched between a woman shouting into her cell phone and a man snoring as loud as thunder, <u>I</u> couldn't possibly get any work done on the train. (A clear referent needs to be added so we know who was *sandwiched* between two loud passengers.)

PRACTICE 6

1. Be sure to chew your food <u>thoroughly</u> before you swallow it. (The infinitive should not be split in this sentence.)

2. Are you ready yet? It's <u>already</u> time to go. (The limiting modifier *already* should precede *time*.)

3. Author of several self-help books and creator of a series of children's workbooks, Renee Yeager will be the keynote speaker at the conference. *Another option is to break this into two sentences*: Renee Yeager will be the keynote speaker at the conference. She is the author of several self-help books and creator of a series of children's workbooks. (The modifier *author . . . workbooks* is too long to interrupt the subject-verb pattern.)

4. I will help <u>only</u> if you promise <u>never</u> to tell anyone what I told you. (The limiting modifier *only* should precede the *if* clause. The adverb *never* should not split the infinitive.)

5. The control group will receive a placebo <u>each week</u>, while the experimental group will be given small doses of the new drug. *Another option is to put the modifier at the beginning*: Each week, the control group will receive a placebo, white the experimental group will be given small doses of the new drug. (The modifier *each week* cannot be between the verb and its object.)

CHAPTER 7 TEST

Choose the best version of the underlined portion of each sentence. If the sentence is correct as written, choose (A).

1. There's nothing <u>gooder</u> than a bowl of hot soup on a cold, rainy day.

   (A) No change
   (B) better
   (C) best
   (D) betterer
   (E) more good

2. The fire is burning <u>bright</u>.

   (A) No change
   (B) more brighter
   (C) brighter
   (D) most brightly
   (E) brightly

3. You are <u>badly</u> mistaken if you think I'm to blame.

   (A) No change
   (B) bad
   (C) worse
   (D) badde-
   (E) most bad

4. Let's go with the <u>least expensive</u> of the two options.

   (A) No change
   (B) lesser expensive
   (C) less expensiver
   (D) less expensive
   (E) least expensiver

5. We have it on <u>well</u> authority that you will win the award.

   (A) No change
   (B) good
   (C) best
   (D) gooder
   (E) more good

6. Yogurt is a much <u>more healthy</u> snack than potato chips.

   (A) No change
   (B) healthy
   (C) healthier
   (D) more healthier
   (E) healthiest

7. There <u>isn't nothing</u> wrong with the phone itself; let me check the wires.

   (A) No change
   (B) is anything
   (C) is nothing
   (D) isn't anything
   (E) is a thing

8. Please <u>give me now that paper</u>.

   (A) No change
   (B) give me that paper now
   (C) give now me that paper
   (D) now give me that paper
   (E) give me that now paper

9. <u>Wilson, unlike all the other governors before him, chose to continue living in his own home.</u>

   (A) No change
   (B) Wilson chose to continue living in his own home, unlike all other governors before him.
   (C) Wilson, choosing to continue living in his own home, was unlike all other governors before him.
   (D) Unlike all the other governors before him, Wilson chose to continue living in his own home.
   (E) Choosing to continue living in his own home, and unlike all the other governors before him, was Wilson.

10. <u>The next step is to carefully hammer the nail into the base.</u>

   (A) No change
   (B) Into the base, the next step is to carefully hammer the nail.
   (C) The next step is into the base to carefully hammer the nail.
   (D) The next step is to hammer carefully into the base the nail.
   (E) The next step is carefully to hammer the nail into the base.

11. <u>I'm going to soundly sleep tonight.</u>

   (A) No change
   (B) Soundly I'm going to sleep tonight.
   (C) I'm soundly going to sleep tonight.
   (D) I'm going soundly to sleep tonight.
   (E) I'm going to sleep soundly tonight.

12. <u>We barely were through the door</u> when the phone rang.

   (A) No change
   (B) We were barely through the door
   (C) Barely we were through the door
   (D) We were through the door barely
   (E) We weren't barely through the door

13. <u>There is one stipulation only in the contract.</u>

   (A) No change
   (B) There is one stipulation in the contract only.
   (C) There only is one stipulation in the contract.
   (D) There is one stipulation in the only contract.
   (E) There is only one stipulation in the contract.

14. Sitting at my computer, the screen suddenly went blank.

    (A) No change
    (B) While sitting at my computer, the screen suddenly went blank.
    (C) As I sat at my computer, the screen suddenly went blank.
    (D) While sitting at my computer, my screen suddenly went blank.
    (E) My screen suddenly went blank while sitting at my computer.

15. I went to the mall with Hannah wearing my new black shoes.

    (A) No change
    (B) Wearing my new black shoes, I went to the mall with Hannah.
    (C) I went to the mall wearing my new black shoes with Hannah.
    (D) I went with Hannah wearing my new black shoes to the mall.
    (E) To the mall I went with Hannah wearing my new black shoes.

16. Being sick, we didn't want to visit Erika.

    (A) No change
    (B) Being sick, we didn't want Erika to visit.
    (C) We didn't want Erika to visit, being sick.
    (D) Because we were sick, we didn't want to visit Erika.
    (E) Because of being sick, we didn't want to visit Erika.

17. The elderly patients we visit every week ask us to stay longer.

    (A) No change
    (B) Every week, the elderly patients we visit ask us to stay longer.
    (C) The elderly patients we visit weekly ask us to stay longer.
    (D) The elderly patients every week we visit ask us to stay longer.
    (E) The elderly patients we visit ask us to stay every week longer.

18. The dreams I have from time to time are disturbing.

    (A) No change
    (B) I have dreams from time to time that are disturbing.
    (C) Being disturbing, I have dreams from time to time.
    (D) From time to time, my dreams are disturbing.
    (E) I have dreams that are disturbing from time to time.

19. Standing in the shower, the water suddenly became ice cold.

    (A) No change
    (B) As I stood in the shower, the water suddenly became ice cold.
    (C) While standing in the shower, the water suddenly became ice cold.
    (D) Suddenly becoming ice cold, I stood in the shower.
    (E) The water suddenly became ice cold while standing in the shower.

20. The novel tells the story of a woman with a dog who is an aspiring painter.

    (A) No change
    (B) of a woman with a dog and an aspiring painter
    (C) of a woman who has a dog and is an aspiring painter
    (D) of a dog, a woman, and an aspiring painter
    (E) of an aspiring painter who is a woman and a dog

**ANSWERS AND EXPLANATIONS
BEGIN ON NEXT PAGE**

Answers and Explanations

1. B

The sentence compares two things: *a hot bowl of soup* and *nothing*; the comparative is correct.

2. E

The underlined word modifies the verb *is burning*, so it should be an adverb.

3. A

The underlined word modifies the verb *mistaken*, so it should be an adverb.

4. D

There are two options, so use the comparative. (B), (C), and (E) incorrectly use two comparative or superlative forms.

5. B

The underlined word modifies the noun *authority*, so it should be an adjective.

6. C

The positive comparative form is needed here. *Healthy* has only two syllables, so it takes the *-er* form, not *more*.

7. C *or* D

A trick question: Both (C) and (D) are acceptable; both avoid the double negative.

8. B

The modifier *now* cannot be between verb and object and is awkward before the verb. It is most logical *after* the object.

9. D

The modifier *unlike ... before him* is too long to safely interrupt the subject (*Wilson*) and verb (*chose*). It's best placed at the beginning, where it clearly modifies *Wilson*.

10. A

This split infinitive is logical, because it helps to emphasize the modifier *carefully*.

11. E

The modifier *soundly* should immediately follow *sleep*.

12. B

The limiting modifier *barely* should be immediately before *through*.

13. E

The limiting modifier *only* should be immediately before *one*.

14. C

This dangling modifier needs a specific referent—*who* was *sitting at my computer*? Only (C) adds the referent.

15. B

The placement of the modifier *wearing . . . shoes* in (A), (D), and (E) means *Hannah* was wearing them. (C) seems to say both the speaker and Hannah were wearing them.

16. D

We can't tell who is sick: *we* or *Erika*. Only (D) correctly adds the needed referent, *we*.

17. B

Do we visit the patients every week, or do they ask us to stay longer every week? Only (B) clarifies the meaning.

18. D

Does the speaker have dreams from time to time, or are the dreams disturbing from time to time? Only (D) clarifies the sentence. (C) is simply illogical.

19. B

We don't know *who* was standing in the shower. Only (B) corrects the problem.

20. C

In the original sentence, the *dog* is an aspiring painter! (C) corrects this. (E) says that the aspiring painter is both a woman and a dog!

CHAPTER 8

SENTENCE FRAGMENTS AND RUN-ONS

Imagine that as you read there are no periods on a page every sentence seems to run together into the next one they are blended into one big sentence you can't really tell where one idea ends and the next begins.

Or imagine. The opposite. That periods keep. Popping up in places. They don't belong. So you are always stopping. Before an idea is. Complete.

Not very pleasant reading, is it? That's because neither paragraph respects sentence boundaries.

UNDERSTANDING SENTENCE BOUNDARIES

Sentence fragments and run-ons are two of the most common writing errors. To recognize and correct these errors, you must identify kinds of phrases and clauses and determine the best way to join them.

Phrases and Clauses

A **phrase** *does not* contain a subject and predicate. It may contain one or the other or neither, but not both:

> to the store   sleeping soundly   once upon a time

A **clause** does contain both a subject and predicate. An **independent clause** expresses a complete thought and can stand alone. A **subordinate** (or **dependent**)

clause cannot stand by itself; it does not express a complete thought and depends upon another clause to complete its idea. These clauses begin with a **subordinating conjunction** or **relative pronoun** (see chapter 1):

Independent: I / <u>went</u> to the store.

Dependent: while I / <u>was</u> at the store

who / <u>likes</u> to go shopping

A **sentence** contains at least one independent clause, so it (1) contains a **subject** and a **predicate** and (2) expresses a **complete thought**. To be grammatically correct, a sentence must meet *both* criteria. (The big exceptions are the **imperative** sentence, which has the unstated but understood subject *you*, and **interjections**; see chapters 1 and 2). If a sentence lacks a subject or a predicate (or both) or does not express a complete thought, it is a **fragment**:

Fragment: Thinking of you.

Complete: <u>I was</u> thinking of you.

A sentence should express only *one* complete thought; it may consist of several clauses, but each clause must be closely related and contribute to a unified idea. When clauses are not properly connected, the result is a **run-on** sentence:

Run-on: I was thinking of you again, I couldn't help it.

Correct: I was thinking of you again; I couldn't help it.

PRACTICE 1

Determine whether each of the following is a phrase or a clause and decide whether each clause is independent or subordinate.

1. Freud divided the mind into three levels.

2. The id, the ego, and the superego.

3. The id is the most important part of our personality.

4. Because it allows us to meet our basic needs.

5. Such as food, drink, and shelter.

6. The id functions on what Freud called "the pleasure principle."

7. Which means it only cares about its own needs and satisfaction.

8. Not the satisfaction or needs of others.

PRACTICE 2

Determine whether each underlined segment is a phrase or a clause; decide whether each clause is independent or subordinate.

On the other hand, the ego functions on the reality principle. The ego is the
      1   **2**   **3**

awareness of the self in relationship to others. Thus, the ego must balance

the needs of the id with the needs and desires of others. As we grow older,
                   4   **5**

e third part of our personality, the superego, develops. The superego is the

oral conscience that helps us determine right from wrong and keeps us
                   6

m seeking too much satisfaction for our id.
                   7

SENTENCE FRAGMENTS

A fragment is either missing an essential part (subject and/or predicate) or does not express a complete idea. Sometimes you may write a fragment because you think of something to add after you've already ended a sentence or because you think that a sentence is already too long.

Types of Fragments

Most fragments will be one of four types:

1. **Subordinate clause.** These fragments have a subject and verb, but they do not express a complete thought. The fragments are underlined in the example below:

   In the futuristic society of *Brave New World*, everyone is happy. Because they all take a drug called soma. Unlike the others, however, Bernard, the protagonist of the novel, refuses to take the drug. So that he can feel both pleasure and pain.

2. **Phrase missing a subject or verb.** These fragments have one essential element but lack the other. They are often a participial phrase or the second part of a compound predicate that got separated from the original sentence:

   <u>Believing that happiness means nothing without unhappiness</u>. Bernard rejects soma. <u>Thereby ostracizing himself from society. Being the only one who is not happy</u>.

3. **Phrase missing both subject and verb.** These fragments can be any kind of phrase, including prepositional phrases, modifiers, lists, and examples:

   In Bernard's world, everyone is predestined to be happy. <u>Through genetic engineering and psychological conditioning. For example, exposing the bottled fetus to cold to condition that person to enjoy cold weather. Also, hypnopedia or "sleep teaching" (brainwashing during sleep)</u>.

4. **Fragment used for effect.** Writers may deliberately use fragments *for effect*—for emphasis, for transitions, or to answer a question. Fragments are also frequently used in advertising, and most interjections are fragments:

   Emphasis: Everyone is happy. <u>Except Bernard</u>.

   Transition: <u>First, a fundamental question</u>.

   Answer to a question: Can we be happy if there is no unhappiness? <u>Probably not</u>.

   Advertisement: <u>Soma: Happiness today, tomorrow, and always</u>.

PRACTICE 3

Determine whether any of the following are fragments and, if so, which type.

1. This brave new world sounds like a scary place. Because people don't have free will.

2. They are born already predestined to be a plumber or pilot or factory worker.

3. And love what they do.

4. Also, the children. They are raised in group homes. Not with their parents.

5. Because emotional attachment is considered dangerous.

How to Correct Fragments

1. **Subordinate clause.** To fix this kind of fragment, (1) attach the subordinate clause to an independent clause or (2) make the clause independent.

   In the futuristic society of *Brave New World*, everyone is <u>happy because</u> they all take a drug called soma. Unlike the others, however, Bernard, the protagonist of the novel, refuses to take the drug. <u>He wants to feel</u> both pleasure and pain.

2. **Phrase missing a subject or verb.** Attach the phrase to an independent clause or add the missing element.

   Believing that happiness means nothing without <u>unhappiness, Bernard</u> rejects soma. <u>He</u> thereby <u>ostracizes</u> himself from society. <u>He is</u> the only one who is not happy.

3. **Phrase missing both subject and verb.** Attach the phrase to an independent clause or add the missing elements.

   In Bernard's world, everyone is predestined to be <u>happy through</u> genetic engineering and psychological conditioning. For example, <u>a fetus may be exposed</u> to cold to condition that person to enjoy cold weather. Also, <u>everyone was subjected to</u> hypnopedia or "sleep teaching" (brainwashing during sleep).

PRACTICE 4

Correct any fragments in the following paragraph.

> Francis Ford Coppola's visually stunning and deeply disturbing film *Apocalypse Now*. Set in Vietnam during the war, it is an adaptation of Joseph Conrad's 1902 novel *Heart of Darkness*. Which takes place in the Belgian Congo. Conrad's novel is based on his own experience as a riverboat captain. During a time of widespread corruption and slaughter. Of both elephants (for their ivory) and natives. Ironically, the most human characters in Conrad's novel are the "savages." While the "civilized" Europeans behave like animals. *Apocalypse Now* adds new characters and makes many significant changes. Such as Marlow's murder of Kurtz. Yet the film remains true to the themes of Conrad's novel. Both are equally haunting. And instead of indicting the Europeans for their imperialism and greed. *Apocalypse Now* indicts America for its wrongheaded and imperialistic involvement in Vietnam.

RUN-ON SENTENCES

Two or more improperly joined independent clauses need to be connected in certain ways so that the boundaries of a sentence and the relationship between its parts are clear.

Think of each sentence as a color. If you paint a red sentence and immediately paint a blue sentence after it—without doing anything to show the boundary between them—you end up with one purple sentence rather than a red one and a blue one. The ideas blur together rather than remaining distinct.

Types of Run-Ons

There are only two types of run-on sentences:

1. **Fused sentences.** Two (or more) independent clauses are run together.

   Japanese anime is Japanese animation there are several important differences between anime and American animated comics and cartoons. For one thing, anime develops the characters as well as the plot over multiple episodes here in America each episode of a cartoon is typically its own story.

2. **Comma splices.** Two (or more) independent clauses are separated only by a comma.

   Another important difference is that anime tends to be more realistic and sophisticated than American versions, our animation often avoids real-life issues such as death or important aspects of daily life such as school and work. And anime characters are more human than the typical American comic book hero, they aren't superhuman exaggerations but people much more like you and me.

MEMORY TIP

Two independent clauses cannot be separated by a comma alone. If you use a comma, you must also have a coordinating conjunction (*and, or, nor, for, so, but, yet*).

PRACTICE 5

Identify any comma splices or fused sentences in the following.

1. Perhaps the greatest comic book superhero of all time, Superman debuted in June of 1938, this "man of steel" was the creation of two young men, Jerry Siegel and Joe Shuster.

2. Siegel and Shuster were still in high school when they created their hero, whom they dubbed the "champion of the oppressed."

3. Their timing couldn't have been better the nation was still suffering from the Great Depression and the world was on the brink of World War II.

4. Part of Superman's appeal was that he was dedicated "to helping those in need," and many in the nation were needy.

5. In fact, nearly a quarter of Americans still lived below the poverty line, in addition unemployment was still near record highs at 15 percent.

How to Correct Run-Ons

There are five ways to correct run-on sentences, depending upon the context of the run-on and the relationship between the independent clauses.

1. **Separate clauses with a period.** Divide the independent clauses into two complete sentences, with or without a transitional word or phrase:

   Japanese anime is Japanese <u>animation. There</u> are several important differences between anime and American animated comics and cartoons. For one thing, anime develops the characters as well as the plot over multiple episodes. <u>Here</u> in America, each episode of a cartoon is typically its own story.

2. **Separate clauses with a comma + coordinating conjunction.** A comma alone cannot separate two independent clauses.

   For one thing, anime develops the characters as well as the plot over multiple episodes, <u>but</u> here in America, each episode of a cartoon is typically its own story. And anime characters are more human than the typical American comic book <u>hero, for</u> they aren't superhuman exaggerations but people much more like you and me.

   Note: Many people confuse coordinating conjunctions with conjunctive adverbs. *But* is a coordinating conjunction and can safely separate two independent clauses with just a comma. *However* has a similar meaning, but it is a conjunctive adverb.

Run-on: For one thing, anime develops the characters as well as the plot over multiple episodes, however here in America, each episode of a cartoon is typically its own story.

Correct: For one thing, anime develops the characters as well as the plot over multiple episodes, but here in America, each episode of a cartoon is typically its own story.

3. **Separate clauses with a semicolon.** If the two independent clauses are closely related to each other, use a semicolon; it means that the two ideas are distinct but important enough to each other that they need a strong physical connection. Semicolons may be followed by a conjunctive adverb such as *however*.

If you use a semicolon to join an independent clause to a phrase or dependent clause, you create a fragment.

Fragment: While anime uses many of the same technological conventions as American animation; it is more advanced and stylistically unique.

Correct: Anime uses many of the same technological conventions as American animation; however, it is more advanced and stylistically unique. (Two independent clauses connected by a semicolon.)

4. **Separate clauses with a colon or dash.** If the second independent clause summarizes or explains the first, then use a colon. If the idea in the second clause is strongly connected to the first and deserves emphasis, use a dash.

And anime characters are more human than the typical American comic book hero: they aren't superhuman exaggerations but people much more like you and me.

5. **Turn one clause into a subordinate clause or modifier.** Add an appropriate subordinating conjunction to one clause or make it a modifying phrase.

Modifier: There are several important differences between anime, or Japanese animation, and American animated comics and cartoons.

Subordinate clause: For one thing, while anime develops the characters as well as the plot over multiple episodes, here in America, each episode of a cartoon is typically its own story.

PRACTICE 6

Correct any run-ons in the following paragraph.

One of the most popular means of transportation for teens and young adults today is the skateboard, it was invented back in the early 1900s, though no one knows exactly who made the first board or when. The earliest skateboards were more like scooters, they were roller skate wheels attached to wooden boxes or boards. These early skateboards were not very safe, many people got hurt in those first years. Skateboards got a big boost in the 1950s, that's when California surfers started to popularize skateboards and refine the design, they wanted to "surf" on the street. In 1963, a surfboard company began mass manufacturing skateboards, in the same year the first skateboard contest was held in California.

SUMMARY

A **sentence** must (1) contain both a subject and predicate and (2) express a complete thought. Sentences must contain both elements; otherwise, they are fragments. **Fragments** come in four types: subordinate clauses, phrases missing a subject or verb, phrases missing a subject and verb, and fragments used for effect (like interjections and imperatives).

Correct a fragment by attaching it to an independent clause or adding the missing element. If the fragment is a subordinate clause, the subordinating conjunction or relative pronoun can be removed to make the clause independent.

Run-ons are independent clauses that are not properly connected. Depending upon the relationship between the clauses, run-ons can be corrected by doing the following:

1. Separate the clauses with a period.

2. Separate the clauses with a comma and coordinating conjunction.

3. Separate the clauses with a semicolon, if the clauses are strongly connected.

4. Separate the clauses with a colon (if the second clause explains the first) or a dash (for emphasis).

5. Turn one of the clauses into a subordinate clause or modifier.

PRACTICE ON YOUR OWN

Advertisements are a great place to find fragments (and occasionally a run-on). Look through a newspaper or magazine to find examples of different kinds of fragments. Practice correcting them using the different strategies outlined in this lesson. You're less likely to find run-ons in published writing, but you can find examples on websites, especially personal sites or chat rooms.

Practice Answers and Explanations

PRACTICE 1

1. Independent clause

2. Phrase

3. Independent clause

4. Dependent clause

5. Phrase

6. Independent clause

7. Dependent clause

8. Phrase

PRACTICE 2

1. Phrase

2. Independent clause

3. Independent clause

4. Phrase

5. Dependent clause

6. Dependent clause

7. Phrase

PRACTICE 3

1. Fragment: *Because...free will* is a dependent clause.

2. No fragment

3. Fragment: *And love what they do* is missing a subject (it's the second part of a compound predicate).

4. Fragment: *Also, the children* and *Not with their parents* are phrases missing subject and verb.

5. Fragment: *Because...dangerous* is a subordinate clause.

PRACTICE 4

Answers may vary. In (A) below, all fragments are underlined, and (B) offers one corrected version.

A. <u>Francis Ford Coppola's visually stunning and deeply disturbing film *Apocalypse Now*</u>. Set in Vietnam during the war, it is an adaptation of Joseph Conrad's 1902 novel *Heart of Darkness*. <u>Which takes place in the Belgian Congo</u>. Conrad's novel is based on his own experience as a riverboat captain. <u>During a time of widespread corruption and slaughter</u>. <u>Of both elephants (for their ivory) and natives</u>. Ironically, the most human characters in Conrad's novel are the "savages." <u>While the "civilized" Europeans behave like animals</u>. *Apocalypse Now* adds new characters and makes many significant changes. <u>Such as Marlow's murder of Kurtz</u>. Yet the film remains true to the themes of Conrad's novel. Both are equally haunting. <u>And instead of indicting the Europeans for their imperialism and greed</u>. *Apocalypse Now* indicts America for its wrongheaded and imperialistic involvement in Vietnam.

B. Set in Vietnam during the war, Francis Ford Coppola's visually stunning and deeply disturbing film *Apocalypse Now* is an adaptation of Joseph Conrad's 1902 novel *Heart of Darkness*, which takes place in the Belgian Congo. Conrad's novel is based on his own experience as a riverboat captain during a time of widespread corruption and slaughter of both elephants (for their ivory) and natives. Ironically, the most human characters in Conrad's novel are the "savages," while the "civilized" Europeans behave like animals. *Apocalypse Now* adds new characters and makes many significant changes, such as Marlow's murder of Kurtz. Yet the film remains true to the themes of Conrad's novel. Both are equally haunting. And instead of indicting the Europeans for their imperialism and greed, *Apocalypse Now* indicts America for its wrongheaded and imperialistic involvement in Vietnam.

PRACTICE 5

1. Run-on: comma splice

2. No run-on

3. Run-on: fused sentence

4. No run-on

5. Run-on: comma splice

PRACTICE 6

Every sentence in this paragraph is a comma splice run-on. The fourth sentence (*Skateboards...street*) has three independent clauses. Answers may vary.

One of the most popular means of transportation for teens and young adults
[*Turned into a modifier.*]

today, the skateboard was invented back in the early 1900s, though

no one knows exactly who made the first board or when. The earliest

skateboards were more like scooters: they were roller skate wheels attached
[*A colon is best here, as the second independent clause explains the first.*]

to wooden boxes or boards. These early skateboards were not very

safe; many people got hurt in those first years. Skateboards got a big boost
[*These closely related independent clauses can be connected with a semicolon, colon, or dash, depending upon desired effect.*]

in the 1950s when California surfers, who wanted to "surf" on the street,
[*Delete subordinating conjunction "that."*] [*Turned independent clause into a modifier.*]

started to popularize skateboards and refine the design. In 1963, a

surfboard company began mass manufacturing skateboards. In the same
[*A period is fine here; a semicolon would also do.*]

year, the first skateboard contest was held in California.

CHAPTER 8 TEST

Read each proverb carefully, correcting punctuation and conjunctions as needed.

1. After three days without reading; talk becomes flavorless. —*Chinese*

2. Don't be too sweet lest you be eaten up, don't be too bitter lest you be spewed out. —*Jewish*

3. A closed mind is like a closed book. Just a block of wood. —*Chinese*

4. Don't run too far you will have to return the same distance. —*Biblical*

5. The eyes believe themselves; the ears believe other people. —*German*

6. From a thorn comes a rose, from a rose comes a thorn. —*Greek*

7. When spiders unite, they can tie down a lion. —*Ethiopian*

8. Goodness shouts, evil whispers. —*Balinese*

9. If you can't go over. You must go under. —*Jewish*

10. Life is not separate from death, it only looks that way. —*Native American*

11. Man has responsibility. Not power. —*Native American*

12. Since we cannot get what we like; let us like what we can get. —*Spanish*

13. To know the road ahead. Ask those coming back. —*Chinese*

14. Vision without action is a daydream, action without vision is a nightmare. —*Japanese*

15. What the heart thinks. The tongue speaks. —*Romanian*

16. When you go to buy, use your eyes. Not your ears. —*Czech*

17. Tell me who your friends are, I'll tell you who you are. —*Russian*

18. You've got to do your own growing. No matter how tall your grandfather was. —*Irish*

19. Shared joy is a double joy shared sorrow is half a sorrow. —*Swedish*

20. Never do anything standing that you can do sitting. Or anything sitting that you can do lying down. —*Chinese*

Answers and Explanations

1. After three days without reading, talk becomes flavorless. (A semicolon can only separate two independent clauses. *After...reading* is a phrase.)

2. Don't be too sweet lest you be eaten up; don't be too bitter lest you be spewed out. (The original is a run-on.)

3. A closed mind is like a closed book: it is just a block of wood. (The original second sentence is a fragment.)

4. Don't run too far, for you will have to return the same distance. (The original is a run-on.)

5. Correct as written.

6. From a thorn comes a rose, and from a rose comes a thorn. (The original is a run-on.)

7. Correct as written.

8. Goodness shouts while evil whispers. (The original is a run-on.)

9. If you can't go over, you must go under. (The original first sentence is a fragment. *If...over* is a subordinate clause.)

10. Life is not separate from death—it only looks that way. (The original is a comma splice.)

11. Man has responsibility, not power. (The original second sentence is a fragment. *Not power* is a phrase.)

12. Since we cannot get what we like, let us like what we can get. (The original first clause is a fragment. *Since...like* is a subordinate clause.)

13. To know the road ahead, ask those coming back. (The original first sentence is a fragment. *To know the road ahead* is a phrase.)

14. Vision without action is a daydream; action without vision is a nightmare. (The original is a run-on.)

15. What the heart thinks, the tongue speaks. (The original first sentence is a fragment. *What the heart thinks* is a subordinate clause functioning as the subject of the sentence.)

16. When you go to buy, use your eyes, not your ears. (The original second sentence is a fragment. *Not your ears* is a phrase.)

17. Tell me who your friends are, and I'll tell you who you are. (The original is a run-on.)

18. You've got to do your own growing, no matter how tall your grandfather was. (The original second sentence is a fragment. *No matter...was* is a phrase.)

19. Shared joy is a double joy, and shared sorrow is half a sorrow. (The original is a run-on.)

20. Never do anything standing that you can do sitting or anything sitting that you can do lying down. (The original second sentence is a fragment. *Or anything...down* is part of the predicate.)

CHAPTER 9

PARALLELISM AND ACTIVE VERSUS PASSIVE VOICE

Congratulations! This is your last lesson in Section I: Grammar and Sentence Structure.

The two subjects of this chapter—parallel structure and the active and passive voice—are not only a fitting conclusion to this section but also an introduction to the next. Both parallelism and active/passive voice are matters of structure *and* style.

PARALLEL STRUCTURE

One of the basic principles of art is **symmetry**: the balancing or mirroring of two sides or parts through repetition of patterns or forms. In writing, symmetry is achieved through **parallel structure**: expressing related ideas in similar form. Many proverbs, like the following Chinese one, are excellent examples of parallel structure:

> Give a man a fish, and you feed him for a day. Teach a man to fish, and you feed him for a lifetime.

Both sentences follow the same grammatical pattern:

Give / a man / a fish, / and   / you / feed / him / for a day.
verb / indirect object / direct object / coordinating conjunction / subject / verb / direct object / prepositional phrase

Teach / a man / to fish, / and   / you / feed / him / for a lifetime.

Consider this proverb without parallel structure; it loses rhythm and rhetorical impact:

> Give a man a fish and you feed him for a day; he'll be fed for the rest of his life if he's taught how to fish.

Parallel structure may be used in a series of sentences or within a single sentence:

> **Not parallel:** Wally is quite a scholar, but he's not very good at teaching.
>
> **Parallel:** Wally is <u>quite a scholar</u> but <u>not much of a teacher</u>.

MEMORY TIP

Parallelism means that two or more sentences (or parts of sentences) have the same grammatical structure.

PRACTICE 1

Determine which version of each sentence uses parallel structure and underline the parallel items.

Example: (a) The computer screen flickered, turned blue, and then it was just blank.

(b) The computer screen <u>flickered</u>, <u>turned blue</u>, and then <u>went blank</u>.

1. (a) There is no eating or drinking, and do not chew gum.
   (b) There is no eating, drinking, or chewing gum.

2. (a) I will either dance or sing, but I will not dance *and* sing.
   (b) I will either dance or sing, but dancing *and* singing together I will not do.

3. (a) The song starts off soft and slow, but by the end it is loud and fast.
   (b) The song starts off soft and slow, but it's different at the end, being loud and fast.

4. (a) In addition to stretching the body, yoga also stretches the mind.
   (b) In addition to stretching the body, yoga is good for mind stretching.

When to Use Parallel Structure

Use parallel structure any time you have two or more comparable or analogous ideas or items.

ITEMS IN A SERIES

Items in a list should be in parallel form:

Not parallel: It will be an evening of singing, dancing, and there will be food to eat.

Parallel: It will be an evening of singing, dancing, and eating.

ITEMS IN PAIRS

Items connected by coordinating or correlative conjunctions or other pairing constructions should be in parallel form:

Not parallel: The test measures reasoning skills as well as students' ability to solve problems.

Parallel: The test measures reasoning skills as well as problem-solving ability.

Remember, **coordinating conjunctions** include *and, or, nor, for, so, but,* and *yet.* They connect grammatically equivalent elements. **Correlative conjunctions** have the same function and include *either...or* and *neither...nor* constructions.

ITEMS COMPARED

When two or more items are compared, they should have parallel structure:

Not parallel: Jin Lee thinks only with her heart; you, however, also use your brain to think.

Parallel: Jin Lee thinks only with her heart; you, however, also think with your brain.

MEMORY TIP

Use parallel structure for items in lists, pairs, or comparisons—whenever two or more items are comparable or analogous.

SIGNPOST READERS

Parallel structure—especially in lists—is often introduced by a signal word such as *that*, *to*, or *of*. Sometimes it's necessary to repeat these signal words to make your parallel structure clear:

> I love you because you're smart and you're compassionate.

> I love you <u>because</u> you're smart and <u>because</u> you're compassionate.

Repeating *because* makes it clear that *I love you* for both characteristics.

Correcting Faulty Parallelism

If just one of several items is faulty, change it to match the structure of the others. If you have two items with different structures, choose the structure that is more concise or eloquent:

> **Not parallel:** I am <u>industrious</u>, <u>creative</u>, and <u>I always tell the truth</u>.

> **Parallel:** I am <u>industrious</u>, <u>creative</u>, and <u>honest</u>.

Here's another example:

> **Not parallel:** Erich von Daniken's book *Chariots of the Gods* sold over 7,000,000 copies; several million copies of its follow-up, *Gods from Outer Space*, were also sold.

The first clause is title–verb–number sold. The second clause is number sold–title–verb. The first clause uses the active voice and is more powerful and concise:

> **Parallel:** Erich von Daniken's book *Chariots of the Gods* sold over 7,000,000 copies; its follow-up, *Gods from Outer Space*, also sold several million.

PRACTICE 2

Correct any faulty parallelism in the following sentences.

1. Before we go, I need to make a few phone calls, and the dishwasher needs to be turned on.

2. According to moral relativism, we each determine for ourselves what is right or wrong; according to utilitarianism, right and wrong is determined by the principle of "the greatest good."

3. The study revealed that most people vote based on a politician's personality, not where the politician stands on issues.

4. If we go to the diner now, we can beat the dinner crowd, and money will be saved with the early bird special.

5. Bob Dylan captivates me with his lyrics, while Neil Young's music is what mesmerizes me.

ACTIVE VERSUS PASSIVE VOICE

In active sentences, the subject directly performs the action. In passive sentences, the active agent is removed or displaced (see chapter 4):

Active: Sherman Alexie wrote my favorite novel, *Reservation Blues*.

Passive: *Reservation Blues*, my favorite novel, was written by Sherman Alexie.

The subject of the active sentence, *Sherman Alexie*, becomes the *object* of the prepositional phrase *by Sherman Alexie* in the passive version, and the object, *Reservation Blues*, becomes the subject. The novel didn't *do* the writing; it *was written*. Hence the term *passive*.

PRACTICE 3

Determine whether the following sentences are active or passive.

1. The judges have selected a winner.

2. The winner will be announced tomorrow.

3. A prize of $10,000 will be given to the winner.

4. The winner will also receive an all-expenses paid trip to Hawaii.

5. Included in the package are scuba-diving lessons.

Because they have a clear agent of action, active sentences are more direct and engaging. They are also more concise—an important element of style you'll review in the next section. Note the significant difference between the active and passive versions of this paragraph:

Passive: In the ancient Greek myth of Icarus, wings of feathers and wax are built by Icarus and his father. Icarus is told by his father not to fly too close to the sun, for the wax will be melted by the heat. Unfortunately, this warning is not heeded. A height too great is reached by Icarus, and the wings are menaced by destruction. Death is then faced by Icarus, who is drowned in the sea below.

Active: In the ancient Greek myth of Icarus, Icarus and his father build wings of feathers and wax. Icarus's father tells him not to fly too close to the sun, for the heat will melt the wax. Unfortunately, Icarus does not heed this warning. He flies too high, the wings disintegrate, and Icarus falls to his death in the sea below.

A NOTE ABOUT WORD COUNT

We just said that one of the reasons the active voice is better than the passive is that it is more concise. But what about word count? What if you're looking at your essay outline on test day and don't think you have enough to say? Why not boost your word count by using the passive voice?

You could, but it's a bad idea. Yes, your essay would be longer, but it would also be much less effective. Using the passive voice won't get you a higher score. In fact, it would probably decrease your score. Instead of using the passive to fill out your essay, add more details or expand an explanation.

PRACTICE 4

How would you make the following passive sentences active?

1. Eugene should be given another chance by the coach.
2. Due to circumstances beyond our control, the brochures can't be delivered until tomorrow.
3. The test will be taken by over 3,000 students statewide.
4. The art school was given a donation of $10,000 from Wilson Banks.
5. Several volunteers are needed for Friday's potluck dinner.

When the Passive Is Preferred

In some cases, the passive tense may be used.

TO MINIMIZE THE SIGNIFICANCE OF THE AGENT OR EMPHASIZE THE RECEIVER

Sometimes, we want to downplay the role of the agent of action or emphasize the receiver. We can accomplish this by using the passive voice:

Active: Henrietta fired Charlotte today.

Passive: Charlotte was fired today.

Henrietta disappears in the passive version; all the emphasis is on Charlotte.

WHEN THE AGENT IS UNKNOWN

When we don't know the agent of action, the passive voice is a logical choice:

Active: Someone found the scrolls in a cave in the desert.

Passive: The scrolls were found in a cave in the desert.

PRACTICE 5

Which version—the active or passive—is most appropriate?

1. **Active:** The noise of the fireworks frightened Hannah.

   Passive: Hannah was frightened by the noise of the fireworks.

2. **Active:** Builders completed the bridge in 1902.

   Passive: The bridge was completed in 1902.

3. **Active:** Investigators found wiretaps on the house telephones.

   Passive: Wiretaps on the house telephones were found by investigators.

4. **Active:** The panel of judges gave Janel top honors.

   Passive: Janel received top honors from the panel of judges.

SUMMARY

Parallel structure means that comparable or analogous items follow the same grammatical pattern. Items in lists, pairs, and comparisons should be expressed in parallel form. Sometimes the word(s) that introduce the parallel items must be repeated for clarity.

In **active** sentences, the subject is a clear agent of action. In **passive** sentences, that agent is displaced or removed. In most cases, the active voice is preferable. However, the passive voice is best when you want to emphasize the receiver, when you want to minimize the significance of the agent of action, or when the agent of action is unknown.

PRACTICE ON YOUR OWN

Find examples of parallel structure and passive versus active voice in news articles. Choose a few articles and find several examples of parallelism. Look for a variety of uses of parallelism—in short phrases, long clauses, and a series of sentences. Then find examples of passive sentences and see if you can determine why the author decided to use the passive voice.

Practice Answers and Explanations

PRACTICE 1

1. (b) There is no <u>eating</u>, <u>drinking</u>, or <u>chewing gum</u>.
2. (a) <u>I will either dance or sing</u>, but <u>I will not dance *and* sing</u>.
3. (a) The song starts off <u>soft and slow</u>, but by the end it is <u>loud and fast</u>.
4. (a) In addition to stretching <u>the body</u>, yoga also stretches <u>the mind</u>.

PRACTICE 2

Answers may vary. The revised portion is underlined.

1. Before we go, I need to make a few phone calls and <u>turn on the dishwasher</u>.
2. According to moral relativism, we each determine for ourselves what is right or wrong; according to utilitarianism, <u>the principle of "the greatest good" determines what is right and wrong</u>.

3. The study revealed that most people vote based on a politician's personality, not <u>the politician's stance on issues</u>.

4. If we go to the diner now, we can beat the dinner crowd and <u>save money</u> with the early bird special.

5. Bob Dylan captivates me with his lyrics, while Neil <u>Young mesmerizes me with his music</u>.

PRACTICE 3

1. Active

2. Passive

3. Passive

4. Active

5. Passive

PRACTICE 4

Answers may vary. The agent of action is underlined.

1. The <u>coach</u> should give Eugene another chance.

2. Due to circumstances beyond our control, <u>we</u> cannot deliver the brochures until tomorrow.

3. Over <u>3,000 students</u> statewide will take the test.

4. <u>Wilson Banks</u> donated $10,000 to the art school.

5. <u>We</u> need several volunteers for Friday's potluck dinner.

PRACTICE 5

1. **Passive.** The emphasis should be on *Hannah*, the receiver.

2. **Passive.** Because the agent of action is the generic *builders*, it's probably best to use the passive and emphasize the receiver—*the bridge*.

3. **Active.** The passive would only be acceptable if the writer wanted to emphasize *wiretaps*.

4. **Passive.** Here, the receiver (*Janel*) should be emphasized, not the agent (*the panel of judges*).

CHAPTER 9 TEST

Choose the version of the underlined portion of the sentence that best corrects any error(s) in the original (including any grammar error covered in Section I). If the original is correct, choose (A). There may be more than one correct answer!

1. Sam likes to spend his Sundays reading the paper, watching sports, and he'll make a gourmet dinner.

   (A) No change
   (B) reading the paper, watching sports; and he'll make a gourmet dinner
   (C) reading the paper, watching sports, and making a gourmet dinner
   (D) to read the paper, watch sports, and to make a gourmet dinner
   (E) reading the paper. Watching sports, and making a gourmet dinner

2. Without electricity and not having any candles, we were stuck in total darkness for hours.

   (A) No change
   (B) Without electricity and not having no candles, we
   (C) Without electricity or candles, we
   (D) Without electricity and no candles; we
   (E) We, without electricity or candles,

3. To be honest, being fair, and being kind are the three principles I try to live by.

   (A) No change
   (B) Being honest, being fair, and being kind are the three principles
   (C) Being honest, being fair, and being kind. Are the three principles
   (D) The three principles, to be honest, fair, and kind, are what
   (E) Honesty, fairness, and being kind are the three principles

4. Nearly 300,000 children in the United States are affected by juvenile arthritis.

   (A) No change
   (B) Juvenile arthritis affects nearly 300,000 children in the United States.
   (C) By juvenile arthritis, nearly 300,000 children in the United States are affected.
   (D) Affected by juvenile arthritis, nearly 300,000 children are in the United States.
   (E) Juvenile arthritis affect nearly 300,000 children in the United States.

5. The keynote speaker seemed <u>nervous; he kept adjusting his tie and shuffling his papers as he spoke.</u>

   (A) No change
   (B) nervous, he kept adjusting his tie and shuffling his papers as he spoke
   (C) nervous; he kept adjusting his tie and shuffling his papers. As he spoke
   (D) nervous, he kept adjusting his tie as he spoke and shuffling his papers
   (E) nervous; he adjusted his tie a lot and was shuffling his papers as he spoke

6. *Or, the Modern Prometheus* <u>was the subtitle given by Mary Shelley to her novel *Frankenstein.*</u>

   (A) No change
   (B) *Or, the Modern Prometheus* was the subtitle of the novel *Frankenstein* given by Mary Shelley.
   (C) *Or, the Modern Prometheus* was the subtitle Mary Shelley gave to her novel *Frankenstein.*
   (D) Mary Shelley gave the subtitle *Or, the Modern Prometheus* to her novel *Frankenstein.*
   (E) To her novel *Frankenstein,* Mary Shelley gave the subtitle *Or, the Modern Prometheus.*

7. Take what Justin says with a grain of salt, <u>for he has been known to embellish his stories and he exaggerates.</u>

   (A) No change
   (B) for he has been known to embellish his stories and exaggerate
   (C) for he has been known to embellishing his stories and exaggerating
   (D) for him has been known to embellish his stories and to exaggerate
   (E) for he has been known to embellish his stories. And exaggerate

8. My five-year-old nephew says he wants to be a <u>firefighter because firefighters help people, they save animals, and he'd get to ride in a fire truck.</u>

   (A) No change
   (B) firefighter. Because firefighters help people, save animals, and he'd get to ride in a fire truck
   (C) firefighter, because firefighters help people, save animals, and get to ride in a fire truck
   (D) firefighter; because firefighters help people, save animals, and get to ride in a fire truck
   (E) firefighter, because people are helped and animals are saved by firefighters, who also get to ride in a fire truck

9. <u>The senator's office was inundated with calls from angry constituents.</u>

   (A) No change
   (B) From angry constituents, the senator's office was inundated with calls.
   (C) Calls from angry constituents inundated the senator's office.
   (D) The senator's office, with calls from angry constituents, was inundated.
   (E) The senator's office were inundated with calls from angry constituents.

10. The witch told Dorothy <u>to click her heels together three times and then "There's no place like home," is what she should say.</u>

   (A) No change
   (B) clicking her heels together three times and saying, "There's no place like home."
   (C) to click her heels together three times. Then say, "There's no place like home."
   (D) to click her heels together three times and say, "There's no place like home."
   (E) her heels should be clicked together three times and then "There's no place like home," should be said.

11. <u>The meal was thoroughly enjoyed by all of us.</u>

   (A) No change
   (B) By all of us, the meal was thoroughly enjoyed.
   (C) The meal was thoroughly enjoyed by all of we.
   (D) Us all thoroughly enjoyed the meal.
   (E) We all thoroughly enjoyed the meal.

12. Renee is definitely a good <u>friend, but she is not my best friend</u>.

   (A) No change
   (B) friend, however, she is not my best friend
   (C) friend, but she is not my most best friend
   (D) friend, but we're not best friends
   (E) friend. Although she is not my best friend

KAPLAN

13. <u>The mansion was home to several original works by Picasso, Van Gogh, and Matisse.</u>

    (A) No change
    (B) The mansion was home to several original works; by Picasso, Van Gogh, and Matisse.
    (C) Several original works by Picasso, Van Gogh, and Matisse were housed in the mansion.
    (D) Housed in the mansion were several original works by Picasso, Van Gogh, and Matisse.
    (E) Housed in the mansion was several original works by Picasso, Van Gogh, and Matisse.

14. When fluoride was first introduced into the water supply in the United <u>States, it was believed to be a government conspiracy by some.</u>

    (A) No change
    (B) States. It was believed to be a government conspiracy by some
    (C) States. Some people believed it was a government conspiracy
    (D) States, some people believed it was a government conspiracy
    (E) States, it was a government conspiracy, some people believed

15. Approximately one-fifth of the world's population lives in <u>China, while in India there is another one-fifth.</u>

    (A) No change
    (B) China. While in India there is another one-fifth
    (C) China, while another one-fifth lives in India
    (D) China, another one-fifth lives in India
    (E) China, while India has another one-fifth

16. As you prepare your résumé, <u>remember that items in lists and pairs should be expressed in parallel form.</u>

    (A) No change
    (B) remember to express items in list and pairs in parallel form
    (C) remember that parallel form should be used for items in lists and pairs
    (D) remember. Items in lists and pairs should be expressed in parallel form
    (E) remember that for items in lists and pairs, parallel form should be used

17. For me, a doctor's bedside manner is as important as <u>his knowledge and experience</u>.

    (A) No change
    (B) their knowledge and experience
    (C) how much he knows and how much experience he has
    (D) the knowledge and expertise they have
    (E) his or her knowledge and experience

18. <u>Feeling fully prepared and having confidence,</u> Elliot entered the courtroom prepared to win the case.

    (A) No change
    (B) Feeling fully prepared and with confidence,
    (C) Feeling fully prepared and confident,
    (D) Feeling fully prepared and confident.
    (E) Feeling fully prepared and confident;

19. College students are a favorite target of credit card companies because students need to establish a credit <u>history but often have little experience managing money</u>.

    (A) No change
    (B) history but often having little experience managing money
    (C) history. But often have little experience managing money
    (D) history, but their experience managing money is often little
    (E) history, but often he or she lacks experience managing money

20. <u>The jury submitted its verdict, and the judge sentenced Carlson to five months of community service.</u>

    (A) No change
    (B) The jury submitted its verdict, and Carlson was sentenced to five months of community service.
    (C) The verdict was submitted by the jury, and Carlson was sentenced to five months of community service.
    (D) Submitted by the jury, the verdict was in, and five months of community service was the sentence received by Carlson.
    (E) The jury submitted its verdict, and Carlson was sentenced. To five months of community service.

**ANSWERS AND EXPLANATIONS
BEGIN ON NEXT PAGE**

Answers and Explanations

1. C

This version corrects the faulty parallelism. (E) is a fragment.

2. C

This is the only version that corrects the faulty parallelism of the original. (B) has a double negative. (D) creates a fragment. (E) awkwardly inserts a modifier between the subject and verb.

3. B

(A) and (E) lack parallel structure. (C) creates a fragment. (D) is parallel but unnecessarily interrupts the subject-verb structure.

4. B

The original is grammatically correct, but the active voice is preferable unless the writer wants to emphasize the children. (C) and (D) misplace modifiers. (E) lacks subject-verb agreement.

5. A

The original is correct, with clear parallel structure. (B) and (D) are run-ons. (C) has a fragment. (E) lacks parallel structure.

6. D

(D) uses the active voice. (A), (B), and (C) are wordy and awkward. (E) awkwardly places the phrase *to her novel* Frankenstein.

7. B

(A) and (C) lack parallel structure. (D) uses the objective pronoun *him* instead of the subjective *he*. (E) creates a fragment.

8. C

(A), (B), and (E) lack parallel structure. (B) and (D) are also fragments. (E) uses the passive voice when the active is better.

9. A or C

(A) is an acceptable use of the passive voice, if the emphasis is on the senator's office. (C) uses the active voice, which is also correct but emphasizes the angry constituents. (B) has a misplaced modifier. (D) inserts a modifier between subject and verb. (E) has an error in subject-verb agreement.

10. D

(A) lacks parallel structure. (B) is a fragment. (C) also contains a fragment. (E) unnecessarily uses the passive voice.

11. E

(A), (B), and (C) use the passive voice inappropriately. (B) misplaces a modifier. (C) and (D) contain pronoun case errors.

12. A

The original has correct parallel structure. (B) creates a run-on. (C) has a double superlative. (D) lacks parallel structure, and (E) is a fragment.

13. A

(A) is best because it is in the active voice. (B) creates a fragment. (C), (D), and (E) are all passive. (E) also has an error in subject-verb agreement.

14. D

The original unnecessarily uses the passive, as does (B), which also creates a fragment. (C) uses the active voice but creates a fragment. (E) awkwardly places the object (what people believed) before the subject and verb.

15. C

(A) and (E) lack parallel structure. (B) is a fragment and lacks parallel structure. (D) is a run-on.

16. B

(A), (C), (D), and (E) all use the passive voice. (B) is the most direct and concise because it is active. (D) is a fragment.

17. E

(A) does have parallel structure, but the pronoun *his* does not acknowledge both genders. (B) and (D) incorrectly use a plural pronoun. (C) has faulty parallelism, and (D) places the object before the subject and verb.

18. C

(A) and (B) lack parallel structure. (D) and (E) correct the faulty parallelism in the same way as (C) but create fragments.

19. A

(B) and (D) lack parallel structure. (C) is a fragment. (E) uses the singular *he or she* to refer to a plural antecedent.

20. A or B

(A) uses the active voice for both clauses. (B) is fine if the writer wants to emphasize Carlson. (C) uses the passive voice, which is awkward and unnecessary. (D) misplaces modifiers, and (E) is a fragment.

SECTION II

Style and Usage

CHAPTER 10

EFFECTIVE WORD CHOICE

Good writing has three characteristics: (1) it has something to say, (2) it says it correctly, and (3) it says it with style. Style refers to the kinds of words and sentences we use to express our ideas. Do you describe a movie as *suspenseful* or *riveting*? Are your sentences compact or long and complex? Do you offer figurative language or stick to unadorned facts? While sentence structure plays a large role in shaping our style, the greatest impact comes from the individual words we use. So we'll begin this section with **diction**.

WHY WORD CHOICE MATTERS

Poor word choice in your GMAT essay is a score killer. You're not going to get points for using simple words over and over again! You're boring the reader, but worse, you're not getting your point across. You may never have thought of it this way before, but writing is a series of decisions. What should you write about? How should you organize your ideas? What is the best punctuation? And the one decision that you make in every part of every sentence is which word to use. Is an experience *moving* or *profound*? Poor word choice distorts your ideas and misleads your readers; the right word leaves no room for misinterpretation, because it is

- precise,
- appropriate,
- concise, and
- correct.

This chapter focuses on the first quality: precision.

PRECISE LANGUAGE

Want to elevate your style to the next level? **Be precise**. Notice how the following sentence is enhanced by substituting one of the precise verbs listed below for the imprecise *looked at*:

Sebastian <u>looked at</u> the woman seated next to him.

stared at	admired	surveyed
glared at	gazed at	regarded
leered at	peered at	scrutinized
studied	watched	inspected

Because they create vivid and exact pictures, exact words are far more powerful than general terms.

EXACT VERBS

Use an exact verb whenever possible. If you have a *verb + modifier* phrase, you can often find a single verb to express that idea more powerfully, precisely, and concisely:

Imprecise: "Hurry up!" Jolene <u>said</u>.

Precise: "Hurry up!" Jolene <u>shrieked</u>.

Precise: "Hurry up!" Jolene <u>begged</u>.

Precise: "Hurry up!" Jolene <u>bellowed</u>.

Imprecise: Xavier <u>drove quickly</u> to the hospital.

Precise: Xavier <u>raced</u> to the hospital.

Precise: Xavier <u>zoomed</u> to the hospital.

Precise: Xavier <u>sped</u> to the hospital.

EXACT NOUNS

Name people, places, and things as precisely as possible: *modifier + noun* combinations can often be replaced by a single, more precise noun:

Imprecise: The <u>flowers</u> are beginning to bloom.

Precise: The <u>geraniums</u> are beginning to bloom.

Imprecise: Ansel's <u>car</u> is in the garage—again.

Precise: Ansel's <u>Volkswagen</u> is in the garage—again.

EXACT MODIFIERS

Describe people, places, things, and actions precisely. You can often replace a modifying phrase or clause with just the right word:

Imprecise: Harold makes me <u>very mad</u>.

Precise: Harold makes me <u>furious</u>.

More precise: Harold <u>infuriates</u> me.

Imprecise: Myra is <u>always coming up with original ideas</u>.

Precise: Myra is very <u>innovative</u>.

Imprecise: Hans is <u>the kind of person who likes to have his own business</u>.

Precise: Hans is <u>an entrepreneur</u>.

PRACTICE 1

In each of the following sentences, replace the underlined section with a more precise word or phrase.

Example: The contract ~~does not have~~ a specific deadline.
lacks

1. It's <u>really cold</u> outside today.

2. I think Hillary would be <u>a good</u> manager.

3. The car <u>made a noise</u>, then stopped.

4. The cake is <u>really good</u>.

5. The <u>lack of light</u> made it difficult to see what I was doing.

The Right Connotation

Each word has a **denotation**—its dictionary meaning—and a **connotation**—the suggested or implied meaning, the set of assumptions or associations carried by that word. You're headed for trouble if you open up a thesaurus and randomly pick a synonym. Words with similar denotations have vastly different connotations. Consider this list of synonyms for *smart*:

intelligent	bright	sharp
clever	brainy	sagacious
gifted	keen	astute

Brainy is the most informal and suggests the person is more comfortable with books than people. *Sagacious* connotes wisdom and insight, while *clever* implies craftiness. A *gifted* person has a special talent and this is not interchangeable with someone who is *sharp* or *keen*. Like the verbs we examined earlier, adjectives convey very specific meanings.

PRACTICE 2

Rank the following word groups according to connotation, with 1 being weakest or most negative, 2 the most neutral, and 3 the strongest or most positive.

1. __ happy	2. __ furious	3. __ exaggerated	4. __ boring
__ ecstatic	__ angry	__ lied	__ routine
__ content	__ upset	__ fibbed	__ tedious

PRACTICE 3

Which choice in parentheses has a connotation that best fits the context?

1. The twins, finally reunited after ten years, stayed up all night (talking/getting reacquainted).

2. Unable to convince Hector to help, Adele (resorted to/tried) begging and pleading.

3. "That's the last straw!" Belinda (hissed/remarked) as she (fled/stormed out of) the room.

4. I admire Kendra's (distinct/peculiar) style.

5. At first, Nadia felt (self-conscious/ashamed) in her new glasses, but now she won't go anywhere without them.

Word Choice and Tone

Word choice is the key factor in establishing **tone**: the mood or attitude conveyed by words or speech—heavy or light, informative or mysterious.

1. I'd like to be alone.

2. Go away.

3. Get lost!

All three examples say essentially the same thing—but each has a different tone and sends a very different message. The first is polite and respectful, the second curt, and the third rude. Tone is very important in the Analytical Writing Assessment of the GMAT. You want the reader to see you as intelligent and professional, so writing with a formal, polished tone is the best way to do just that.

PRACTICE 4

Match the following sentences with the word that best describes their tone.

Sentence	Choice	Tone
1. "Hurry up!" Jolene demanded.		a. angry
2. "Hurry up!" Jolene seethed.		b. cheerful
3. "Hurry up!" Jolene shrieked.		c. impatient
4. "Hurry up!" Jolene snapped.		d. serious
5. "Hurry up!" Jolene sang.		e. fearful

SUMMARY

Style is controlled largely by **word choice** (diction) and sentence structure. Effective diction means that words are exact, appropriate, concise, and correct. **Exact language** means using precise verbs, nouns, and modifiers. A precise word can often replace a bulky, imprecise verb, noun, or modifying phrase.

Effective word choice also requires sensitivity to **connotation**. Words have positive or negative connotations and a range of social and cultural associations. Word choice also controls the **tone**.

PRACTICE ON YOUR OWN

Books (either fiction or nonfiction), major magazines, and newspapers are great places to look for examples of effective word choice. Find instances of precise language as you look through chapters or articles. Alternatively, find examples of writing that lacks precise language—perhaps a workplace memo, the draft of an essay, or an email you received. How much can you improve that text?

Practice Answers and Explanations

PRACTICE 1

Answers will vary. We provide two options for each question below.

1. freezing, frigid
2. an effective, a motivating
3. sputtered, hissed
4. delicious, buttery
5. darkness, shadows

PRACTICE 2

1. 2, 3, 1
2. 3, 2, 1
3. 1, 3, 2
4. 2, 1, 3

PRACTICE 3

1. *getting reacquainted.* If the twins have been separated for ten years, they'll want to do more than just *talk* about anything.

2. *resorted to.* The context tells us that Adele already *tried* other means; *resorted to* tells us that she's moving to an option she didn't want to use but has to.

3. *hissed, stormed out of.* The quote tells us that Belinda is angry, so *hissed* is appropriate. *Fled* connotes fear instead of anger, and anger is clearly implied by *stormed out*.

4. *distinct.* If Kendra's style is something we admire, we need a positive word. *Peculiar* has a slightly negative connotation.

5. *self-conscious.* The connotation of *ashamed* is too strong for the context of the sentence. *Self-conscious* is more accurate and appropriate.

PRACTICE 4

1. **d.** *Demanded* suggests the situation is serious.

2. **a.** *Seethed* suggests anger.

3. **e.** *Shrieked* suggests fear.

4. **c.** *Snapped* suggests impatience.

5. **b.** *Sang* suggests cheerfulness.

CHAPTER 10 TEST

Choose the answer that best fills the blank in the sentence.

1. The id is always there, ___ just under the surface of our consciousness.

    (A) being
    (B) hiding
    (C) lurking
    (D) hanging out
    (E) waiting

2. With holes in his shirt, pants, and shoes, Connor looked ___.

    (A) messy
    (B) unpolished
    (C) sloppy
    (D) bedraggled
    (E) untidy

3. Irfan's ___ makes him unpleasant to be around.

    (A) negative attitude
    (B) pessimism
    (C) unoptimistic nature
    (D) bleak outlook
    (E) feelings of negativity

4. I enjoy the ___ of the lake.

    (A) tranquility
    (B) quiet
    (C) peace and quiet
    (D) lack of noise
    (E) muteness

5. The car ___ out of control.

    (A) swerved back and forth
    (B) went
    (C) swiveled
    (D) zigzagged
    (E) careened

6. Rajesh was feeling so ___ that he went to the hospital.

    (A) unwell
    (B) ill
    (C) under the weather
    (D) unhealthy
    (E) bad

7. I like that Ike is ___ when it comes to getting what he wants.

    (A) a person who always keeps trying
    (B) obstinate
    (C) persistent
    (D) relentless
    (E) single-minded

8. When I leaned closer, I could hear the old man ___, "Thank you."

    (A) say quietly
    (B) say in a hushed tone of voice
    (C) hiss
    (D) request
    (E) whisper

9. I don't like Ed's ___ attitude; he thinks he's better than everyone else.

   (A) superior
   (B) confident
   (C) self-assured
   (D) overbearing
   (E) unpleasant

10. Cody refuses to sleep without a light on because he ___ the dark.

    (A) doesn't like
    (B) is terrified of
    (C) dislikes
    (D) gets nervous in
    (E) is alarmed by

11. Ahmed is so ___ that I'm afraid he'll have a heart attack.

    (A) excitable
    (B) uptight
    (C) tense
    (D) preoccupied
    (E) stressed out

12. Jasmine's outfit ___ the new dress code.

    (A) violates
    (B) does not accord with
    (C) counters
    (D) breaks
    (E) disagrees with

13. Lowell's office is so ___ with papers that you literally can't see the floor.

    (A) messy
    (B) bursting
    (C) littered
    (D) replete
    (E) full

14. According to the letter, James will not be ___ until the disputed balance is paid in full.

    (A) gratified
    (B) pleased
    (C) content
    (D) satiated
    (E) satisfied

15. The 1994 ___ of Tutsis in Rwanda left an estimated 800,000 dead.

    (A) ethnic cleansing
    (B) termination
    (C) selective elimination
    (D) mass murder
    (E) purging

16. American Sign Language translators will be available for the ___.

    (A) hard of hearing
    (B) deaf
    (C) hearing impaired
    (D) unhearing
    (E) auditorily disadvantaged

17. The acoustics in Stan's new ____ are quite amazing.

    (A) place
    (B) apartment
    (C) loft
    (D) residence
    (E) abode

18. The overwhelming success of the experiment ____ even Jing Lee, who had been the most optimistic about the results.

    (A) startled
    (B) alarmed
    (C) flabbergasted
    (D) surprised
    (E) dumbfounded

19. What happened to the ____ you left on the table?

    (A) thing
    (B) instrument
    (C) tool
    (D) equipment
    (E) hammer

20. Because of my consistently low grades in math, my parents have decided to send me to a ____.

    (A) learning consultant
    (B) tutor
    (C) educational assistant
    (D) academic counselor
    (E) achievement aide

ANSWERS AND EXPLANATIONS
BEGIN ON NEXT PAGE

Answers and Explanations

1. C

Lurking is the most precise word with the most appropriate connotation.

2. D

Bedraggled is the most precise word with the strongest connotation (required here given the context).

3. B

Pessimism is most precise and concise. *Bleak* has a very strong connotation, and *bleak outlook* is less concise than *pessimism*.

4. A

Tranquility is most precise, concise, and appropriate. *Muteness* has an inappropriately negative connotation, and *lack of noise* is not positive enough.

5. E

Careened is the most precise verb with the strongest connotation.

6. B

Ill carries the strongest connotation and is the most precise of the choices.

7. C

The correct word must have a positive connotation. (A) is wordy and imprecise; (B), (C), (D), and (E) are all precise, but only (C) is positive.

8. E

Whisper is the most precise and concise choice. Because the speaker has to *lean close*, neither *hiss* nor *request* is appropriate.

9. A

The best word will be negative and show Ed's sense of being better than others. *Superior* is best. *Confident* and *self-assured* are positive; *overbearing* and *unpleasant* are negative but don't convey the specific idea of being above others.

10. B

Cody feels strongly about the dark, so we need a word or phrase with a strong connotation. *Terrified* is powerful and precise.

11. E

We need a strong word—something powerful enough to send Ahmed to the hospital. *Stressed out* has the strongest connotation.

12. A

Violates is clearly the most precise word with the strongest connotation (and note how wordy (B) is in comparison).

13. C

Littered is the most precise choice. (A), (B), and (E) have appropriate connotations, but (A) and (E) are not as precise, and (B) doesn't fit the context. (D) has an inappropriate connotation.

14. E

Though all the words are precise and have similar meanings, *satisfied* best fits the context. (A), (B), and (C) are too positive. (D) has too strong a connotation.

15. D

Only *mass murder* is clear, straightforward language (and the only concrete noun). All other choices offer euphemisms.

16. B

Deaf is the most straightforward choice.

17. C

Loft is the most precise choice. *Residence* and *abode* are more sophisticated but not as precise. *Apartment* is specific, but *loft* is a precise kind of apartment. (A) is imprecise.

18. D

Surprised is precise and fits the context. (A) and (B) both suggest fear and are negative. (C) and (E) suggest an inability to understand.

19. E

Hammer is the only specific, concrete choice. (A) is about as imprecise as you can get. (B), (C), and (D) offer only categories of things, not specific items.

20. B

Tutor is the only honest and precise choice.

CHAPTER 11

BEING APPROPRIATE

So, it's like, we were talking about word choice and stuff in the last lesson, and we covered exact language, because that was numero uno on our list. Now we're gonna do number two, being appropriate—which this here intro sure ain't!

Effective style means that your word choice is **appropriate**: your language *suits* your subject, audience, and purpose.

LEVEL OF FORMALITY

As mentioned in the previous chapter, a high level of formality is essential to getting a top score on the writing section of the GMAT, and formality can be conveyed with appropriate words. For example, you'd say *celebration* or *festivities* instead of *party*, *persist* instead of *keep at it*, *attempt* instead of *try*, or *evaluate* rather than *size up*.

In most writing, there are two word choice pitfalls to avoid: slang and jargon.

PRACTICE 1

For each writing task below, determine the appropriate level of formality on the following scale:

1 very informal   3 middle ground   5 very formal

2 somewhat informal   4 somewhat formal

__ 1. An essay for your sociology class

__ 2. A letter informing the Department of Motor Vehicles of an address change

__ 3. A note thanking your neighbor for taking care of your cats while you were away

__ 4. A note thanking your landlord (whom you know well but with whom you aren't friendly) for getting the kitchen sink fixed promptly

__ 5. A memo to your new boss requesting a schedule change

Slang

In normal conversation, you probably use **slang**: the very casual and often playful language used by a particular group. It is prone to frequent change.

While slang has its place, it should be avoided in your GMAT writing for two reasons. First, it is highly informal, so it is not the way to score points with the reader. Second, it has a limited accessibility (not everyone knows what many slang terms mean):

> **Slang:** Jules, <u>I've gotta give you props</u> for how you handled that situation.

> **Standard English:** Jules, <u>congratulations</u> on how you handled that situation.

The Standard English version lacks the vitality of everyday speech, but *all* readers can understand it—and that's essential for effective GMAT writing.

REGIONALISMS AND DIALECTS

Like slang, **regional expressions** and **dialects** have their place but in general should be avoided because they are not familiar to all readers. If you want to convey the nature of your characters' speech, that's one thing—but for test day, stick to Standard English:

> **Regional Expression:** My dad <u>saws gourds</u> so loudly <u>ain't no one can</u> sleep at night.

> **Standard English:** My dad <u>snores</u> so loudly that <u>no one can</u> sleep at night.

PRACTICE 2

Revise the following sentences to eliminate slang.

1. I love your idea, Hank, but it'll never fly.

2. Please tell me straight up what's going on.

3. You wouldn't know it from the clothes he wears, but Antonio has really deep pockets.

4. We've been on a roll since Hendricks stepped up to the plate.

5. I totally bombed the math test—my mom's gonna kill me.

Jargon

Jargon is technical language shared by those engaged in a shared activity—members of a certain profession or people who share a hobby. Computer experts can toss around such terms as *jpeg* and *firewall*, and economists can speak to each other of *aggregate demand*, but average readers are likely to be lost.

In your GMAT writing, use plain English that all readers can understand. If you must use a technical or specialized term, define it:

> **Jargon:** The patient has an <u>internal rotation ROM of the shoulder</u> of 15 degrees.

> **Plain English:** The patient <u>can rotate his arm in from the shoulder</u> by 15 degrees.

> **Defined:** The patient has an internal rotation <u>ROM (range of motion)</u> of the shoulder of 15 degrees.

PRACTICE 3

Revise the following sentences to eliminate the underlined jargon.

1. Paul's two <u>periorbital hemotomas</u> made him look like a raccoon.

2. Before we got our jobs at the mall, Irma and I just <u>IMed</u> each other all afternoon.

3. The newspaper's <u>byline</u> attributed the article to the wrong author.

4. The <u>PA system</u> wasn't working, so Gus's band had to reschedule the show.

5. Olga's convinced we need a <u>hired gun</u>, but I don't think an outsider can solve our problems.

PRACTICE 4

Revise these pretentious or inflated sentences using simple, familiar words.

1. Avoid placement of the wheeled medium of transportation anterior to the mammal of the equine family.

2. The experience of temporality elapses at an expeditious rate while one is enjoying diversions.

3. Purveyors of benevolent deeds perpetually terminate in the rearmost position.

SEXIST AND OFFENSIVE LANGUAGE

We've come a long way in eliminating bias in our language, and it definitely does not have a place in your GMAT essays. That's a first-class ticket to getting a low score.

Sexist language includes any word or phrase that reflects a disrespect or contempt for women *or* men. This includes blatantly sexist terms and sentences that reflect stereotypical roles or behaviors.

Use Gender-Free Terms

Any word with *man* or *woman* in it can be revised to eliminate the inherent gender reference. Similarly, most words that have a masculine and feminine version are no longer acceptable; use a gender-neutral version instead. The chart offers a short list of sexist terms and their gender-free counterparts.

Sexist	Gender-Free
businessman	executive
chairman, chairwoman	chairperson, chair, coordinator
congressman, congresswoman	member of Congress, representative
fireman	firefighter
foreman	supervisor
mailman	mail carrier, letter carrier
mankind	people, humans
policeman, policewoman	police officer
salesman, saleswoman	sales clerk, sales representative
stewardess, steward	flight attendant
waitress, waiter	server, wait staff
weatherman	forecaster, meteorologist

SUMMARY

Appropriate language comes from having the right level of formality and avoiding sexist or otherwise offensive language. To find the appropriate level of formality, consider the following: (1) What style does your subject deserve? (2) What style best fits your purpose? (3) Who is your audience? (4) What is your relationship to that audience?

Slang and **jargon** are appropriate only when the audience consists solely of readers who will understand it *and* it is suitable to the subject.

Avoid **sexist** or **biased language**. Avoid stereotypes (positive and negative) based on sex, ethnicity, race, or culture.

PRACTICE ON YOUR OWN

Browse through a variety of texts and identify their level of formality. Consider *why* each author used that level of formality. Search for examples of slang and jargon in the texts you read. Is it appropriate? Did you have difficulty understanding it?

Practice Answers and Explanations

PRACTICE 1

1. **4 or 5**. Somewhat to very formal is called for in an academic assignment for a general reader. Write at the highest level of formality, but try not to sound too stuffy.

2. **5**. Because you have no relationship with the reader and the reader is in a position of authority, your letter should be highly respectful.

3. **1 or 2**. Depending upon just how close you and your neighbor are, this note can be somewhat to very informal.

4. **3**. Because you do have a relationship with your landlord, even if it is not particularly friendly, and because the message is positive, the note can be somewhere in the middle.

5. **4 or 5**. We can assume you don't have a particularly close relationship with your new boss, so it's best to show distance and respect.

PRACTICE 2

Answers will vary. We've provided one sample revision for each.

1. *it'll never fly*. I love your idea, Hank, but <u>it'll never work</u>.
2. *straight up*. Please tell me <u>honestly</u> what's going on.
3. *has really deep pockets*. You wouldn't know it…but Antonio <u>is really rich</u>.
4. *on a roll, stepped up to the plate*. We've been <u>very successful</u> since Hendricks <u>began doing his share</u>.
5. *totally bombed, gonna kill me*. I <u>failed</u> the math test—my mom <u>will be furious</u>.

PRACTICE 3

Answers may vary.

1. Paul's two <u>black eyes</u> made him look like a raccoon.
2. Before we got our jobs at the mall, Irma and I just <u>sent electronic instant messages to</u> each other all afternoon.
3. The newspaper's <u>byline, which names the author of the article, was incorrect</u>.
4. The <u>sound system</u> wasn't working, so Gus's band had to reschedule the show. (*PA* means *public address*.)
5. Olga's convinced we need a <u>consultant</u>, but I don't think an outsider can solve our problems.

PRACTICE 4

1. Don't put the cart before the horse.
2. Time flies when you're having fun.
3. Good guys always finish last.

CHAPTER 11 TEST

Read the following sentences carefully to identify inappropriate language. If the sentence is correct, choose (D).

1. Vanessa has been down in the dumps since her best friend moved to California.

    (A) Slang (including regionalisms or dialect)

    (B) Jargon

    (C) Sexist or biased language

    (D) No error

2. Someone jacked Jordan's backpack.

    (A) Slang (including regionalisms or dialect)

    (B) Jargon

    (C) Sexist or biased language

    (D) No error

3. Listen, I'm going to just lay my cards on the table here and tell you I love you.

    (A) Slang (including regionalisms or dialect)

    (B) Jargon

    (C) Sexist or biased language

    (D) No error

4. From the beginning of time, mankind has wondered about his place in the universe.

    (A) Slang (including regionalisms or dialect)

    (B) Jargon

    (C) Sexist or biased language

    (D) No error

5. Miko was flustered by the interviewer's inappropriate question.

    (A) Slang (including regionalisms or dialect)

    (B) Jargon

    (C) Sexist or biased language

    (D) No error

6. We don't have nothin' to say to ya'll, so skedaddle!

    (A) Slang (including regionalisms or dialect)

    (B) Jargon

    (C) Sexist or biased language

    (D) No error

7. FYI, your boyfriend is not welcome in this house!

   (A) Slang (including regionalisms or dialect)
   (B) Jargon
   (C) Sexist or biased language
   (D) No error

8. I still think Wendell is the best man for the job.

   (A) Slang (including regionalisms or dialect)
   (B) Jargon
   (C) Sexist or biased language
   (D) No error

9. "The girls from my office are always asking me to join them for lunch," Hayden bragged.

   (A) Slang (including regionalisms or dialect)
   (B) Jargon
   (C) Sexist or biased language
   (D) No error

10. Unfortunately, the company's assets didn't amount to a hill of beans, and the owners had to call it quits.

    (A) Slang (including regionalisms or dialect)
    (B) Jargon
    (C) Sexist or biased language
    (D) No error

11. Though the pain was excruciating, Eunice didn't cry.

    (A) Slang (including regionalisms or dialect)
    (B) Jargon
    (C) Sexist or biased language
    (D) No error

12. I googled my high school sweetheart and found out he married my best friend from grade school.

    (A) Slang (including regionalisms or dialect)
    (B) Jargon
    (C) Sexist or biased language
    (D) No error

13. All of the freshmen are invited to an ice cream social in the student center.

    (A) Slang (including regionalisms or dialect)
    (B) Jargon
    (C) Sexist or biased language
    (D) No error

14. This product will finally put us on the map.

    (A) Slang (including regionalisms or dialect)
    (B) Jargon
    (C) Sexist or biased language
    (D) No error

15. After a harrowing drive up the mountain in a rickety cart, Kurt decided to hike back down.

    (A) Slang (including regionalisms or dialect)
    (B) Jargon
    (C) Sexist or biased language
    (D) No error

16. When the market is bullish again, I will sell my stocks and invest in real estate instead.

    (A) Slang (including regionalisms or dialect)
    (B) Jargon
    (C) Sexist or biased language
    (D) No error

17. With her wicked song list, Eloise is sure to keep everyone dancing at the party.

    (A) Slang (including regionalisms or dialect)
    (B) Jargon
    (C) Sexist or biased language
    (D) No error

18. With all of his accounts in the red, Andres decided it was time to get a job.

    (A) Slang (including regionalisms or dialect)
    (B) Jargon
    (C) Sexist or biased language
    (D) No error

19. The boisterous sounds of the party echoed down the hallway and into my apartment.

    (A) Slang (including regionalisms or dialect)
    (B) Jargon
    (C) Sexist or biased language
    (D) No error

20. These are all man-made materials. How about something natural?

    (A) Slang (including regionalisms or dialect)
    (B) Jargon
    (C) Sexist or biased language
    (D) No error

**ANSWERS AND EXPLANATIONS
BEGIN ON NEXT PAGE**

Answers and Explanations

1. A

The phrase *down in the dumps* is slang for *depressed* or *upset*.

2. A

The word *jacked* is slang; *stole* would be more appropriate.

3. A

The phrase *lay my cards on the table* is slang for *be honest*.

4. C

The use of *mankind has* and *his* is sexist; *humans have* and *their* would correct the problem.

5. D

Flustered is a precise, effective verb; there is no inappropriate language.

6. A

This sentence includes regionalisms (*y'all, skedaddle*) and dialect (a double negative).

7. B

FYI is jargon. It is an abbreviation of the phrase *for your information*.

8. C

The word *man* excludes the possibility that a woman could be best for the job. Change *man* to *person*.

9. C

Calling the women in his office *girls* is sexist.

10. A

The phrases *a hill of beans* (*small amount*) and *call it quits* (*stop* or *quit*) are slang.

11. D

The sentence is correct; *excruciating* is precise and effective.

12. B

The word *googled* is jargon for using the Internet search engine Google.

13. C

Freshmen is a sexist term that acknowledges only one gender. Use *first-year students* instead.

14. A

The phrase *put us on the map* is slang for *gain us recognition*.

15. D

The sentence is correct. *Harrowing* and *rickety* are precise words.

16. B

Bullish is financial jargon for rising stock prices.

17. A

The term *wicked* is slang. Terms like *excellent* or *fun* would be more appropriate.

18. B

The phrase *in the red* is financial jargon for *in debt* or *operating at a deficit*.

19. D

The sentence is correct. *Boisterous* is an effective, precise word choice.

20. C

The word *man-made* is sexist. Replace it with *manufactured* or *synthetic*.

CHAPTER 12

BEING CONCISE

In the Analytical Writing section of the GMAT, you only have 30 minutes to write an essay. That means that you'll spend 8 minutes developing your ideas, 20 minutes on the actual composition, and the last 2 minutes proofreading. Not a lot of time!

Take the following sentence as an example of what can happen:

> *In my opinion, I believe that the fact that Frankenstein abandons his creature is the main reason that causes him (that is, the creature) to become violent and hurt people. (30 words)*

Essays that are wordy have exactly the same problem as the sentence above: they're loaded with repetition and full of clutter. Note how much more effective this version of the Frankenstein sentence is:

> *I believe the creature becomes violent because Frankenstein abandons him. (10 words)*

Therefore, being concise is the key to completing your essay in the allotted amount of time *and* getting a good score.

LESS IS MORE

Wordy sentences waste your reader's time, and clutter often clouds the meaning. Less is more. Concise writing shows that you have control over your ideas and that you have respect for your readers. That means a better score!

There are five specific strategies for writing clear, concise sentences:

1. Be precise.

2. Use active action verbs.

3. Simplify structure.

4. Eliminate clutter.

5. Avoid unnecessary repetition.

BE PRECISE

You've heard this one before. Exact words are often also concise:

> After Wynona <u>took all the stuff out of</u> her closet, she gave it a fresh coat of paint.

> After Wynona <u>emptied</u> her closet, she gave it a fresh coat of paint.

Avoid Intensifiers; Don't Be Wishy-Washy

Such intensifiers as *really*, *very*, *quite*, *totally*, and *extremely* add little but unnecessary bulk. Find the right word, instead, for a more powerful sentence:

> **Imprecise:** The desert was <u>totally empty</u> as far as we could see.

> **Precise and concise:** The desert was <u>barren</u> as far as we could see.

Likewise, such wishy-washy and informal modifiers as *sort of*, *pretty*, and *kind of* suggest uncertainty. Find a more precise word to replace the modifier and modified word:

> **Wishy-washy:** Sheila was <u>pretty upset</u> when she found out that Janell was lying to her.

> **Precise and concise:** Sheila was <u>livid</u> when she learned that Janell lied to her.

PRACTICE 1

Use more precise wording to make each sentence more concise.

1. The way Nina kept walking back and forth across the room made Tula nervous, too.

2. Everyone on the island was ordered to get away from the area because of the approaching hurricane.

3. Cheyenne was pretty embarrassed when her mom told everyone at the party her middle name.

4. The Tigers beat the Ravens by a lot.

USE ACTIVE ACTION VERBS

Whenever possible, use action verbs in the active voice. It's more direct, powerful, and concise than the passive:

Passive: Aboriginal art <u>has finally been given</u> the respect it deserves <u>from art critics</u>.

Active: <u>Art critics have finally given</u> aboriginal art the respect it deserves.

Action Verbs

Don't rely too much on the verb *to be*. Use vigorous, active verbs wherever possible:

Indirect (*be*) verb: Charles Darwin's trip to the Galapagos Islands <u>is what inspired</u> him to develop his theory of evolution. (17 words)

Direct verb: Charles Darwin's trip to the Galapagos Islands <u>inspired</u> him to develop his theory of evolution. (15 words)

AVOID *IT IS/THERE IS* CONSTRUCTIONS

Notorious word wasters include the *it is (was)* and *there is/are (was/were)* constructions:

Indirect (*be*) verb: <u>There are many factors that</u> contribute to weight gain, not just a poor diet.

Direct verb: <u>Many factors</u> contribute to weight gain, not just a poor diet.

PRACTICE 2

Use active voice and action verbs to make the following sentences more concise.

1. Several artists were commissioned by the State Council on the Arts to create a series of murals for the subway.

2. Carly's report is what I will use as a model for other students.

3. It was Nanny's chicken noodle soup that made me feel better when I was sick.

4. There is still a chance that I'll win the poetry contest.

SIMPLIFY STRUCTURE

Wordiness is often the result of unnecessarily bulky sentence constructions.

Turn Clauses and Phrases into Modifiers

Many clauses and phrases can be reduced to modifiers, especially *that, who,* and *which* clauses and prepositional phrases:

> **Wordy:** The school <u>that I go to</u> is undergoing major renovations. (10 words)
>
> **Concise:** <u>My</u> school is undergoing major renovations. (6 words)
>
> **Wordy:** <u>People who visit Internet chat rooms regularly</u> are familiar with chat room slang. (13 words)
>
> **Concise:** <u>Chat room regulars</u> are familiar with Internet jargon. (8 words)

Combine Sentences

When one sentence adds a detail to the preceding one, it can often be turned into a modifier:

> **Wordy:** <u>One of the problems</u> in early childhood education is high turnover among teachers and <u>assistants. This high turnover is</u> due primarily to long hours and low wages. (27 words)
>
> **Concise:** <u>One problem</u> in early childhood education is high turnover among teachers and <u>assistants due</u> primarily to long hours and low wages. (21 words)

PRACTICE 3

Simplify the structure of the following sentences to eliminate wordiness.

1. There are 40 children registered for the class. However, the classroom can only accommodate 35 people.

2. My sociology class meets at 8 o'clock, which is unfortunate.

3. I was shocked to learn that 130 pounds of sugar are consumed by the average American each year.

4. A typical can of soda contains about nine teaspoons of refined white sugar. Refined white sugar is so chemically processed that it contains no vitamins, minerals, protein, fiber, or water.

ELIMINATE CLUTTER

Some words merely add clutter. The word *that* is a frequent offender:

> **Cluttered:** The face <u>that</u> is on the $20 bill <u>is that of</u> Andrew Jackson.

> **Concise:** The face on the $20 bill is Andrew Jackson's.

Cluttered	Concise	Cluttered	Concise
in the event that	if	for the purpose of	for
in spite of the fact that	although	due to the fact that	because
until such time as	until	for the reason that	because
at that point in time	then	at this point in time	now
in the neighborhood of	about	has the appearance of	looks like, seems like

PRACTICE 4

Cross out clutter in the following sentences.

1. I hope that you find that these accommodations are acceptable.

2. In spite of the fact that he can't see without his glasses, Ted almost never wears them.

3. I have always believed that the here and now is more important than the future or the past.

4. I will keep this job until such time as I complete my degree, at which point I will look for an internship.

AVOID UNNECESSARY REPETITION

Repetition is a common cause of wordy sentences:

Redundant: As a bonus, you'll receive a <u>free</u> pen <u>at no extra charge</u>! (12 words)

Concise: As a bonus, you'll receive a <u>free</u> pen! (8 words)

Redundant	Concise
red in color	red
circular in shape	circular
large in size	large
refer back to	refer to
return back to	return to
completely unanimous	unanimous
circle around	circle
end result	result
cooperate together	cooperate
true fact	fact

Redundant	Concise
12 midnight	midnight
2 A.M. in the morning	2 A.M. *or* 2 in the morning
shorter in length	shorter
repeat again	repeat
revert back to	revert to
In my opinion, I believe	In my opinion *or* I believe
surrounded on all sides	surrounded
each and every	each *or* every
biography of his life	biography
personal opinion	opinion

Some abbreviations can lead to unnecessary repetition. For example: *There are no ATM machines around here.* ATM stands for *automated teller machine*—so the sentence states *machine* twice.

PRACTICE 5

Eliminate repetition in the following sentences.

1. I worked until 3 A.M. in the morning, but I still didn't finish my report.

2. These statistics refer back to the chart on page 181.

3. Carmen is a pianist who plays the piano with great skill.

4. Under different circumstances, if we weren't in the situation we're in now, I'd quit my job and go back to school.

5. The airplane circled around the airport several times before it received clearance to land.

SUMMARY

Effective writing is **concise**: it conveys its ideas without unnecessary words. To be concise, do the following:

1. **Be precise.** Use exact words and phrases. Avoid weak intensifiers and wishy-washy language. Find an exact word instead.

2. **Use active action verbs.** Most sentences should be in the active voice. When possible, choose a vigorous action verb over the state of being verb *be*. Avoid *there is* and *it is* constructions.

3. **Simplify structure.** Turn clauses and phrases into modifiers, especially *that, who*, and *which* clauses and prepositional phrases. Combine sentences that have repeating elements.

4. **Eliminate clutter.** *That* often unnecessarily clutters sentences, and common clutter phrases should be replaced by clearer alternatives.

5. **Avoid unnecessary repetition.** Common redundant phrases include *end result* and *in my opinion, I believe*. Watch out for redundancies when using abbreviations.

PRACTICE ON YOUR OWN

Wordy writing is everywhere, so you're bound to find examples now that you know what to look for. Amateur publications or websites and everyday communications such as workplace memos are good places to search. Think about how you'd make the writing more concise.

Practice Answers and Explanations

PRACTICE 1

Answers may vary. We underlined the word that replaces an imprecise word or phrase.

1. The way Nina <u>paced</u> the room made Tula nervous, too.

2. Everyone on the island was ordered to <u>evacuate</u> because of the approaching hurricane.

3. Cheyenne was <u>mortified</u> when her mom told everyone at the party her middle name.

4. The Tigers <u>crushed</u> the Ravens.

PRACTICE 2

Answers may vary.

1. The State Council on the Arts commissioned several artists to create a series of murals for the subway.

2. I will use Carly's report as a model for other students.

3. Nanny's chicken noodle soup made me feel better when I was sick.

4. I still have a chance to win the poetry contest.

PRACTICE 3

Answers may vary.

1. Forty children are registered for the class, but the room can only accommodate 35.

2. Unfortunately, my sociology class meets at 8 A.M.

3. I was shocked to learn that the average American consumes 130 pounds of sugar per year.

4. A typical can of soda contains about nine teaspoons of refined white sugar, which is so chemically processed that it contains no vitamins, minerals, protein, fiber, or water.

PRACTICE 4

Answers may vary.

1. I hope you find these accommodations acceptable.

2. Although he can't see without his glasses, Ted almost never wears them.

3. I have always believed the present is more important than the future or past.

4. I will keep this job until I complete my degree; then I will look for an internship.

PRACTICE 5

1. I worked until 3 A.M. ~~in the morning~~, but I still didn't finish my report.

2. These statistics refer ~~back~~ to the chart on page 181.

3. Carmen is a pianist ~~who plays the piano with~~ <u>of</u> great skill.

4. Under different circumstances, ~~if we weren't in the situation we're in now,~~ I'd quit my job and go back to school.

5. The airplane circled ~~around~~ the airport several times before it received clearance to land.

CHAPTER 12 TEST

Choose the version that has precise, concise, and appropriate language as well as correct grammar. If the original is the best, choose (A).

1. Because of the fact that he was surrounded on all sides, Cody decided to surrender.

   (A) No change
   (B) Because of the fact that he was surrounded on all sides, Cody decided to call it quits.
   (C) Because he was surrounded on all sides; Cody decided to surrender.
   (D) Because he was surrounded, Cody decided to surrender.
   (E) Due to the fact that he was surrounded, Cody decided to surrender.

2. Guy de Maupassant wrote the short story "The Necklace." This is one of the most famous short stories ever written.

   (A) No change
   (B) The short story "The Necklace" was written by Guy de Maupassant, and this story is one of the most famous stories ever written.
   (C) Guy de Maupassant wrote "The Necklace," one of the most famous short stories ever written.
   (D) Composed by the writer Guy de Maupassant, the short story "The Necklace" is one of the most famous ever written.
   (E) Guy de Maupassant wrote "The Necklace," one of the phattest stories ever written.

3. Did you know the fact that the first motion pictures were created and developed by Louis Aimé Augustin Le Prince back in the year 1888?

   (A) No change
   (B) Did you know the first motion pictures were created by Louis Aimé Augustin Le Prince back in 1888?
   (C) Were you aware of the fact that Louise Aimé Augustin Le Prince developed the first motion pictures? He did this back in the year 1888.
   (D) Did you know the fact that back in the year 1888, the first motion pictures were created and developed by Louis Aimé Augustin Le Prince?
   (E) Created by Louis Aimé Augustin Le Prince, did you know that the first motion pictures were developed back in the year 1888?

4. Dragonflies are the "helicopters" of the insect world. They are like helicopters in that they can hover, fly forward and backward, and change direction rapidly.

    (A) No change

    (B) Dragonflies are the "helicopters" of the insect world. This is because they can hover, fly forward and backward, and change direction rapidly.

    (C) Dragonflies are the "helicopters" of the insect world, this is so because they can hover, fly forward and backward, and have the ability to change direction rapidly.

    (D) Dragonflies are the "helicopters" of the insect world; they can hover, fly forward and backward, and change direction rapidly.

    (E) Dragonflies can be deemed the "helicopters" of the insect realm; exhibiting a striking resemblance to these hover craft, the dragonfly can hover, aviate forward and backward, and change trajectory rapidly.

5. A law passed in England in 1865 limited the speed of steam cars to two miles per hour.

    (A) No change

    (B) A law which was passed in England in the year 1865 limited the speed of steam cars to two miles per hour.

    (C) In England, a law passed in 1865 restricted the speed of steam cars, allowing them to travel no more than two miles per hour.

    (D) In 1865, British lawmakers passed a law that allowed steam cars to travel at no more than two miles per hour.

    (E) Restricted to the speed of no more than two miles per hour were steam cars, according to a law passed in England in 1865.

6. The babies of most animal species are hatched from eggs, and the newborns are not taken care of by their parents after they hatch.

    (A) No change

    (B) The progeny of the majority of zoological creatures are hatched from eggs, and these descendants are not nurtured by their progenitors upon emergence.

    (C) Most animal species hatch their offspring from eggs and do not nurture the hatchlings after they are born.

    (D) Not taken care of upon birth are the majority of babies of animal species, which are hatched from eggs.

    (E) The babies of most animal species are born from eggs, and these new beings do not get any care from their parents after they come out.

7. Mozart composed his first symphony when he was only at the age of eight years old.

   (A) No change
   (B) Mozart composed his first symphony when he was only eight years old.
   (C) Mozart, when he was only eight years old, composed his first symphony.
   (D) Only at the age of eight years old was when Mozart composed his first symphony.
   (E) The first symphony of Mozart was composed by him when he was at the age of eight.

8. Requests will be taken by the deejay during dinner.

   (A) No change
   (B) During dinner is when requests will be taken by the deejay.
   (C) The deejay will take requests during dinner.
   (D) During the repast, the deejay shall accept requests.
   (E) Tell the deejay what you want to hear while we chow.

9. The longest fangs of any snake are on the gaboon viper, whose fangs are up to two inches long.

   (A) No change
   (B) With fangs that are up to two inches long, the gaboon viper has the longest fangs of any snake.
   (C) The gaboon viper's fangs—the longest of any snake—can grow up to two inches long.
   (D) Having the longest fangs of any snake is the gaboon viper, whose fangs are up to two inches in length.
   (E) At two inches long, the gaboon viper has the longest fangs of any snake.

10. I'm pretty hungry, so you should get two pizzas.

   (A) No change
   (B) I'm sort of starving, so you should get two pizzas.
   (C) I'm famished, so you should order two pizzas.
   (D) I'm hungry, order two pizzas.
   (E) As I am in a ravenous state, I recommend that you request two pizzas.

11. In the event that the baby wakes up before I return back, please give her a bottle.

    (A) No change

    (B) In the event the baby awakens before I return, please feed her with the bottle.

    (C) Should the baby wake up before I return, she should be given a bottle.

    (D) If the baby wakes before I get back, please give her a bottle.

    (E) If I am not back before the baby wakes, the bottle should be given to her.

12. Zizi said she's just dying for a pedicure for her birthday.

    (A) No change

    (B) Zizi said that she would really like a pedicure for her birthday.

    (C) Zizi has articulated an intense desire for a pedicure for her birthday.

    (D) Zizi said she wants a pedicure for her birthday.

    (E) Zizi said she'd love a pedicure for her birthday.

13. There are few American writers as prolific as Mark Twain.

    (A) No change

    (B) There are few American writers who are or were as prolific as Mark Twain.

    (C) Most American writers have not written as much as Mark Twain did.

    (D) The number of American writers achieving the status of Mark Twain in terms of the number of texts they have written is very few.

    (E) Not many American writers share being prolific with Mark Twain.

14. Fossils show that the stegosaurus was in the neighborhood of about six feet tall in height.

    (A) No change

    (B) Fossils indicate that the stegosaurus was about six feet tall.

    (C) According to fossil evidence, the height of the stegosaurus was in the neighborhood of six feet.

    (D) Shown by fossils is the fact that the stegosaurus reached a height of approximately six feet.

    (E) Fossils show that stegosaurus dinos maxed out around six feet up.

15. This is the email that I have been waiting for.

    (A) No change
    (B) I have been anticipating the arrival of this email.
    (C) I have been waiting for this email.
    (D) The arrival of this email is what I have been awaiting.
    (E) This email is what I have been waiting for.

16. Chelsea is an area in Manhattan that is located in the area of the Lower West Side in the 20s.

    (A) No change
    (B) Located in the Lower West Side in the 20s, Manhattan has the area known as Chelsea.
    (C) Found in the 20s on the Lower West Side of Manhattan is the area known as Chelsea.
    (D) On Manhattan's Lower West Side, you'll find the neighborhood called Chelsea, in the 20s.
    (E) The area known as Cheslea is located in the 20s on Manhattan's Lower West Side.

17. The ETA for the arrival of Chad's flight is 8:15.

    (A) No change
    (B) The ETA for Chad's flight is 8:15.
    (C) Chad's flight's arrival has an ETA of 8:15.
    (D) The arrival of Chad's flight has an ETA of 8:15.
    (E) Eight-fifteen is the approximate ETA of Chad's flight.

18. A thick, wooly coat protected mammoths from subzero temperatures.

    (A) No change
    (B) Enveloped in a coat of thick wool, mammoths were protected from subzero temperatures.
    (C) It was a thick, wooly coat that protected mammoths from subzero temperatures.
    (D) A thick, wooly coat kept mammoths warm despite subzero temperatures.
    (E) Mammoths had thick, wooly coats. These protected them from subzero temperatures.

19. Missy's poem is what inspired me to start writing my own poetry.

    (A) No change
    (B) Missy's poem is what inspired me starting to write my own poetry.
    (C) Missy's poem inspired me to start writing my own poetry.
    (D) Missy's poem gave me the inspiration to start writing my own poetry.
    (E) Missy's poem gave me the inspiration and motivation to begin to write poetry of my own.

20. The office that is in the corner is finally up for grabs.

    (A) No change
    (B) The office that is in the corner is finally available.
    (C) At last, the office in the corner is finally available.
    (D) Finally available is the corner office.
    (E) The corner office is finally available.

Answers and Explanations

1. D

Because of the fact that is wordy and *surrounded on all sides* is repetitious. (E) replaces it with an equally wordy phrase.

2. C

Combine the sentences as concisely as possible. (A) and (B) both repeat *story* and use the unnecessary *this … is*. (D) uses *composed* instead of *written*, a diction error. (E) uses slang.

3. B

The original sentence is wordy, as are (D) and (E). (B) eliminates the problems. (C) adds unnecessary words.

4. D

The original sentences can be combined, as (D) does. (C) and (E) are wordy, and (C) is also a run-on.

5. A

(A) is the most concise. (B) adds unnecessary words. (C) and (D) are wordy. (E) is awkward and passive.

6. C

(A) and (D) are wordy and passive. (B) is pretentious. (E) doesn't use precise verbs.

7. B

The original is redundant. (B) is the most clear and concise. (C) inserts a clause between subject and verb. (D) is awkward. (E) is passive and wordy.

8. C

The original sentence is passive, as is (B). (C) is the most direct and concise. (D) is pretentious, and (E) uses slang.

9. C

(A) and (B) are grammatically correct but not concise. (D) is awkward and uses *in length* instead of *long*. (E) has a misplaced modifier.

10. C

(A) and (B) use wishy-washy intensifiers. (C) uses the precise verb *order*. (D) is a run-on. (E) is wordy and pretentious.

11. D

(A) and (B) use the clutter phrase *in the event*. (A) also uses the redundant phrase *return back*. (B) is awkward and imprecise. (C) and (E) use the passive voice.

12. E

(A) uses slang. (B) uses a weak intensifier and verb. (C) is pretentious. (D)'s word choice is not as precise as (E)'s.

13. A

Here, the *there are* construction is the most effective way to convey the idea. (B) unnecessarily adds a *who* clause. (C) uses *have not written as much* instead of the precise *prolific*. (D) is wordy and pretentious. (E) is awkward, indirect, and unclear.

14. B

(A) uses the clutter phrase *in the neighborhood of* and the redundant *in height*. (C) is passive. (D) uses several wordy constructions. (E) uses slang.

15. C

(C) has only one clause; (A) and (E) have two clauses. (B) has one clause but is wordy. (D) keeps the indirect *be* verb of the original.

16. E

(E) is the clearest and most concise version. (C) also uses the passive voice.

17. B

ETA stands for estimated time of arrival; (A), (C), and (D) repeat *arrival*. (E) adds *approximate*, which repeats *estimated*.

18. A

(B) is passive. (C) uses an unnecessary *it was* clause. (D) is less precise, and (E) causes unnecessary repetition.

19. C

(A) and (B) use a wordy *be* construction. (D) and (E) use the wordy phrase *gave me the inspiration*, and (E) also uses the redundant *inspiration and motivation*.

20. E

(E) turns *the office that is in the corner* into *the corner office*. (C) turns the clause into a prepositional phrase, while (D) is awkward.

CHAPTER 13

COMMONLY CONFUSED WORDS

Usage refers to the proper *use* of words, phrases, and expressions. Certain aspects of usage can vary by region. For example, an American would say, "I'm going *to the* hospital," while someone in England, Australia, or India would say, "I'm going *to* hospital." Neither is wrong. The standard usage in British English is simply different from the American.

Usage also includes idioms (specific word combinations and expressions such as *dream about* and *keep an eye on*) or colloquialisms (informal expressions). This will be the focus of the chapter—commonly confused and misused words. Your knowledge of these words will be tested in Sentence Correction questions, and you should use them correctly in your Analytical Writing Assessment essay. In fact, we've arranged 101 of these words into manageable groups for you to use in your review.

HOMOPHONES

Homophones *sound* the same but *mean* different things, and they are often (but not always) spelled differently. So you may hear both words used all the time in everyday speech, but when it comes to reading or writing them, you need to know the differences!

Here's a list of the most commonly confused homophones, with sample sentences using the words in context:

> **accept** (v.): to take or receive. *Camille <u>accepted</u> a job offer in Singapore.*
>
> **except** (prep.): leave out. *I love everything about my job <u>except</u> the commute.*

MEMORY TIP

Accept and *affect* are verbs or actions. They both begin with the letter *a*.

affect (v.): to have an impact or influence on. *The amount of sleep you get directly affects your ability to concentrate.*

effect (n.): result, impact. *One effect of sleep deprivation is an inability to focus.* (v.): to cause, implement. *Irfan effected several changes in his sleep schedule.*

altar (n.): an elevated structure, typically intended for religious rituals. *Determined to get married despite the storm, the couple exchanged vows at a makeshift altar.*

alter (v.): to change. *If the ship does not alter its course, it will head straight into the hurricane.*

ascent (n.): climb, upward movement. *Vanessa's rapid ascent up the corporate ladder impressed us all.*

assent (v.): to agree; (n.): agreement. *Peter has given his assent to the plan.*

bazaar (n.): a market consisting of various shops; a fair selling miscellaneous items. *I found these fantastic bracelets at the school bazaar.*

bizarre (adj.): very strange, weird. *No one knew how to respond to the bizarre question.*

capital (n.): a seat of government; accumulated assets; (adj.) first-rate; extremely serious; involving the death penalty. *It's near the state capital, Harrisburg.*

capitol (n.): the building(s) in which lawmakers meet. *Security at the state capitol is tight.*

cite (v.): to quote, to refer to. *The article cited our school's test scores.*

sight (n.): something seen or visible; the faculty of seeing. *Manolo's sight was restored after the operation.*

site (n.): location; (v.): to place or locate. *This is the perfect site for a picnic.*

coarse (adj.): rough to the touch, large grained; crude, vulgar; of low quality. *Lou's coarse language offended everyone.*

course (n.): path, route, direction; mode of action or behavior; series of classes on a subject; (v.): to move swiftly through or over. *You've chosen a wise course of action.*

PRACTICE 1

Circle the correct word(s) within the parentheses.

1. Julio needs the client's (ascent/assent) to use this (coarse/course) fabric instead of the twill.

2. This is the most (bazaar/bizarre) (cite/sight/site) I have ever seen!

3. There will be a (bazaar/bizarre) on the steps of the state (capital/capitol) tomorrow.

4. I had to (altar/alter) my intended (coarse/course) to avoid traffic.

5. There's nothing we can do now (accept/except) wait to see how the medication (affects/effects) Kelly's condition.

Now back to our list of homophones:

complement (n.): something that completes; (v.): to go with or complete. *That shirt complements your eyes.*
compliment (n.): a flattering remark; (v.): to flatter. *I'm not sure that compliment was sincere.*

counsel (v.): to advise or recommend; (n.):advice or guidance; a lawyer. *I try to keep my own counsel.*
council (n.): a body called together for consultation or discussion; an assembly of officials or advisers. *The town council discussed the impact of the proposed landfill.*

elicit (v.): to call forth or draw out. *Raul was provocative to elicit a response from the apathetic audience.*
illicit (adj.): unlawful. *He accepted illicit contributions to his campaign.*

passed (v.): simple past or past participle of the verb *to pass. Thank goodness that time has passed!*
past (n.): time before the present; (adj.): pertaining to time before the present; (prep., adv.): going by or beyond. *In the past, phones couldn't be carried around easily.*

principal (n.): head of a school or organization; primary participant; main sum of money; (adj.): main, most important. *Joshua is one of the principals of the company.*

principle (n.): a basic truth or law. *I run my business based on the principle that honesty is the best policy.*

reign (n.): period in which a ruler exercised power; (v.): to exercise power. *Under the reign of Mrs. Walker, the students became studious and kind.*

rein (n.): a means of restraint or guidance; (v.): to restrain, control. *You need to rein in your temper before it gets you in trouble.*

stationary (adj.): not moving; not capable of moving. *Jojo rides a stationary bike each morning.*

stationery (n.): writing paper. *I've ordered stationery with my name and address on it.*

MEMORY TIP

Use another "a" memory trick: *station<u>a</u>ry* with an *a* is the <u>a</u>djective.

weather (n.): climatic conditions. *The bad weather will keep people away from our fund-raiser.*

whether (conj.): refers to a choice between alternatives. *I am not sure whether I will attend the fund-raiser or not.*

PRACTICE 2

Circle the correct word(s) within the parentheses.

1. I can't tell (weather/whether) these fabrics will (complement/compliment) the decor in my room.

2. The (council/counsel) (passed/past) the proposal to renovate the existing meetinghouse rather than build a new one.

3. If Hannah ever sought my (advice/advise), I'd (council/counsel) her to (reign/rein) in her jealousy.

4. We just (passed/past) the (weather/whether) station.

5. I must (complement/compliment) you on your beautiful selection of (stationary/stationery).

CONTRACTIONS AND OTHER TROUBLEMAKERS

This list includes frequently confused pairs such as *it's/its* and *lose/loose*.

One Word or Two?

In each set below, the meaning of the term depends upon whether it's one word or two:

a lot (adv.): very many or much. *I have a lot of studying to do.*

allot (v.): to give out or distribute, parcel out. *We were each allotted 15 minutes to defend our position.*

all ready (adj.): completely prepared. *I am all ready for my interview.*

already (adv.): prior to a specific time. *I have already read* Fahrenheit 451.

all together (adj. or adv.): everyone gathered; all members of a group acting collectively. *All together now: 1, 2, 3, pull!*

altogether (adv.): entirely; all included or counted. *I am altogether lost; I've no idea where we are!*

its (pn.): third-person, singular, possessive pronoun. *This computer is on its last legs.*

it's (pn. + v.): contraction of *it* + *is*. *It's time to get a new one.*

their (pn.): third-person, plural, possessive pronoun. *Is that their bag or yours?*

there (adv.): at or in that place; (n.) that place or point. *I'll meet you over there.*

they're (pn. + v.): contraction of *they* + *are*. *They're going to meet us as well.*

whose (pn.): the possessive form of the pronoun *who*. *Whose car should we take?*

who's (pn. + v.): contraction of *who* + *is*. *Who's going to drive?*

your (pn.): second-person, singular, possessive pronoun. *Your drawings are quite impressive.*

you're (pn. + v.): contraction of *you + are. You're going to be a famous artist someday.*

MEMORY TIP

If you want to express <u>action</u>, you need a cont<u>raction</u>, which includes both a subject and a verb.

PRACTICE 3

Choose the correct word(s) within the parentheses.

1. Since (your/you're) (already/all ready) here, let's go ahead and get started.
2. (Your/You're) car—if you can even call it that—is (altogether/all together) a lost cause.
3. I hope (your/you're) (already/all ready) to go, because we have (a lot/allot) of work to do today.
4. (Its/It's) a shame that (its/it's) too late for you to join the team this year.
5. I have (already/all ready) decided (whose/who's) going to get the award.

Other Troublemakers

Whether they're similar in sound or meaning, these pairs frequently cause writers trouble:

advice (n.): recommendation. *Ask Eton for <u>advice</u> about writing a good résumé.*

advise (v.): to recommend what should be done. *He will be happy to <u>advise</u> you.*

MEMORY TIP

When you *advise* someone, you *say* your advice. *Advise* and *say* both have the letter *s*.

Pronunciation note: The *s* in *advise* is pronounced like a *z*.

allusion (n.): an indirect reference. *The story makes an <u>allusion</u> to* Moby Dick.

illusion (n.): erroneous perception; false impression; misleading or deceptive image. *Captain Ahab's dream of catching the great white whale was an <u>illusion</u>.*

among (prep.): in the midst of. [**Usage note:** Use *among* for <u>three or more</u> items or entities.] *Anthropologist Margaret Mead lived <u>among</u> the Samoans for many years.*

between (prep.): in an intermediate position or interval. [**Usage note:** Use *between* for <u>two</u> items or entities.] *Many immigrants feel they must choose <u>between</u> their native culture and American culture.*

amount (n.): number or quantity; (v.) to add up in number or quantity. [**Usage note:** Use *amount* with quantities that <u>cannot</u> be counted.] *She has a great <u>amount</u> of courage.*

number (n.): symbol representing a mathematical unit; total, sum; quantity of units or individuals; (v.) to count; add up to. [**Usage note:** Use *number* with quantities that <u>can</u> be counted.] *She has auditioned for a <u>number</u> of plays.*

conscience (n.): awareness of moral principles, together with preference for right over wrong. *My <u>conscience</u> has been bothering me since I cheated on the exam.*

conscious (adj.): aware, alert; perceiving one's surroundings and existence. *I was very <u>conscious</u> of the fact that Colette kept staring at me.*

fewer (adj.): consisting of a smaller number. [**Usage note:** Use *fewer* with items that <u>can</u> be counted.] *We received <u>fewer</u> votes than I'd expected.*

less (adj.): not as great in quantity or amount; of lower rank or importance. [**Usage note:** Use *less* with quantities that <u>cannot</u> be counted.] *My bowl contained <u>less</u> soup than my sister's.*

incidence (n.): instance of happening; frequency of occurrence. *There is a high <u>incidence</u> of accidents at this corner.*

incident (n.): an occurrence or event. *There have been several <u>incidents</u> involving disorderly fans.*

loose (adj.): not securely fastened; not taut or rigid. *In the* _loose_ *atmosphere of the writing workshop, April was able to be more creative.*

lose (v.): to misplace; to fail to win or maintain. *Please be quiet so I don't* _lose_ *my train of thought.*

personal (adj.): private or pertaining to the individual. *My* _personal_ *trainer is helping me.*

personnel (n.): employees. *As a human resources intern, I help maintain the files on* _personnel_.

MEMORY TIP

The a̲djective, *personal*, is spelled with an *a*.

quotation (n.): a passage cited from a person or text; a statement of a price or bid. *I have a great* _quotation_ *by John Wayne in my essay about early Westerns.*

quote (v.): to repeat a passage from; to state a price for services or goods. *I* _quote_ *John Wayne in my essay about stereotypes in early Westerns.* [**Usage note:** Using *quote* as a short form of *quotation* is considered informal and should be avoided in formal writing.]

than (conj.): used to compare. *I have more experience* than *Marie.*

then (adv.): at that time; therefore. *I was very naïve back* _then_.

PRACTICE 4

Circle the correct word(s) within the parentheses.

1. I would (advice/advise) you to take a (coarse/course) in statistics even if you aren't majoring in business.

2. If you don't tighten that (loose/lose) knot, (your/you're) going to (loose/lose) your balloon.

3. As Dakota wandered (among/between) the numerous displays, she wished (their/there/they're) were (fewer/less) choices.

4. Don't forget to use (quotation/quote) marks whenever you (quotation/quote) somebody.

5. Yesterday's shouting (incidence/incident) has been troubling my (conscience/conscious).

ADJECTIVE PAIRS AND VERB PAIRS

These can be particularly tricky since they share the same part of speech.

Adjectives

adverse (adj.): unfavorable. *Not doing your homework will have an adverse impact on your grades.*

averse (adj.): opposed or reluctant. *I am averse to doing homework.* [**Usage note:** *Averse is almost always followed by the preposition to.*]

amoral (adj.): without a sense of moral judgment. *Claire was upset with the amoral discussion of terrorist acts.*

immoral (adj.): morally wrong. *Claire said, "All terrorist acts are immoral."*

continual (adj.): repeated regularly and frequently. *Meditation should be a continual practice.*

continuous (adj.): extended or prolonged without interruption. *The continuous banging from the construction site gave me a severe headache.*

discreet (adj.): modest, having discretion; not allowing others to notice. *I must be very discreet about looking for a new job.*

discrete (adj.): separate, not connected. *They look connected but are actually two discrete panels.*

disinterested (adj.): impartial, objective. *We need a disinterested person to act as an arbitrator.*

uninterested (adj.): not interested. *My nephew is uninterested in anything that doesn't have wheels.*

eminent (adj.): outstanding, distinguished. *The eminent Judge Blackwell will teach a seminar.*

imminent (adj.): about to happen, impending. *Warned of imminent layoffs, Loretta began looking for another job.*

explicit (adj.): fully and clearly expressed or defined. *Please leave* <u>*explicit*</u> *instructions for your substitute.*

implicit (adj.): implied or understood though not directly expressed. <u>*Implicit*</u> *in John's letter was the reason he wasn't coming home: he didn't want to see Nell.*

ingenious (adj.): very clever; showing great inventiveness or skill. *It was* <u>*ingenious*</u> *of him to protect the window so effectively.*

ingenuous (adj.): frank, candid; not cunning or deceitful; naive. *Her compliment was not entirely* <u>*ingenuous*</u>.

sensual (adj.): sensory; gratifying to the physical and especially sexual appetites.

sensuous (adj.): pleasing to or gratifying the senses.

[**Usage note:** *Sensual* is used primarily to describe physical gratification, while *sensuous* describes aesthetic enjoyment as of art and music.]

PRACTICE 5

Circle the correct word(s) within the parentheses.

1. Don't ask Quinn for (advice/advise); he is not a (disinterested/uninterested) party.

2. What an (ingenious/ingenuous) idea, Erik. You're brilliant!

3. The (sensual/sensuous) sound of a Chopin sonata drifted down the hall to my apartment.

4. Our (continual/continuous) friendship is one of the most important things in my life.

5. You can't see the cell walls, but you can see two nuclei, which means these are two (discreet/discrete) cells, not one.

Verbs

adapt (v.): to change to suit a new purpose or conditions. *Hasaan has* <u>*adapted*</u> *well to his new country.*

adopt (v.): to legally take a child into one's family; to accept as if one's own; to accept formally and put into effect. *The English faculty voted to* <u>*adopt*</u> *a new grammar book.*

assure (v.): to convince or guarantee. *Cole* <u>*assures*</u> *me there's nothing wrong with this car.*

ensure (v.): to make certain. *Please ensure that there's nothing wrong with this car before I buy it.*

insure (v.): to guard against loss. *The "lemon law" helps insure the rights of used car buyers.*

censor (v.): to remove or suppress objectionable material; (n.) one who censors. *Parents protested when the principal censored Anthony's article.*

censure (v.): to criticize severely, rebuke formally. *The principal was later censured for his actions.*

emigrate (from) (v.): to leave one country or region and settle in another. *My great grandfather emigrated from Ireland in 1880.*

immigrate (to) (v.): to enter another country or region and settle there. *He immigrated to Canada, then to the United States.*

imply (v.): to suggest or state indirectly. *Are you implying that I can't handle the job?*

infer (v.): to draw a conclusion based on reasoning or evidence. *Katrina inferred from Aaron's comments that he didn't think she could handle the job.*

precede (v.): to come before. *In your book report, the summary should precede your analysis.*

proceed (v.): to go forward. *The weather is not ideal, but we will proceed as planned.*

PRACTICE 6

Circle the correct word(s) within the parentheses.

1. We cannot (precede/proceed) without your (ascent/assent).

2. I (assure/ensure/insure) you that I was not (implying/inferring) that you don't know what you're doing.

3. I would like to (adapt/adopt) a new policy that will (assure/ensure/insure) that our patient data is properly protected.

4. We plan to (emigrate/immigrate) to Australia to be closer to our families.

5. The senator was (censored/censured) for his sexist remarks.

COMMON GMAT IDIOMS

All of the following idioms have been known to appear on the GMAT. For each idiom, we have provided a sample sentence using the idiom in context. Entries with double ellipses (such as *between...and...*) indicate that the idiom also sets up a parallelism (between *A* and *B*):

able to (ability to): *No one has been <u>able to</u> prove that the person who wrote Shakespeare's plays was named Shakespeare.*

among *versus* between: Use *between* when referring to two items or groups, *among* when referring to three or more.

Don't make me choose <u>between</u> Tweedledum and Tweedledee.

<u>Among</u> all five candidates, he's by far the best qualified.

amount *versus* number: Use *amount* when referring to an uncountable quantity, like soup or love, and *number* when referring to countable things, like jelly beans or people.

The <u>amount</u> of work you put into your studies will affect the <u>number</u> of points you will add to your GMAT score.

as *versus* like: Use *like* to compare nouns; use *as* to compare actions—in other words, use *as* when what follows is a clause.

<u>Like</u> fine wine, fruitcake tastes better after it has aged.

Dogs don't scratch up furniture <u>as</u> cats often do.

as...as: *She actually is <u>as</u> naive <u>as</u> she appears.*

associate with: *Many people <u>associate</u> the smell of vinegar <u>with</u> coloring Easter eggs.*

at least as...as: *The Eiffel Tower is <u>at least as</u> tall <u>as</u> the Statue of Liberty.*

attribute to: *I <u>attribute</u> his success <u>to</u> having good friends in high places.*

believe to be: *The expert <u>believes</u> the painting <u>to be</u> a fraud.*

between...and...: *You must decide <u>between</u> privacy <u>and</u> fame.*

both *versus* each: Use *both* when pointing out similarities; use *each* when pointing out differences. Note that *each* is always singular.

Although <u>both</u> cooks enjoy making goulash, <u>each</u> has a different take on this classic dish.

both...and...: *He is <u>both</u> an artist <u>and</u> a rogue.*

compare to *versus* **compare with:** On the GMAT, *compare with* is the generally preferred form. Use *compare to* to point out an abstract or figurative likeness and *compare with* to consider likenesses and differences in general.

Shall I <u>compare</u> thee <u>to</u> a summer's day? <u>Compared with</u> a summer's day, it's cold outside.

connection between: *I saw little <u>connection between</u> her words and her deeds.*

consequence of: *One <u>consequence of</u> the Supreme Court decision was increased public distrust of the judicial system.*

consider: Although *consider to be* is acceptable in everyday spoken English, it's not proper usage and will never be correct on the GMAT.

I <u>consider</u> you a very good friend.

continue to: *Do not <u>continue to</u> deny the obvious.*

contrast with: *I like to <u>contrast</u> my plaid pants <u>with</u> a lovely paisley jacket.*

credit with: *James Joyce is often <u>credited with</u> the invention of the literary form called stream of consciousness.*

debate over: This idiom only applies when *debate* is used as a noun.

They held a lively <u>debate over</u> whom to invite to the party.

decide to: *She <u>decided to</u> go to the party after all.*

define as: *My dictionary <u>defines</u> a clause <u>as</u> group of words containing a subject and a verb.*

different from: *John Major's policies were not very <u>different from</u> those of Margaret Thatcher.*

difficult to: *It's <u>difficult to</u> disagree with such a persuasive argument.*

dispute over: This idiom applies only when *dispute* is used as a noun.

The <u>dispute over</u> how to read the punch cards was never properly resolved.

distinguish between...and...: *Some color-blind people cannot <u>distinguish between</u> red <u>and</u> green.*

distinguish...from...: *Other color-blind people find it difficult to <u>distinguish</u> blue <u>from</u> purple.*

double *versus* **twice** (*triple* versus *three times*, etc.): On the GMAT, *double* (*triple, quadruple,* etc.) is only used as a verb; when making a comparison, the preferred form is *twice* (*three times,* etc.).

He promised to <u>double</u> the company's profits in less than a year.

I ate <u>twice</u> as much as you did.

each (see **both** *versus* **each**)

each other *versus* **one another:** In GMAT English, *each other* is used to refer to two things, and *one another* is used for three or more.

Those two theories contradict <u>each other.</u>

Those three theories contradict <u>one another</u>.

either…or…: *Today I will <u>either</u> look for a job <u>or</u> watch the Boston Marathon on TV.*

-er than: *Winston Churchill was a bett<u>er</u> dancer <u>than</u> Neville Chamberlain ever was.*

estimate to be: *The oldest cave paintings known to exist are <u>estimated to be</u> over 50,000 years old.*

extent to which: *You should appreciate the <u>extent to which</u> the same idioms repeatedly appear on the GMAT.*

fewer *versus* **less:** Use *fewer* to describe countable things, like jelly beans or people, and *less* to describe an uncountable quantity, like soup or love.

I ate <u>fewer</u> hotdogs and <u>less</u> potato salad than I did at last year's picnic.

forbid to: *I was <u>forbidden to</u> discuss politics at the dinner table.*

from…to…: *<u>From</u> the redwood forest <u>to</u> the Gulf Stream waters, this land was made for you and me.*

if *versus* **whether:** If you're ever given a choice on the GMAT, choose *whether*. The actual rule is that if you're discussing a choice between alternatives, you should use *whether* (as in *whether or not to do something*) rather than *if*. On the GMAT, *if* is reserved for conditional "if-then" statements.

Let me know <u>if</u> I behave inappropriately in front of the royal family.

(Translation: *I may or may not behave inappropriately, but if I do, I should be informed*).

Tell me <u>whether</u> I behaved inappropriately in front of the royal family.

(Translation: *Either I behaved inappropriately or I didn't; tell me the truth.*)

in danger of: *Conservationists fear that the West Indian manatee is <u>in danger of</u> becoming extinct.*

just as...so too...: *<u>Just as</u> sand flows through an hourglass, <u>so too</u> flow the days of our lives.*

less (see **fewer** *versus* **less**)

like *versus* such as: If you're ever given a choice, choose *such as* when there are items or examples in a list. On the GMAT, *like* means similar to.

I prefer salty snacks <u>such as</u> potato chips to sweet snacks <u>such as</u> candy bars.

I've never met anyone <u>like</u> him before.

likely to: *You're <u>likely to</u> do well on the GMAT Verbal section.*

link to: *Exposure to classical music has been <u>linked to</u> improved performance on mathematical aptitude tests.*

model after: *Louisiana's legal system is <u>modeled after</u> the Napoleonic Code.*

more than: *I was <u>more</u> prepared this time <u>than</u> I was the last time I took the test.*

native: Use *native to*, meaning indigenous to, when discussing plants, animals, etc. Use a *native of* when discussing people and where they were born.

The sugar maple is <u>native to</u> Canada.

My wife is a <u>native of</u> Canada.

neither...nor...: Note that when a sentence has a *neither...nor...* subject, whatever follows *nor* determines whether the verb is singular or plural. (The same thing is true of *either...or...* subjects.)

<u>Neither</u> the coach <u>nor</u> the fans were surprised by the team's victory.

not...but [rather, merely]...: *It's <u>not</u> a bother <u>but rather</u> an honor to serve you.*

not only...but also...: *I am <u>not only</u> charming <u>but also</u> modest to a fault.*

not so...as: *It's <u>not so</u> bad <u>as</u> it seems.*

not so much...as...: *The company's recent success is due <u>not so much</u> to better management <u>as</u> to an improved economy.*

number: Also note that on the GMAT, *the number of* will always be singular, while *a number of* will always be plural.

<u>The number of</u> stars in our galaxy <u>is</u> huge.

<u>A number of</u> guests <u>are</u> waiting in the foyer.

one another (see **each other** *versus* **one another**)

opposition to: *There has been far less <u>opposition</u> in the United States than in Europe <u>to</u> the use of genetically modified foods.*

perceive as: *I didn't mean for my comments to be <u>perceived as</u> criticism.*

prohibit from: *People are <u>prohibited from</u> entering the park after 10 P.M.*

range from…to…: *Scores on the GMAT <u>range from</u> 200 <u>to</u> 800.*

regard as: *I <u>regard</u> him <u>as</u> little more than a common criminal.*

require to: *The laws in some states <u>require</u> couples <u>to</u> have their blood tested before getting married.*

resistance to: *Stress can lower one's <u>resistance to</u> cold and flu viruses.*

same as: *I got the <u>same</u> score <u>as</u> he did.*

seem to: *He <u>seemed to</u> be at a loss for words.*

so…as to be…: *My new computer game is <u>so</u> entertaining <u>as to be</u> genuinely addictive.*

so…that: *In fact, it's <u>so</u> addictive <u>that</u> I spend several hours every day playing it.*

such as (see **like** *versus* **such as**)

superior to: *Superman's powers are clearly <u>superior to</u> those of Batman.*

target at: *I sometimes suspect that junk food ads are <u>targeted at</u> children.*

the -er…the -er…: *<u>The</u> bigg<u>er</u> they come, <u>the</u> hard<u>er</u> they fall.*

try to: *<u>Try to</u> write a short story based on your travel experiences.*

twice (see **double** *versus* **twice**)

use as: *Lacking cooking implements, we <u>used</u> a hubcap <u>as</u> a makeshift pan.*

view as: *Many <u>view</u> the former publishing magnate <u>as</u> a con artist extraordinaire.*

whether (see **if** *versus* **whether**)

worry about: *There's no need to <u>worry about</u> idioms on the GMAT; just study the ones you don't recognize.*

PRACTICE 7

For each item, circle the correct idiom to use in that sentence.

1. The actor skillfully portrays not only a politician (and also/and as well/but also) a father in this film.

2. She is widely respected both as an athlete (and also/and as/but also as) a role model.

3. I must have either a sandwich (or else/or/and) a salad for lunch.

4. You must decide (between/among) the hot and sour soup (or/and) the egg drop soup.

5. (Between/Among) the three professors, Steiner is generally (considered/considered to be/considered as) the (more/most) entertaining lecturer.

6. There were (less/fewer) immigrants entering the country last year than the previous year.

7. The (number/amount) of students in my class (has/have) gone up.

8. I regard the movies of Orson Welles (as/to be/as being) superior (when compared to/over/to) those of Alfred Hitchcock.

9. Zeppo is often perceived (as/to be/as being) the least talented of the Marx Brothers.

10. According to exit polls, a majority of those who voted for the winning candidate viewed him (as/to be/as being) the lesser of two evils.

SUMMARY

Unless you use these commonly confused words regularly, review them often before test day. That way you can use them with confidence!

PRACTICE ON YOUR OWN

After you complete the Chapter 13 Test, check your answers carefully. Make a list of the words you still confuse. Add a definition and sample sentence for each. As you work, try to think of mnemonic devices to help you remember their differences.

Practice Answers and Explanations

PRACTICE 1

1. assent, coarse

2. bizarre, sight

3. bazaar, capitol

4. alter, course

5. except, affects

PRACTICE 2

1. whether, complement

2. council, passed

3. advice, counsel, rein

4. passed, weather

5. compliment, stationery

PRACTICE 3

1. you're, already

2. Your, altogether

3. you're, all ready, a lot

4. It's, it's

5. already, who's

PRACTICE 4

1. advise, course

2. loose, you're, lose

3. among, there, fewer

4. quotation, quote

5. incident, conscience

PRACTICE 5

1. advice, disinterested
2. ingenious
3. sensuous
4. continuous
5. discrete

PRACTICE 6

1. proceed, assent
2. assure, implying
3. adopt, ensure
4. immigrate
5. censured

PRACTICE 7

1. The actor skillfully portrays not only a politician <u>but also</u> a father in this film.
2. She is widely respected both as an athlete <u>and as</u> a role model.
3. I must have either a sandwich <u>or</u> a salad for lunch.
4. You must decide <u>between</u> the hot and sour soup <u>and</u> the egg drop soup.
5. <u>Among</u> the three professors, Steiner is generally <u>considered</u> the <u>most</u> entertaining lecturer.
6. There were <u>fewer</u> immigrants entering the country last year than the previous year.
7. The <u>number</u> of students in my class <u>has</u> gone up.
8. I regard the movies of Orson Welles <u>as</u> superior <u>to</u> those of Alfred Hitchcock.
9. Zeppo is often perceived <u>as</u> the least talented of the Marx Brothers.
10. According to exit polls, a majority of those who voted for the winning candidate viewed him <u>as</u> the lesser of two evils.

CHAPTER 13 TEST

Part A: For questions 1–10, which word matches the definition?

1. Frank, candid, not cunning or deceitful
   - (A) Adverse
   - (B) Averse
   - (C) Ingenious
   - (D) Ingenuous
   - (E) Explicit

2. An indirect reference
   - (A) Allusion
   - (B) Illusion
   - (C) Counsel
   - (D) Quotation
   - (E) Quote

3. To draw a conclusion based on reasoning, evidence, or circumstances
   - (A) Imply
   - (B) Infer
   - (C) Censor
   - (D) Censure
   - (E) Advise

4. Impartial, objective
   - (A) Sensual
   - (B) Sensuous
   - (C) Discrete
   - (D) Discreet
   - (E) Disinterested

5. Opposed or reluctant
   - (A) Illicit
   - (B) Stationary
   - (C) Amoral
   - (D) Averse
   - (E) Implicit

6. To go with or complete
   - (A) Compliment
   - (B) Complement
   - (C) Adapt
   - (D) Adopt
   - (E) Proceed

7. To criticize severely, rebuke formally
   - (A) Infer
   - (B) Imply
   - (C) Elicit
   - (D) Reign
   - (E) Censure

8. Prudent, modest, having discretion
   - (A) Discrete
   - (B) Discreet
   - (C) Disinterested
   - (D) Adverse
   - (E) Averse

9. Unlawful

   (A) Illicit
   (B) Elicit
   (C) Eminent
   (D) Ingenuous
   (E) Amoral

10. About to happen, impending

   (A) Explicit
   (B) Implicit
   (C) Imminent
   (D) Eminent
   (E) Continual

Part B: For questions 11–20, which set of words best fills in the blanks?

11. The __ you __ here __ that there's a direct correlation between this medication and obesity.

   (A) quotation, sight, infers
   (B) quote, cite, infers
   (C) quotation, cite, implies
   (D) quote, site, implies
   (E) quotation, cite, infers

12. __ is no evidence that dying __ hair during pregnancy will have any negative __ on the fetus.

   (A) Their, you're, affect
   (B) There, your, effect
   (C) They're, your, effect
   (D) There, your, affect
   (E) Their, your, effect

13. Please __ my apologies for my __ behavior in the __.

   (A) accept, bizarre, past
   (B) except, bizarre, passed
   (C) accept, bazaar, passed
   (D) except, bazaar, past
   (E) accept, bazaar, past

14. The __ has agreed to __ __ procedures for appointing new members.

   (A) counsel, altar, it's
   (B) counsel, alter, it's
   (C) council, altar, its
   (D) council, alter, it's
   (E) council, alter, its

15. __ __ were 250 __ from schools across the country at the conference.

   (A) All together, their, principles
   (B) Altogether, there, principals
   (C) Altogether, they're, principals
   (D) All together, there, principles
   (E) Altogether, their, principals

16. I wish you would spend __ time giving me __ and more time worrying about your own __ problems.

   (A) less, advice, personal
   (B) less, advise, personnel
   (C) fewer, advice, personnel
   (D) fewer, advise, personal
   (E) less, advise, personal

17. I __ you, an __ person cannot have a clear __.

    (A) ensure, amoral, conscience
    (B) assure, amoral, conscious
    (C) insure, immoral, conscience
    (D) assure, immoral, conscious
    (E) assure, immoral, conscience

18. The __ of __ involving __ language in the classroom has declined.

    (A) number, incidents, coarse
    (B) amount, incidents, course
    (C) amount, incidence, coarse
    (D) number, incidence, course
    (E) amount, incidence, course

19. In the __, the __ was __ more predictable.

    (A) past, whether, allot
    (B) passed, weather, a lot
    (C) past, weather, a lot
    (D) passed, whether, a lot
    (E) past, weather, allot

20. Once you provide __ instructions, __ we can __.

    (A) explicit, then, precede
    (B) explicit, then, proceed
    (C) implicit, than, proceed
    (D) implicit, then, precede
    (E) explicit, than, proceed

**ANSWERS AND EXPLANATIONS
BEGIN ON NEXT PAGE**

Answers

1. D
2. A
3. B
4. E
5. D
6. B
7. E
8. B
9. A
10. C
11. C
12. B
13. A
14. E
15. B
16. A
17. E
18. A
19. C
20. B

SECTION III

Punctuation and Mechanics

CHAPTER 14

COMMAS

A GMAT essay that is otherwise powerful and clear can be mangled by incorrect use of punctuation—the subject of this final section. Many writers consider punctuation an instrument of torture, but it really *is* designed to help express ideas clearly.

a. I know who did it, Winston.

b. I know who did it: Winston.

Punctuation clarifies ideas and signals relationships between them. In **a**, the speaker tells Winston that she knows who did it; in **b**, the speaker says *Winston* did it.

WHEN TO USE A COMMA

The comma is the most common punctuation mark; it gently separates sentence elements from each other or from the main clause. Here are its nine uses.

1. Between Two Independent Clauses Connected by a Coordinating Conjunction

Place the comma at the end of the first clause *before* the coordinating conjunction. If both clauses are short and there's no chance for confusion, you can omit the comma. On the other hand, you may want to keep that comma for effect:

Anuj always loved animals, so I'm not surprised that he is a veterinarian.

I love you and you love me.

I love you, but you don't love me.

2. After an Introductory Word, Phrase, or Clause

Introductory words, phrases, and clauses are typically adverbs that tell us the when, where, why, how, or under what conditions the action of the sentence took place. They should always be followed by a comma:

Unfortunately, the roster is already full.

Without a cup of coffee, I'm useless in the morning.

Because she was so quiet, everyone forgot that little Ellen was there.

In the last example, a subordinate clause introduces the main clause. But be careful: a subordinate clause at the beginning of a sentence does not always serve that function:

Incorrect: Whoever ate my lunch, is going to pay!

This subordinate clause is the subject of the main clause, so the comma is wrong.

PRACTICE 1

Insert any necessary commas in the following sentences.

1. I wanted to call you right away but I didn't want to wake you so I decided to wait until the morning.
2. Whatever you decide I will support you for you are my best friend.
3. Early Monday morning a main transformer was hit by lightning and city residents spent the next 32 hours without power.
4. Much to my dismay you're right and I'm wrong.

3. Between Items in a Series

Three or more items in a series should be separated by commas. This includes a comma between the last two items (but *not* a comma after the last item). Some consider this penultimate comma optional, but it's best to play it safe and use the comma to clearly separate the two items:

The <u>sandhill crane, American alligator,</u> and West Indian manatee are all endangered Florida wetland species.

When one or more items in the series itself has a comma, use semicolons to separate the items in the list.

I have been to New York, Boston, and Providence in the Northeast; Las Vegas, Phoenix, and Santa Fe in the Southwest; and Minneapolis, Milwaukee, and Chicago in the Midwest.

4. Between Adjectives That Modify the Same Word

Coordinate adjectives modify the same noun or pronoun; they must be separated by commas:

The <u>dark, dingy room</u> could use a coat of bright paint.

MEMORY TIP

If you can logically insert the word *and* between two consecutive adjectives, there should be a comma between them.

Cumulative adjectives build up to one modifying phrase and do not take commas:

The <u>light blue paint</u> really brightens the room.

Cumulative: The <u>fierce north wind</u> threatened to knock over the old barn.

Coordinate: The <u>fierce, steady wind</u> threatened to knock over the old barn.

PRACTICE 2

Insert any necessary commas in the following sentences.

1. Not rain sleet hail or a plague of grasshoppers will keep me from Miller's one-day sale.

2. The only thing we had to eat was watery vegetable soup.

3. Rescue workers were ecstatic to find that the frightened shivering child was unharmed by the blast.

4. Bekah's constant, unequivocal support gave me the strength to overcome my depression.

5. To Set Off Nonessential Modifiers

Appositives and adjective phrases or clauses should be set off with commas if they are not essential to the meaning of the sentence. An **appositive** is a modifier that defines or renames another noun (much as a subject complement defines or renames the subject):

> **Adjective phrase:** Henry Ford, openly challenging his own role as a history maker, once said, "History is bunk."
>
> **Adjective clause:** Henry Ford, who is one of the most important figures in American history, once said, "History is bunk."
>
> **Appositive:** Henry Ford, one of the most important figures in American history, once said, "History is bunk."

Essential elements are *not* set off by commas. Without the information in the phrase, clause, or appositive, the sentence loses its specific meaning:

> The documents signed by Henry Ford fetched $2,000 each at the auction.
>
> The dusty pile of papers that I found in the corner of the attic turned out to be original blueprints signed by Henry Ford.

MEMORY TIP

Any information that is essential (that limits the meaning of the sentence) should **not** be set off by commas.

PRACTICE 3

Insert any necessary commas in the following sentences.

1. My cousin Mikala who has been suffering from back pain for years swears that acupuncture has cured her.

2. The package that I needed for the meeting had been delivered to the wrong address.

3. Jasmine my best friend since grade school is moving to Montana.

4. Remember the book that you're borrowing is very special and I want it back as soon as possible.

6. To Set Off Transitional and Parenthetical Expressions, Question Tags, Affirmatives and Negatives, and Mild Interjections

TRANSITIONAL EXPRESSIONS

Transitional words and phrases link sentences or parts of sentences, showing the relationship between them (e.g., comparison and contrast or cause and effect):

Wolhee's grandfather, for example, was a master potter in Korea.

Similarly, the newt's diet also consists primarily of worms and insects.

PARENTHETICAL EXPRESSIONS

A parenthetical expression offers ancillary information or acts as an afterthought that interrupts or concludes the sentence:

The wipers need to be replaced, you know.

Sometimes you just have a run of bad luck, I guess.

QUESTION TAGS

Question tags are exactly that: questions we tack on to the end of a sentence:

You're coming with us, aren't you?

This is a perfect gift for Mojca, don't you think?

AFFIRMATIVES AND NEGATIVES

Words or phrases indicating acceptance or rejection should also be set off from the main sentence:

On second thought, no, Haily and Jules would not make good lab partners.

Sure, you can come along.

MILD INTERJECTIONS AND OTHER INTERRUPTERS

Strong interjections stand alone as short sentences ending in an exclamation point (e.g., *Back off!*), but mild interjections are usually part of a sentence and are separated by a comma. Mild or casual interrupters such as *um, like,* and *well* follow the same rule:

> Hey, isn't that Old Man Morrison's dog running down the street?
>
> We were, like, totally exhausted.

Note that you will not see or use interjections such as these on the GMAT; they are far too informal.

7. To Set Off a Direct Address or Direct Quotation

DIRECT ADDRESS

In a direct address, the specific person being addressed should be set off by commas:

> We should grill Andy since it's such a nice day outside.
>
> We should grill, Andy, since it's such a nice day outside.

This is essential for clarity; without the commas, we might cook Andy and eat him with barbecue sauce.

DIRECT QUOTATION

When you quote someone else's words, set them off with commas as well as quotation marks (see chapter 15). *Indirect* quotes should have neither commas nor quotation marks:

> **Direct:** Omar said, "Lucy, I really need your help."
>
> **Indirect:** Omar told Lucy he really needs her help.

Quotations consisting of more than four lines are usually introduced by colons instead of commas (see chapter 15).

MEMORY TIP

Direct addresses and direct quotations get commas; indirect addresses and indirect quotations do not.

PRACTICE 4

Insert any necessary commas in the following sentences.

1. We have lots of time to kill Eddie so what should we do?

2. "Please excuse me" Joel said and then he raced out of the room.

3. No it doesn't sound like a very good idea does it?

4. "Wow that really is great news" said Victor.

8. To Separate Parts of Dates, Numbers, Addresses, and Titles

DATES

Place commas around the year, unless the date is inverted or only the month and year are stated:

On February 11, 1998, Lukas was born.

April 2000 was the rainiest month in this town's history.

Applications are due 1 May 2006.

NUMBERS

Numbers with more than four digits are separated into groups of three, except in street addresses, telephone numbers, ZIP codes, and dates:

Hasaan bought his house for $26,000, renovated it, and sold it for $274,000.

ADDRESSES

Use commas to separate the street from the town, the town from the state or province, and the state or province from the country:

His mailing address is 2234 Vine Street, Oak Ridge, PA 19042.

TITLES

When a title follows a noun, set it off with commas:

Katarina Nagy, PhD, has agreed to chair the committee.

9. As Needed to Prevent Confusion

Occasionally, a comma is needed to clarify meaning or prevent confusion, such as when a word or phrase is repeated or omitted:

Sometimes what you believe is true, is.

PRACTICE 5

Insert any necessary commas in the following sentences.

1. I met my husband at Waterloo Lounge in Watertown New York in January 2001.
2. I was very very disappointed by that movie.
3. Noam Feighter AIA was the chief architect for the building at 3305 Main Street in Red Rock Arkansas.
4. For lunch we ordered lobster ravioli and for dinner glazed duck.

WHEN *NOT* TO USE A COMMA

Here are some reminders to help you avoid superfluous commas. Following are eight situations in which a comma should *not* be used.

1. Between a Subject and Its Verb, a Verb and Its Object, or a Linking Verb and Subject Complement

Incorrect: The cotton crops, were destroyed by boll rot.

Incorrect: Grandpa gave Wiley, a lecture about respecting one's elders.

2. Between Parts of a Compound Predicate

Predicates can have compound verbs or other compound parts. Do not put a comma between these compound elements:

Incorrect: The water <u>overflowed, and quickly covered </u>the bathroom floor.

Incorrect: I always believed that you <u>were innocent, and would be acquitted.</u>

PRACTICE 6

Cross out any unnecessary commas in the sentences below.

1. Cyan, is a color between green and blue on the spectrum.
2. Standing before a crowded courtroom, the defendant stated, his name, and swore to tell the truth.
3. I'm sorry, but the map is missing the page, that we need.
4. Indigo, an intense shade of blue, has always been, my favorite color.

3. After a Coordinating or Subordinating Conjunction

Commas may be necessary *before* a coordinating or subordinating conjunction, but commas do not go after conjunctions:

Incorrect: Dr. Chan tried for years, <u>but, he</u> never succeeded in recording his dreams.

4. Before the First Item in a Series or after the Last

Commas belong *between* items in a series but not *around* them:

Incorrect: The children <u>collected, feathers,</u> pine cones, and <u>pebbles, during</u> their nature walk.

5. Between a Modifier and What It Modifies

Do not put commas between modifiers and their referents:

Incorrect: The <u>red, door</u> needs another coat of paint.

PRACTICE 7

Cross out any unnecessary commas in the sentences below.

1. My nightmares have subsided, but, I still have trouble, falling asleep at night.

2. I'd rather stay home tonight because, I have an important meeting early tomorrow, remember?

3. The fans cheered wildly as the Olympians passed by in a long, slow, procession.

4. You're an obnoxious, overbearing, boss, and, I refuse to work here any longer.

6. Before Parentheses

Parentheses themselves are enough to set off information; adding a comma is overkill:

Incorrect: Your computer is short on <u>RAM,</u> (random access memory).

7. After Such As, Like, or Including

These words should not be separated from the examples and lists that they introduce:

Incorrect: My favorite restaurants, <u>including,</u> Sushi Roku and Balboa, are in Los Angeles.

8. With an Exclamation Point or Question Mark

The exclamation point and question mark are end marks and do not need to be followed by a comma in dialogue:

Incorrect: "Did you try the <u>quiche?",</u> Annette asked.

PRACTICE 8

Cross out any unnecessary commas in the sentences below.

1. "It felt like, I would never get out of there!", Rachel complained.

2. *The Catcher in the Rye,* (which is my favorite novel, by the way), was first published in July, 1951.

3. Well, Harold told me, I'm supposed to be in charge, while he's gone.

4. "Are you ready yet?", Piotr asked, impatiently.

SUMMARY

DO use a comma:

1. Between two independent clauses connected by a coordinating conjunction

2. After an introductory word, phrase, or clause

3. Between items in a series

4. Between adjectives that modify the same word

5. To set off nonessential modifiers

6. To set off transitional and parenthetical expressions, question tags, affirmatives and negatives, and mild interjections

7. To set off a direct address or direct quotation

8. To separate parts of dates, numbers, addresses, and titles

9. As needed to prevent confusion

DO NOT use a comma:

1. Between a subject and its verb, a verb and its object, or a linking verb and subject complement

2. Between parts of a compound predicate

3. After a coordinating or subordinating conjunction

4. Before the first item in a series or after the last

5. Between a modifier and what it modifies

6. Before parentheses

7. After *such as*, *like*, or *including*

8. With an exclamation point or question mark

PRACTICE ON YOUR OWN

Choose a magazine or book and look for examples of each comma rule. You can also search for examples of superfluous commas. Check samples of your own writing, emails you receive, or websites such as blogs.

Practice Answers and Explanations

PRACTICE 1

1. I wanted to call you right away, but I didn't want to wake you, so I decided to wait until the morning. [Comma between independent clauses; it would be acceptable to omit the first comma as both clauses are short.]

2. Whatever you decide, I will support you, for you are my best friend. [Comma after the introductory clause and between the two independent clauses]

3. Early Monday morning, a main transformer was hit by lightning, and city residents spent the next 32 hours without power. [Comma after the introductory phrase and between the two independent clauses]

4. Much to my dismay, you're right and I'm wrong. [Comma after introductory phrase; no comma is needed between the independent clauses since both are short.]

PRACTICE 2

1. Not rain, sleet, hail, or a plague of grasshoppers will keep me from Miller's one-day sale. [Comma between items in the series]

2. The only thing we had to eat was watery vegetable soup. [No comma between cumulative adjectives]

3. Rescue workers were ecstatic to find that the frightened, shivering child was unharmed by the blast. [Comma between two coordinate adjectives]

4. Bekah's constant, unequivocal support gave me the strength to overcome my depression. [No additional comma; the comma between *constant* and *unequivocal* is correct as both adjectives modify support.]

PRACTICE 3

1. My cousin Mikala, who has been suffering from back pain for years, swears that acupuncture has cured her. [Commas around nonessential clause]

2. The package that I needed for the meeting had been delivered to the wrong address. [No comma; the clause is essential]

3. Jasmine, my best friend since grade school, is moving to Montana. [Commas around nonessential phrase]

4. Remember, the book that you're borrowing is very special, and I want it back as soon as possible. [Comma after introductory word and between independent clauses; no commas around an essential clause]

PRACTICE 4

1. We have lots of time to kill, Eddie, so what should we do? [Commas around direct address and between independent clauses]

2. "Please excuse me," Joel said, and then he raced out of the room. [Comma after direct quotation and between independent clauses]

3. No, it doesn't sound like a very good idea, does it? [Comma after negation and before question tag]

4. "Wow, that really is great news," said Victor. [Comma after mild interjection and after direct quotation]

PRACTICE 5

1. I met my husband at Waterloo Lounge in Watertown, New York, in January 2001. [Commas around the state; no comma between month and year when no day is included]

2. I was very, very disappointed by that movie. [Comma to avoid confusion]

3. Noam Feighter, AIA, was the chief architect for the building at 3305 Main Street in Red Rock, Arkansas. [Commas around title and between town and state]

4. For lunch, we ordered lobster ravioli and for dinner, glazed duck. [Comma to prevent confusion]

PRACTICE 6

1. Cyan is a color between green and blue on the spectrum. [No comma between subject and verb]

2. Standing before a crowded courtroom, the defendant stated his name and swore to tell the truth. [No comma between the verb and object; no comma before the second verb in compound predicate; the first comma sets off introductory phrase]

3. I'm sorry, but the map is missing the page that we need. [No comma sets off essential information. The first comma is between independent clauses connected by a coordinating conjunction. (Though the first clause is very short, the length of the second makes it unwise to omit the comma.)]

4. Indigo, an intense shade of blue, has always been my favorite color. [No comma between verb and complement; the first two commas set off an appositive.]

PRACTICE 7

Commas that should be deleted are enclosed in brackets.

1. My nightmares have subsided, but[,] I still have trouble[,] falling asleep at night.

2. I'd rather stay home tonight because[,] I have an important meeting early tomorrow, remember?

3. The fans cheered wildly as the Olympians passed by in a long, slow[,] procession.

4. You're an obnoxious, overbearing[,] boss, and[,] I refuse to work here any longer.

PRACTICE 8

Commas that should be deleted are enclosed in brackets.

1. "It felt like[,] I would never get out of there!"[,] Rachel complained.

2. *The Catcher in the Rye* [,] (which is my favorite novel, by the way)[,] was first published in July[,] 1951.

3. Well, Harold told me[,] I'm supposed to be in charge[,] while he's gone.

4. "Are you ready yet?"[,] Piotr asked[,] impatiently.

CHAPTER 14 TEST

For questions 1–10, determine where in the sentence a comma(s) needs to be inserted.

1. A kiss can be_ a comma_ a question mark_ or an exclamation point.
           (A)   (B)   (C)

    —*Mistinguett*

2. That_ must be fine_ for_ I don't understand a word. —*Molière*
      (A)   (B) (C)

3. All meanings_ we know_ depend_ on the key of interpretation.
           (A)   (B)   (C)

    —*George Eliot*

4. The first rule for a good style is_ to have something to say; in fact_ this in
                        (A)   (B)

    itself_ is almost enough. —*Schopenhauer*
     (C)

5. In good writing_ words_ become one_ with things. —*Ralph Waldo Emerson*
            (A)   (B)   (C)

6. Everything_ that is written_ merely to please the author_ is worthless.
       (A)   (B)   (C)

    —*Pascal*

7. Sticks and stones_ may break my bones_ and_ words can sting_ like
            (A)   (B)   (C)   (D)

    anything. —*Anonymous*

8. George Santayana_ once said_ "Words_ are weapons."
            (A)   (B)   (C)

9. After many_ long_ challenging years_ I am finally Alyssa Jones_ MD.
        (A)   (B)   (C)   (D)

10. Congratulations_ Alyssa_ on your remarkable_ achievement.
        (A)   (B)   (C)

For questions 11–20, determine which commas, if any, are superfluous.

11. Is it possible for contestants on a reality show, to be themselves, or are they
                                                (A)   (B)

   always acting?", Joachim asked.
                (C)

12. With tears in his eyes, the defendant told the jurors, he was deeply sorry, for
                          (A)   (B)   (C)

   what he'd done.

13. The course, that I most wanted to take, Civilizing Society, is already full.
              (A)   (B)   (C)

14. Though, advice about which foods we should eat may vary, experts always
           (A)   (B)

   agree, that exercise is an essential part of a healthy lifestyle.
        (C)

15. The house at 310 Riley Lane needs several, major repairs, including,
                                            (A)   (B)   (C)

   a new roof.

16. After ripping up the carpet, Elian sanded the floor, and stained it a dark,
                              (A)   (B)   (C)

   cherry color.

17. We agreed that, we will meet at 1,700 Wilson Avenue on July, 14.
                   (A)   (B)   (C)

18. The cake is ready, but, I'm still working on the cookies, that you added to
                     (A)   (B)   (C)

   the order.

19. "Yes, you *are* crazy, Maurice!", Stefan yelled.
          (A)   (B)   (C)

20. Wow, you really *do* love, me, don't you?
        (A)   (B) (C)

**ANSWERS AND EXPLANATIONS
BEGIN ON NEXT PAGE**

Answers and Explanations

1. B and C

Items in a series should be set off by commas.

2. B

Insert a comma between independent clauses connected by a coordinating conjunction.

3. A and B

The parenthetical expression *we know* interrupts the sentence and should be set off by commas.

4. B

The transitional phrase *in fact* should be set off by commas.

5. A

The introductory phrase *in good writing* should be set off by commas.

6. No commas are needed.

7. B

Use a comma between independent clauses connected by a coordinating conjunction.

8. B

Use a comma before a direct quotation.

9. B, C, and D

Two adjectives modifying the same word should be separated by a comma (B). The introductory phrase should also be set off by a comma (C), and titles that follow a name should be set off by a comma (D).

10. A and B

Direct address should be set off by a comma.

11. A and C

(A) has a superfluous comma between a subject and verb. (C) is an unnecessary comma after a question mark. The second comma correctly separates independent clauses connected by a coordinating conjunction.

12. B and C

The clause *he was deeply sorry* should not be set off by commas; it serves as the object (B). The comma between *sorry* and *for* (C) unnecessarily sets off the prepositional phrase. The first comma sets off an introductory phrase.

13. A

The clause *that I . . . to take* is essential. The comma after the clause sets off nonessential information (the course name).

14. A and C

Do not use commas after subordinating conjunctions (A). The clause *that exercise . . . lifestyle* is essential (C). The second comma sets off an introductory clause.

15. A and C

Do not put a comma between a modifier and the word it modifies (A). Do not use a comma after *including* (C). The second comma sets off nonessential information.

16. B and C

Do not use a comma to separate compound parts of a predicate (B). A comma only belongs between two consecutive adjectives if they modify the same word. *Dark* modifies *cherry*. The first comma sets off an introductory phrase.

17. A, B, and C

All of these commas are superfluous. The first sets off essential information, the second breaks up a long number in an address, and the third separates a month from a day.

18. B and C

Do not use commas after coordinating conjunctions (B). (C) sets off essential information. The first comma sets off an independent clause.

19. C

Do not use a comma after an exclamation point. The first comma sets off an affirmative; the second marks direct address.

20. B

Do not insert a comma between a verb and its object. The first comma sets off a mild interjection; the third sets off a question tag.

CHAPTER 15

SEMICOLONS, COLONS, DASHES, AND QUOTATION MARKS

If you felt a bit overwhelmed by the number of comma rules, take heart: the other punctuation marks have far fewer rules.

SEMICOLONS

The semicolon's form actually reflects its function. Like a period, the semicolon separates two independent clauses; like a comma, it keeps them connected. Two closely related independent clauses can be joined by a semicolon (with or without a conjunctive adverb or other transitional word or phrase):

> *You* tell Sidney; he's less likely to be angry if he hears it from you.

> The polls suggest we are losing ground with young voters; however, our level of support from all other demographic groups remains strong.

If one clause is independent and the other subordinate, a semicolon will create a sentence fragment. If the clauses are not closely related, they should not be connected:

> **Incorrect:** The first Oscars were awarded in 1927; this year, the nominees for best picture include three historical films.

In this case, even a coordinating conjunction isn't appropriate. The best punctuation between these two clauses is a period.

PRACTICE 1

Determine whether the semicolon is correct and appropriate in each of the following sentences.

1. You don't get ulcers from what you eat; you get ulcers from what's eating you. —*Anonymous*

2. Without risk; faith is an impossibility. —*Sören Kierkegaard*

3. A failure is not always a mistake; it may simply be the best one can do under the circumstances. —*B. F. Skinner*

4. When we know how to understand our own hearts; we acquire wisdom of the hearts of others. —*Denis Diderot*

MEMORY TIP

Note that the key to correct use of the semicolon is twofold: (1) *both* clauses must be independent, and (2) the sentences must be closely related.

Generally, items in a series should be separated by commas, but if one or more items in a list contain a comma, use semicolons to separate each item:

> Bela's list of favorite cities includes New York City; Denver, Colorado; and New Orleans, Louisiana.

When Not to Use a Semicolon

Semicolons are easy to misuse. **Do not** use a semicolon in the following situations:

1. Between independent clauses joined by a coordinating conjunction. Use a comma (see chapter 14) or change the coordinating conjunction to a conjunctive adverb.

   Incorrect: I usually drink coffee; but today I'm drinking tea.

2. Between a subordinate and independent clause. Semicolons join grammatically equivalent parts. A subordinate clause and independent clause are not grammatically equal. Use a comma or make both clauses independent.

   Incorrect: Although I usually drink coffee; today I'm drinking tea.

3. To introduce a list. If there's any punctuation at all, it should be a colon (see the next section).

> **Incorrect:** Bela's list of favorite cities <u>includes;</u> New York City; Denver, Colorado; and New Orleans, Louisiana.

PRACTICE 2

Determine whether each space should be filled by a comma or a semicolon or if it should be left blank.

1. Never be haughty to the humble_ never be humble to the haughty.
   —*Jefferson Davis*

2. It's great to be great_ but it's greater to be human. —*Will Rogers*

3. Truth must be preached again and again_ because error is constantly being preached round about. —*Johann Wolfgang von Goethe*

4. If it is not seemly_ do it not_ if it is not true_ speak it not. —*Marcus Aurelius Antoninus*

COLONS

The colon's main function is to introduce quotations, lists, summaries, or explanations.

Introducing Quotations

Quotations introduced by an independent clause should be preceded by a colon:

> According to Maria Tatar, the power of fairy tales lies in their ability to help us cope: "Fairy tales register an effort to develop maps for coping with personal anxieties."

If the quotation is introduced by a phrase or subordinate clause, use a comma if necessary; otherwise, no punctuation is needed:

> According to Maria Tatar, "Fairy tales register an effort to develop maps for coping with personal anxieties."

> Maria Tatar states that "[f]airy tales register an effort to develop maps for coping with personal anxieties."

If the quotation is introduced with *said* or other words of dialogue, use a comma, not a colon, even if the introduction is a full sentence.

> **Incorrect:** Professor Grimes said: "Pay particular attention to word choice in this poem."

Introducing Lists

If a list is introduced by an independent clause, separate the clause and list with a colon:

> Be sure to pack the following items: a sleeping bag, a flashlight, bug spray, and a canteen.

However, do not use a colon to introduce (1) a series of objects or complements following a verb, (2) a series of objects following a preposition, or (3) a list introduced by *such as*, *including*, or *for example* (these words already introduce, so a colon is redundant):

> **Incorrect:** Be sure to <u>pack: a sleeping bag</u>, a flashlight, bug spray, and a canteen. [The colon incorrectly separates the verb from its objects.]

> **Incorrect:** You will find that I <u>am: outgoing</u>, intelligent, kind, and modest. [The colon incorrectly separates the linking verb from its complement.]

PRACTICE 3

Determine whether the colons in the following sentences are correct.

1. Henry L. Doherty said: "It is the studying that you do after your school days that really counts."

2. I like what Henry L. Doherty has to say about education: "It is the studying that you do after your school days that really counts."

3. According to Henry L. Doherty: "It is the studying that you do after your school days that really counts."

4. If you think education ends when you graduate, consider this thought by Henry L. Doherty: "It is the studying that you do after your school days that really counts."

5. According to Henry L. Doherty, our formal education is the least important part of our learning: "It is the studying that you do after your school days that really counts."

Introducing Summaries or Explanations

Use a colon to introduce a word, phrase, or clause that summarizes or explains the preceding sentence. When what follows a colon is a complete clause, the first letter should be capitalized:

> The Allies' mission was twofold: to halt the advance of German troops near the capital and to open up a safe supply route to the city.

> If you smoke, I have but one word of advice: quit.

Don't insert a colon before a summary or explanation that is a subject complement:

> **Incorrect:** Luck is: an accident that happens to the competent. *—Albert M. Greenfield*

Minor Uses of the Colon

1. To separate salutation from body in a formal or business letter: *Dear Eleanor:*

2. To separate hours and minutes: *We'll meet at 2:45.*

3. To show ratios or proportions: *The chances of winning the lottery are 1:10,000,000.*

4. To separate titles from subtitles: *The most-taught novel on college campuses continues to be Mary Shelley's masterpiece* Frankenstein: Or, the Modern Prometheus.

5. To separate city and publisher in a bibliography: *Shelley, Mary.* Frankenstein: Or, the Modern Prometheus. *New York: Penguin Putnam, 1994.*

PRACTICE 4

Correct any colon, semicolon, or comma errors in the following sentences.

1. The tongue is: more to be feared than the sword. *—Japanese proverb*

2. Life is like a game of poker: if you don't put any in the pot; there won't be any to take out. *—Moms Mabley*

3. Experience is the worst teacher, it gives the test before presenting the lesson. *—Vernon Law*

4. Complacency is: the enemy of progress. *—Dave Stutman*

EM DASHES

A favorite punctuation mark of many writers, the em dash is often used for phrases, although it can also correctly replace a comma, semicolon, colon, or parenthesis. Writers usually choose the em dash when the phrases are parenthetical—that is, it offers extra information or acts as an interruption or conclusion.

Look at the sentences below. They are the same, except one uses em dashes and the other commas:

> We were alone—all alone at last!—and I was too nervous to tell her how I feel.

> We were alone, all alone at last, and I was too nervous to tell her how I feel.

Don't overuse the dash: doing so defeats its purpose and makes your writing choppy. Unless you have a specific reason for using it, stick to the more conventional punctuation marks.

To Set Off Appositives with Commas

Appositives—nouns or noun phrases that rename nearby nouns—should be set off by commas. But if the appositives contain commas, use dashes:

> Everything that I'd packed—my suitcases, my golf clubs, and a box of presents—was lost by the airline.

PRACTICE 5

Correct any inappropriate uses of the dash in the following sentences.

1. You do not lead by hitting people over the head—that's assault, not leadership. —*Dwight D. Eisenhower*

2. Delegating work works—providing the one delegating works, too. —*Robert Half*

3. Conscience is the inner voice that warns us—that someone may be looking. —*H. L. Mencken*

4. The three parts of the mind—the id, the ego, and the superego—are often in conflict; it is our task to manage them properly.

QUOTATION MARKS

Quotation marks have three main functions:

1. To Set Off Direct Quotations

Any **direct** quotation—of a person, book, article, song, etc.—should be enclosed in quotation marks:

> Eric Hoffer said, "We lie loudest when we lie to ourselves."

DIRECT VERSUS INDIRECT QUOTATIONS

Be sure to distinguish between direct and indirect quotations. Indirect quotations *are not* enclosed in quotation marks:

> **Direct:** Ivy said, "Did you know a 10-minute shower uses 50 gallons of water?"
>
> **Indirect:** According to Ivy, a 10-minute shower uses 50 gallons of water.

LONG QUOTATIONS

When quoting poetry or prose and when the quotation is more than four full lines of text or more than three lines of poetry, omit the quotation marks. Instead, indent the quotation.

> In Anne Sexton's version of "Little Red Riding Hood," deception itself, not the wolf, is the true villain:
>
> The wolf, they decided, was too mean
> to be simply shot so they filled his belly
> with large stones and sewed him up.
> He was as heavy as a cemetery
> and when he woke up and tried to run off
> he fell over dead. Killed by his own weight.
> Many a deception ends on such a note.

QUOTATIONS WITHIN QUOTATIONS

A quotation that appears within a quotation is set off using single quotes:

> In his August 2003 article in *The Nation*, Joe Conason explains the term "compassionate conservative": "'compassionate' softens 'conservative,' a word that tends to be associated with smug stinginess."

PRACTICE 6

Correct any quotation mark errors in the following sentences.

1. According to Juanita Lawes, "Frankenstein's greatest error was not in creating the creature but in abandoning him, leaving him a "miserable wretch" forever."

2. Piu said "his favorite novel is *Frankenstein*."

3. Piu said, "My favorite novel is *Frankenstein*."

4. There is no failure, "said Elbert Hubbard," except in no longer trying.

2. Around Titles

Titles of short works or portions of long works should appear in quotation marks. Short works include newspaper and magazine articles, short stories, poems, chapters or sections of books, songs, and episodes of television or radio programs.

Thus, the title of Bob Dylan's song "Tangled Up in Blue" should be in quotation marks while the album title, *Blood on the Tracks*, belongs in italics.

3. Words Used in Special Ways

When you want to discuss a particular word (e.g., what it means, how it is used, etc.), enclose it in quotation marks.

The word "fiction" comes from the Latin verb "fingere," which means to make or shape. Italics may also be used for this purpose (as we've done throughout this book). Either option is acceptable, as long as you are consistent.

When a word is being used sarcastically or ironically, however, only quotation marks will do:

> My "free" vacation ended up costing me over $2,000.

Only put slang or common expressions in quotation marks to call attention to those words:

Incorrect: Hendrix tries too hard to "play it cool."

Quotation Marks and Other Punctuation Marks

One common area of confusion is where to place other punctuation marks when you have a quotation. Fortunately, there are only two rules:

1. In American usage, periods and commas always go **inside** the quotation marks.

    "I need a new job," Juno said. "This one is driving me crazy."

2. Colons, semicolons, dashes, question marks, and exclamation marks go **inside** if they are part of the quotation and **outside** if they apply to the whole sentence.

    Colin said excitedly, "There it is!"—and there it was, barely visible: the Statue of Liberty.

    Harrison wrote, "Dear Jane: I cannot tell you how deeply you hurt me"; then he tore up the paper and threw it away, deciding it was best to speak to Jane in person.

PRACTICE 7

Insert quotation marks where needed in the following sentences.

1. Do not say illicit when you mean elicit.

2. Read Chapter 3: Invertebrates for next class.

3. The Love Song of J. Alfred Prufrock is one of T. S. Eliot's most famous poems.

4. The 1951 film *The Day the Earth Stood Still* is based on the short story Farewell to the Master by Harry Bates.

5. Charlotte's big secret was something we all already knew.

SUMMARY

Semicolons are used primarily to separate independent clauses that are closely related. They can be used with or without a transitional word or phrase. Semicolons should also be used to separate items in a series if one or more of those items contains a comma.

Colons have three major functions: to introduce quotations, lists, and summaries or explanations that are introduced by an independent clause. If the quotation is introduced by *said*, use a comma. Never use a colon between a verb and its objects or complement; between a preposition and its object; or after *such as*, *including*, and *for example*.

Minor functions of the colon include separating a salutation from the body of the letter, separating hours and minutes, showing ratios or proportions, separating titles and subtitles, and separating city and publisher in a bibliography.

The **em dash** sets off words, phrases, or clauses for emphasis. It should be used sparingly, only when an idea really deserves to be set off.

Finally, **quotation marks** set off direct quotations, titles of short works, and words being used in a special way within sentences. Long quotations should be indented and the quotation marks omitted. If you have a quotation within a quotation, use single quotation marks (') for the internal quotation. Periods and commas always go inside quotation marks; semicolons, colons, dashes, question marks, and exclamation points go inside the quotation marks only if they are part of the quotation.

PRACTICE ON YOUR OWN

Imitation is the best form of flattery. Look through some of your favorite novels or stories or your favorite magazine or newspaper for sentences that use the punctuation marks discussed in this chapter. Try to find examples of all the different uses (e.g., the three different functions of the colon). Using those sentences as models, craft your own sentences following a similar sentence structure.

Practice Answers and Explanations

PRACTICE 1

1. Yes. Both clauses are independent and directly related.

2. No. The semicolon incorrectly separates a phrase (*without risk*) from an independent clause.

3. Yes. Both clauses are independent and directly related.

4. No. The first clause is subordinate, so the semicolon should be a comma.

PRACTICE 2

1. Semicolon. Both clauses are independent and there is no coordinating conjunction, so a comma would create a sentence fragment.

2. Comma. The independent clauses are connected by a coordinating conjunction, so a comma is the correct punctuation mark.

3. No punctuation is necessary. If the subordinate clause preceded the independent clause, a comma would be required, but the sentence as it stands is correct.

4. The correct punctuation is as follows: *If it is not seemly, do it not; if it is not true, speak it not.* The subordinate *if* clauses should be set off by commas, and the two *if...not* complex sentence pairs should be connected by a semicolon.

PRACTICE 3

1. No. Use a comma with the *he said* construction.

2. Yes. The quotation is introduced by a full sentence.

3. No. The introduction is only a phrase, so the punctuation mark should be a comma.

4. Yes. The introduction is a complete sentence.

5. Yes. The introduction is a complete sentence.

PRACTICE 4

1. Delete the colon; do not use a colon to introduce an explanation that is a subject complement.

2. The colon correctly introduces an explanation, but the semicolon should be a comma (*if... pot* is a subordinate clause, not an independent clause).

3. The comma creates a sentence fragment because it stands alone between two independent clauses. A semicolon would be correct since the clauses are closely related. A colon is even more correct, as the second clause explains the first (telling us *why* experience is the worst teacher).

4. Delete the colon; it incorrectly separates the linking verb *is* from its complement *the enemy of progress*.

PRACTICE 5

1. The dash is appropriate.

2. The dash is appropriate.

3. The dash is unnecessary. Why separate the subordinate clause? The dash is especially awkward because the clause is essential to the sentence.

4. The dashes appropriately set off the appositive, which contains commas.

PRACTICE 6

1. The quotation marks around *miserable wretch* should be single quotation marks (') since these words are a quotation within a quotation.

2. This is an indirect quotation, so there shouldn't be any quotation marks.

3. Correct.

4. The quotation marks are around the speaker tag (*said Elbert Hubbard*), not around what Hubbard said. The correct placement is as follows: "There is no failure," said Elbert Hubbard, "except in no longer trying."

PRACTICE 7

1. Do not say "illicit" when you mean "elicit." [Period goes inside quotation mark.]

2. Read "Chapter 3: Invertebrates" for next class.

3. "The Love Song of J. Alfred Prufrock" is one of T. S. Eliot's most famous poems.

4. The 1951 film *The Day the Earth Stood Still* is based on the short story "Farewell to the Master" by Harry Bates.

5. Charlotte's big "secret" was something we all already knew.

CHAPTER 15 TEST

Correct punctuation errors, if any, in the following sentences.

1. If we are ever to enjoy life, now is the time; not tomorrow, nor next year, nor in some future life after we have died. *—Thomas Dreier*

2. The Jester Brothers' new song Ice Cold is getting a lot of radio play lately.

3. Love is blind; friendship closes its eyes. *—Anonymous*

4. Life is the greatest bargain, we get it for nothing. *—Yiddish proverb*

5. Doing what you like is freedom, liking what you do is happiness. *—Frank Tyger*

6. Some people grow under responsibility: others merely swell. *—Carl Hubbell*

7. Never mind your happiness, do your duty. *—Will Durant*

8. Thinking well is wise, planning well, wiser, doing well, wisest and best of all. *—Persian proverb*

9. No is always a door-closing word: yes is a door-opening word. *—Thomas Dreier*

10. According to Desiderius Erasmus: "Every definition is dangerous".

11. My grandfather once told me that there are two kinds of people: those who do the work and those who take the credit. *—Indira Gandhi*

12. Amateurs hope, professionals work. *—Garson Kanin*

13. What did Lindsay mean when she said "We need to take a break?"

14. The editorial Justice for Mall is worth reading.

15. Never to have changed—what a pitiable thing of which to boast! *—Johann Wolfgang von Goethe*

16. If you look closely, you will see, that the numbers increase at a ratio of 1–3.

17. A friend is a person who knows all about you: and still likes you.
     —*Elbert Hubbard*

18. My favorite episode of *Seinfeld* is The Parking Garage, when Kramer spends the whole day trying to find his car.

19. Hey guys listen to this, Dear Miss Manners, How can I get my husband to stop barking when he's hungry?

20. Happiness is not a reward, it is a consequence. —*Robert G. Ingersoll*

**ANSWERS AND EXPLANATIONS
BEGIN ON NEXT PAGE**

Answers and Explanations

1. A dash would set off the list for emphasis. *If we are ever to enjoy life, now is the time—not tomorrow, nor next year, nor in some future life after we have died.*

2. Song titles are enclosed in quotation marks, and because the title is not essential, it should be set off by commas. *The Jester Brothers' new song, "Ice Cold," is getting a lot of radio play lately.*

3. No correction needed.

4. The colon correctly sets off the explanation for why life "is the greatest bargain." *Life is the greatest bargain: we get it for nothing.*

5. The two independent clauses are closely related and should be connected by a semicolon. *Doing what you like is freedom; liking what you do is happiness.*

6. These two independent clauses are also closely related and should be separated by a semicolon. *Some people grow under responsibility; others merely swell.*

7. Again, the two independent clauses are closely related and should be connected by a semicolon. A pair of dashes would make the quotation choppy. *Never mind your happiness; do your duty.*

8. The items in the series contain commas, so they should be separated by semicolons. *Thinking well is wise; planning well, wiser; doing well, wisest and best of all.*

9. The two words are being discussed, so they should be enclosed in quotation marks. The two clauses are closely related and should be connected by a semicolon. *"No" is always a door-closing word; "yes" is a door-opening word.*

10. The quotation is introduced by a phrase, so a comma and quotation marks are correct. The period belongs inside the quotation marks. *According to Desiderius Erasmus, "Every definition is dangerous."*

11. No correction needed. The colon correctly introduces the explanation of the two kinds of people. It is an indirect quotation.

12. The two independent clauses are closely related, so they should be separated by a semicolon. Dashes would make the sentence choppy. *Amateurs hope; professionals work.*

13. The direct quotation should be introduced by a comma and enclosed in quotation marks. The question mark is part of the whole sentence and should be outside the quotation marks. *What did Lindsay mean when she said, "We need to take a break"?*

14. The title of the editorial should be enclosed in quotation marks. The title is essential to the meaning of the sentence, so it should not be set off by commas. *The editorial "Justice for Mall" is worth reading.*

15. No correction needed. The dash effectively sets off the introduction from the main clause. The exclamation point indicates emotion.

16. The introductory clause needs to be set off by a comma, but the comma between *see* and the object (the *that* clause) is incorrect. The ratio is correctly expressed by a colon between the numbers. *If you look closely, you will see that the numbers increase at a ratio of 1:3.*

17. The dash effectively sets off the phrase *and still likes you*, highlighting the implied idea that there are things about each of us that are not necessarily likeable. Colons should never be inserted between the parts of a compound verb. *A friend is a person who knows all about you—and still likes you.*

18. The title of the episode needs to be enclosed in quotation marks, and the comma belongs inside the marks. *My favorite episode of* Seinfeld *is "The Parking Garage," when Kramer spends the whole day trying to find his car.*

19. Direct address (*guys*) should be set off by commas and the quotation from the letter introduced by a colon. The quotation needs to be enclosed in quotation marks with the question mark inside the quotation marks. *Hey, guys, listen to this: "Dear Miss Manners, How can I get my husband to stop barking when he's hungry?"*

20. The best choice for punctuation between these independent clauses is the dash, which highlights the idea that happiness is the result of our actions. *Happiness is not a reward—it is a consequence.*

CHAPTER 16

END MARKS, APOSTROPHES, AND THE REST

This chapter answers some of those burning questions you've had about punctuation: When can you use an exclamation point? How do you use an ellipsis? And just what are brackets for?

END MARKS

There aren't many rules for the period, question mark, or exclamation point.

The Period

All sentences except direct questions and exclamations should end in a period:

Statement: It's getting late.

Statement (indirect question): Géza wants to know if you're ready to go.

The Question Mark

A direct question should be followed by a question mark. If you have a series of questions, each question can be followed by a question mark, even if each question is not a complete sentence:

Indirect: Cameron asked who is in charge around here.

Direct: "Who is in charge around here?" Cameron asked.

Series: Did you pack your pajamas? Your toothbrush? Your medication?

If a sentence ends in a question mark, do not add a period. A question mark *is* an end mark, so no other punctuation is necessary. (The same is true for the exclamation point.)

Incorrect: What time is it?.

Correct: What time is it?

The Exclamation Point

Genuine exclamations—words, phrases, or clauses that express strong emotions or forceful commands—take the exclamation point as their end mark:

This is the most exciting day of my life!

"Duck!" Melinda yelled as Chet threw an icy snowball toward my head.

In the second example, the quotation gets the exclamation point, not the entire sentence, and the exclamation point is inside the quotation marks.

The exclamation point is generally considered informal (it is commonly used in comic strips, for example), so think very carefully about using it in your GMAT essays.

PRACTICE 1

Correct any errors in end mark punctuation in the sentences below.

1. The results are in! We won!
2. You don't know where you're going, do you.
3. Juanita asked me whether I thought it was a good idea?
4. Are you absolutely certain you turned off and unplugged the iron.
5. "Hey. It's my turn" Genevieve wailed!

Periods in Abbreviations

The period is also used in many abbreviations. Generally, abbreviations for some titles, time references, and common Latin terms have periods; abbreviations for names of states and organizations do not.

Period(s)	No Period(s)
Social and professional titles: **Mr., Mrs., Ms., Jr., Sr., Dr., Sgt.**	State names: **PA, CA, TX**
Time references: **a.m., p.m.**	Organization names: **UN, FTC, NASA, NAACP, CIA, YMCA**
Latin abbreviations: **i.e., e.g., vs., et al., etc.**	Academic degrees: **RN, DDS, MD, PhD, BA**
Quantities or measurements: **lb., in., oz., no.**	Era references and time zones: **BCE, AD, CE; GMT, EST**

There are no spaces after the periods in abbreviations. When in doubt about an abbreviation, consult a dictionary or style guide. Following are some notes on using abbreviations correctly:

1. If a sentence ends in an abbreviation that uses a period, do not add another period.

    Incorrect: Let's meet at 3 A.M..

    Correct: Let's meet at 3 A.M.

2. Do not abbreviate titles *unless* they appear with a name.

    Incorrect: My <u>Dr.</u> said I should stay in bed for about a week.

    Correct: <u>My doctor</u> said I should stay in bed for about a week.

3. To use an abbreviation that isn't familiar to your readers, write out the full word(s) followed by the abbreviation in parentheses; thereafter, you may use the abbreviation.

    Incorrect: The <u>AFWA</u> reports an unusual weather pattern over the North Pole.

    Correct: The <u>Air Force Weather Agency (AFWA)</u> reports an unusual weather pattern over the North Pole.

4. Use time and number abbreviations only with specific numbers.

    Incorrect: Kobe wakes early every <u>A.M.</u>

    Correct: Kobe wakes at <u>6:00</u> A.M. every morning.

5. Avoid informal abbreviations of days of the week, months, measurements, names, states, company names, and academic subjects.

Incorrect: Ty <u>Bros.</u> <u>Co.</u> has a big <u>Xmas</u> sale each <u>Dec.</u>

Correct: Ty <u>Brothers</u> <u>Company</u> has a big <u>Christmas</u> sale each <u>December</u>.

PRACTICE 2

Correct any errors in abbreviations in the following sentences.

1. Tamar earned her B.S. degree in just three yrs.
2. The rev. roused the sleepy congregation with a soaring homily.
3. Maj Wrubleski has a reputation for being especially tough on new recruits.
4. Representatives of the local S.P.C.A. will be soliciting donations outside the store tomorrow.
5. The SLCS (submarine laser communication system) is still under development.

THE APOSTROPHE

The apostrophe has two uses: to show possession and omission.

Possessives

Most nouns and indefinite pronouns (e.g., *someone, anybody*) show possession by adding the apostrophe and -*s*:

> <u>Uncle Ming's</u> homemade dumplings were the hit of the party.

NOUNS ENDING IN -S

For singular nouns ending in -*s*, add both the apostrophe and -*s* unless the pronunciation will be awkward:

> The <u>witness's</u> statement sounded forced.

For plural nouns ending in -s, only add the apostrophe:

The <u>witnesses'</u> statements corroborated the defendant's story.

JOINT POSSESSION AND COMPOUND NOUNS

When two or more nouns share possession of an item, add the apostrophe only to the last noun. However, if each individual possesses the item, show possession for each noun:

Individual: <u>Roxanne's</u> and <u>Ravi's</u> dogs won prizes in the dog show.

[Roxanne and Ravi each own dogs.]

Joint: <u>Roxanne and Ravi's</u> dogs won prizes in the dog show.

[Roxanne and Ravi jointly own the dogs.]

To Show Omission

Use the apostrophe when you omit one or more letters from a word or numbers from a date:

I <u>can't</u> believe <u>you're</u> going without me.

Say what you like about disco; I still love the music of the <u>'70s</u>.

Incorrect Uses

Avoid the following common misuses of the apostrophe.

1. **To form plurals.** Plurals are formed *only* with -s (or -es)—not with an apostrophe.

   Incorrect: That was a helpful list of <u>do's</u> and <u>dont's</u>.

2. **With possessive pronouns.** The possessive pronouns (*mine, yours, his, whose,* etc.) already show possession; to add an apostrophe is both incorrect and redundant.

   Incorrect: Is this jacket <u>your's</u> or <u>her's</u>?

3. **With plural numbers and letters.** Don't use the apostrophe to make plural numbers and letters. Use only the plural -s or -es for numbers. To make a letter

plural, italicize or capitalize the letter and add -*s* or -*es* unless the result is a word. In that case, use the apostrophe to prevent confusion.

Incorrect: There are two <u>10's</u> missing from this deck of cards.

Correct: There are two <u>10s</u> missing from this deck of cards.

Incorrect: Both of the <u>*M's*</u> had faded, so the sign read "Toy's" instead of "Tommy's."

Correct: Both of the <u>*M*s</u> had faded, so the sign read "Toy's" instead of "Tommy's."

Correct: There are four <u>*i's*</u> and four <u>*s's*</u> in *Mississippi*.

[Without the apostrophe, readers might mistake *is* for *is*; use the apostrophe for both letters for consistency.]

4. **With plural abbreviations and words used specially.** Abbreviations and words used specially don't need an apostrophe for the plural (unless the word is in quotation marks).

    Incorrect: There are no <u>ATM's</u> around here.

    Correct: There are no <u>ATMs</u> around here.

    Incorrect: You can bury me in *please's*, but I still won't let you go to that party.

    Correct: You can bury me in *pleases*, but I still won't let you go to that party.

PRACTICE 3

Correct any apostrophe errors in the following sentences.

1. Alanas résumé is very impressive, isnt it?

2. The past three winters' have been colder than normal.

3. The 1980's is known as the "me" decade.

4. Who's keys are these—your's or their's?

5. My mother keeps complaining that people in their 20's are so impatient.

ALL THE REST

Parentheses

Parentheses set off information that is supplemental or tangential—a minor example, a digression, an afterthought. In that sense, they are the opposite of the dash, which sets off ideas for emphasis. Parentheses are also used for numbering items in a list as well as for citations of other sources:

> My brother has many nicknames (including Bullfrog, Tadpole, and T-Man, to name a few), but he only ever answers to the name Eugene.

> Which would you rather have: (A) $1,000,000 in one lump sum or (B) $100,000 a year for life?

> The fiscal crisis that ensued was due "solely to the greed of a few top managers" (Jacobs 113).

Do not use a period at the end of a statement inside of parentheses unless the parenthetical statement is a complete sentence *and* the final parenthesis comes after a full stop:

> **Incorrect:** My favorite versions of the Grimm fairy tales are in Roald Dahl's collection *Revolting Rhymes* (his baby bear, for example, eats up the bratty Goldilocks.).

> **Correct:** My favorite versions of the Grimm fairy tales are in Roald Dahl's collection *Revolting Rhymes*. (His baby bear, for example, eats up the bratty Goldilocks.)

Formal writing like your GMAT essay should contain few parenthetical thoughts. As you revise, see how many of your parenthetical ideas can be worked into the text or omitted.

Brackets ([ ])

Brackets indicate that you have added words to, or changed words in, a quotation:

> In his memoir, Carlson confessed that he "never knew just how devoted [his] mother was to her music until after she died." [The original text was in the first person, so the author changed *my* to *his* for clarity.]

Brackets indicate stage directions in a play. (These lines are from Henrik Ibsen's 1879 play *A Doll's House*.)

> NORA [*looking incredulously at her*] But Kristine, how could that be?
>
> MRS. LINDE [*smiling wearily and smoothing her hair*] Oh, sometimes it happens, Nora.

As you've seen over and over in this text, brackets can also set off special instructions or explanations.

PRACTICE 4

Correct any errors in the use of parentheses or brackets in the following sentences.

1. Do you want to 1. go to the movies, 2. go out to dinner, or 3. both?

2. Charles meets Lulu [his sister] at the grocery store (But he doesn't find out she's his sister until the end of the play.).

3. In the final scene, Joy [crying softly] confesses to Hitch (her dying son), "Dylan (Hitch's coach) is your real father, and he's loved you more than you'll ever know."

4. The committee meets biweekly (twice a month) in the library conference room.

Ellipsis (. . .)

An ellipsis has two uses: (1) to indicate that you have deleted one or more words from a quotation and (2) to indicate hesitation, interruption, or unfinished thought in speech. If you delete a full sentence or more from a quotation, use an additional period after the ellipsis.

In his memoir *Factory of Facts*, Luc Sante acknowledges that

> the theme of loss is a constant for exiles … My parents lost friends, lost family ties and patterns of mutual assistance, lost rituals and habits and favorite foods, lost any link to an ongoing social milieu.… We lost connection to a thing larger than ourselves, and as a family failed to make any significant new connection in exchange.

The first ellipsis indicates that only part of a sentence was omitted. The second (four periods) indicates that a full sentence or more was omitted.

Slash (/)

Finally, the slash has two main uses: (1) to separate lines of poetry (with a space before and after the slash) and (2) to separate words that are paired (in which case, there is **no** space before or after the slash).

Another use of the slash (seen below) is generally considered informal and should be used sparingly, if at all. Instead, use *and* or *or* and write out the word pair if possible:

> **Incorrect:** Every student must cast his/her vote by noon.

> **Correct:** Every student must cast his or her vote by noon.

PRACTICE 5

Here is a paragraph from the introduction to Ralph Waldo Emerson's essay "Nature."

> All science has one aim, namely, to find a theory of nature. We have theories of races and of functions, but scarcely yet a remote approach to an idea of creation. We are now so far from the road to truth, that religious teachers dispute and hate each other, and speculative men are esteemed unsound and frivolous. But to a sound judgment, the most abstract truth is the most practical. Whenever a true theory appears, it will be its own evidence. Its test is, that it will explain all phenomena.

1. How would you punctuate the following, which omits part of one sentence?

   But the most abstract truth is the most practical.

2. How would you punctuate the following, which omits the second, third, and fourth sentences?

   All science has one aim, namely, to find a theory of nature. Whenever a true theory appears, it will be its own evidence. Its test is, that it will explain all phenomena.

SUMMARY

Most sentences should end in a **period**. A sentence that asks a direct question should end in a **question mark**. Sentences that express strong emotion (e.g., interjections) or forceful commands should end in an **exclamation point**.

Periods are used in many **abbreviations**. In general, abbreviations of social and professional titles, time references, Latin abbreviations, and quantities or measurements should have periods. Sentences ending in an abbreviation with a period do not take another period. Titles should only be abbreviated if used with names. Unfamiliar abbreviations should be written out first, with the abbreviation in parentheses. Time and number abbreviations should only be used with specific numbers. Informal abbreviations (e.g., *Mon.* or *phys. ed.*) should be avoided.

Apostrophes show possession and omission. To show possession, add an apostrophe and *-s* (if the noun is plural and ends in *-s*, or if adding *-s* to a singular noun ending in *-s* makes for awkward pronunciation, add only the apostrophe). To show joint possession, add the apostrophe only to the last noun. Do not use the apostrophe to make plurals or with possessive pronouns, except to prevent confusion.

Parentheses set off supplemental or tangential information. **Brackets** indicate added words or changed words in a quotation and set off stage directions in a play.

An **ellipsis** indicates omitted words in a quotation or hesitation or interruption in speech. A **slash** separates lines of poetry and paired words such as *either/or*.

Practice Answers and Explanations

PRACTICE 1

1. The results are in. We won! [The exclamation point is overused when it ends both sentences; it is much more effective if left only in the second sentence.]

2. You don't know where you're going, do you? [This is a direct question and should end in a question mark. (Note the comma setting off the question tag.)]

3. Juanita asked me whether I thought it was a good idea. [This is a statement, not a question, so it should end in a period.]

4. Are you absolutely certain you turned off and unplugged the iron? [This is a direct question and should end in a question mark.]

5. "Hey<u>!</u> It's my turn<u>!</u>" Genevieve wailed<u>.</u> [The wailing merits exclamation points, so set the exclamation points after the statements in the quotation marks. The sentence itself should end in a period.]

PRACTICE 2

1. Tamar earned her <u>BS</u> degree in just three <u>years</u>. [Do not use periods in academic degrees and avoid informal abbreviations.]

2. The <u>reverend</u> roused the sleepy congregation with a soaring homily. [Only abbreviate titles if they appear with names.]

3. <u>Maj.</u> Wrubleski has a reputation for being especially tough on new recruits. [Use periods for title abbreviations.]

4. Representatives of the local <u>SPCA</u> will be soliciting donations outside the store tomorrow. [Do not use periods in abbreviations for organizations.]

5. The <u>submarine laser communication system (SLCS)</u> is still under development. [State the full name of an unfamiliar organization or item first, then its abbreviation in parentheses.]

PRACTICE 3

1. <u>Alana's</u> résumé is very impressive, <u>isn't</u> it? [*Alana's* is possessive, not plural; *isn't* is a contraction needing an apostrophe.]

2. The past three <u>winters</u> have been colder than normal. [*Winters* is plural, not possessive.]

3. The <u>1980s</u> is known as the "me" decade. [No apostrophes for decades or other numbers.]

4. <u>Whose</u> keys are these—<u>yours</u> or <u>theirs</u>? [No apostrophes in possessive pronouns.]

5. My mother keeps complaining that people in their <u>20s</u> are so impatient. [No apostrophe with plural numbers.]

PRACTICE 4

1. Do you want to <u>(1)</u> go to the movies, <u>(2)</u> go out to dinner, or <u>(3)</u> both? [Put parentheses around the numbers; the periods create confusion.]

2. Charles meets Lulu <u>(his sister)</u> at the grocery store<u>,</u> but he doesn't find out she's his sister until the end of the play<u>.</u> [Brackets aren't used to set off supplemental

information; the parentheses in the original version set off important information that should be incorporated into the sentence.]

3. In the final scene, Joy, crying softly, confesses to Hitch, her dying son, "Dylan [Hitch's coach] is your real father, and he's loved you more than you'll ever know." [The brackets are incorrect; though the sentence discusses a play, these are not stage directions. The first parentheses can be replaced by commas for an appositive. The parentheses in the quotation should be brackets because they are being used to indicate that these words are added as explanation and are not part of the actual quotation.]

4. The sentence is correct as written.

PRACTICE 5

1. To omit part of a sentence, use a single ellipsis: "But . . . the most abstract truth is the most practical." If you are using Modern Language Association (MLA) format, the ellipsis should be in brackets: "But [. . .] the most abstract truth is the most practical." Do not start or end a quotation with an ellipsis.

2. To omit a full sentence or more, use the ellipsis plus a period for a total of four periods: "All science has one aim, namely, to find a theory of nature. . . . Whenever a true theory appears, it will be its own evidence. Its test is, that it will explain all phenomena."

CHAPTER 16 TEST

Identify which change, if any, is needed to correct each sentence.

1. Today's "smart home" technologies enable homeowners to remotely access and control audio, video, telephone, and/or computer networks from anywhere in the home.

   (A) Delete the apostrophe in *today's*.
   (B) Change *and/or* to *and*.
   (C) Change commas to semicolons.
   (D) Add an apostrophe before the *s* in *homeowners*.
   (E) No change

2. The looting of archeological treasures is a serious problem worldwide, not just in war-torn region's, although countries at war are particularly at risk for losing their cultural and historical treasures.

   (A) Delete the apostrophe in *region's*.
   (B) Add an apostrophe before the *s* in both *treasures*.
   (C) Change the second comma to a semicolon.
   (D) Change the period to an exclamation point.
   (E) No change

3. Is it ethical to release a drug that could help hundreds of thousands of people if a small enough percentage of users risk serious side effects. What percentage is "small enough"?

   (A) Add an apostrophe before the *s* in *users*.
   (B) Change the period to a question mark.
   (C) Change the question mark to a period.
   (D) Put the question mark inside the quotation marks.
   (E) No change

4. The question you need to answer is whether or not the attorney has a conflict of interest in accepting this case?

   (A) Delete *or not.*
   (B) Set *of interest* off with commas.
   (C) Insert a colon after *is.*
   (D) Change the question mark to a period.
   (E) No change

5. As Picasso puts it, art ". . . is a lie that makes us realize the truth . . ."

   (A) Change the comma to a colon.
   (B) Delete the quotation marks.
   (C) Delete the ellipses before and after the quote.
   (D) Delete only the ellipsis after the quote.
   (E) No change

6. In James Finn Garner's number one best seller (*Politically Correct Bedtime Stories*), "Cinderella" ends with all the men at the ball killing each other in a "macho dance of destruction."

   (A) Move the period outside the quotation marks.
   (B) Delete the parentheses.
   (C) Move the parentheses to around *number one best seller.*
   (D) Change the period to an exclamation point.
   (E) No change

7. The women (spelled *womyn* throughout the text to avoid having *men* in the word) live happily ever after, "set[ting] up a clothing co-op that produce[s] only comfortable, practical clothes for womyn."

   (A) Delete the parentheses.
   (B) Delete the first brackets.
   (C) Delete both sets of brackets.
   (D) Insert an ellipsis before *set[ting].*
   (E) No change

8. The class of 96 will present a special gift to the university at its ten-year reunion in April.

    (A) Change *April* to *Apr.*
    (B) Insert an apostrophe before *96*.
    (C) Change *its* to *it's*.
    (D) Put parentheses around *to the university*.
    (E) No change

9. Our cat UFO (short for Unique Feline Organism) licked it's paws and curled up on the pillow, purring contentedly.

    (A) Put *UFO* in the parentheses.
    (B) Change *it's* to *its*.
    (C) Change *paws* to *paw's*.
    (D) Insert periods in *UFO*.
    (E) No change

10. Dear Mr. Holmes: Enclosed please find a copy of my invoice from Sept. Please remit ASAP as the invoice is now several months past due. Thx.

    (A) Write out *Sept., ASAP,* and *Thx.*
    (B) Write out only *ASAP*.
    (C) Insert periods between letters in *ASAP*.
    (D) Change *Thx* to *thank you*.
    (E) No change

11. Carlito tried to open the door, but it was locked! So was the other one! How was he going to enter?

    (A) Change the question mark to an exclamation mark.
    (B) Change the first exclamation point to a period.
    (C) Change both exclamation points to periods.
    (D) Change both exclamation points to question marks.
    (E) No change

12. After Shaban's and Beti's house sold for 25 percent more than their asking price, several other families in the neighborhood decided to put their houses up for sale, too.

    (A) Delete the 's on *Shaban's*.
    (B) Delete the apostrophe in both *Shaban's* and *Beti's*.
    (C) Change *their* to *they're*.
    (D) Change *families* to *family's*.
    (E) No change

13. Javan still writes his b's and d's backwards, but otherwise he has mastered the alphabet much more quickly than I'd expected.

    (A) Change the comma to a semicolon.
    (B) Change *b's and d's* to *B's and D's*.
    (C) Change *b's and d's* to *Bs and Ds*.
    (D) Change *he* to *he's*.
    (E) No change

14. In the opening lines of the poem "Blessing for the Liver," David Keplinger writes that "the heart with its lies, is a lesser thing."

    (A) Insert ellipses before and after the quotation, inside the quotation marks.
    (B) Change the comma in the quotation to a slash.
    (C) Insert slashes at the beginning and end of the quotation.
    (D) Insert brackets around the quotation.
    (E) No change

15. It doesn't really matter what you decide, because I am going with/without you—Celeste needs me!

    (A) Change the exclamation point to a period.
    (B) Change the dash to a colon.
    (C) Change *with/without* to *with or without*.
    (D) Change *with/without* to *with…or without*.
    (E) No change

16. I just have one question for you, Irving: How much are you willing to sacrifice to make this dream a reality.

    (A) Change the colon to a semicolon.
    (B) Put *How . . . reality* in quotation marks.
    (C) Change the colon to a question mark.
    (D) Change the period to a question mark.
    (E) No change

17. I want a car that gets at least 18 m.p.g. and that I can finance at a reasonable APR.

    (A) Change *APR* to *A.P.R.*
    (B) Change *m.p.g.* to *mpg.*
    (C) Change *APR* to *A.P.R.* and add a period at the end of the sentence.
    (D) Change *m.p.g.* to *miles per gallon* and *APR* to *rate.*
    (E) No change

18. After surveying both crime scenes, Det. Mombasa had no doubt that the two robberies were the work of the same thief.

    (A) Change *Det.* to *det.*
    (B) Change *Det.* to *detective.*
    (C) Change *scenes* to *scene's.*
    (D) Change *were* to *we're.*
    (E) No change

19. "Were going fishing," Bubba said. "Do you want to come?"

    (A) Move the comma outside the quotation mark.
    (B) Change *Were* to *We're.*
    (C) Change the question mark to an exclamation point.
    (D) Move the question mark outside the quotation mark.
    (E) No change

20. "Giles needs to take his P.M. medicine," Patricia told the R.N. on duty.

    (A) Change *P.M.* to *evening* and *R.N.* to *nurse*.

    (B) Change *P.M.* to *pm* and *R.N.* to *RN*.

    (C) Change *P.M.* to *P.M.*

    (D) Move the comma outside of the quotation mark.

    (E) No change

**ANSWERS AND EXPLANATIONS
BEGIN ON NEXT PAGE**

Answers and Explanations

1. B

Avoid informal uses of the slash.

2. A

Regions should be plural, not possessive, so the apostrophe must be deleted.

3. B

Both sentences are direct questions, so both should end in question marks.

4. D

This sentence is an indirect question and should end in a period.

5. C

Do not use ellipses at the beginning or end of a quotation, even if the quotation is only part of a sentence.

6. B

The title of the book is not supplementary information and should not be enclosed in parentheses.

7. E

This sentence is correct.

8. B

The year 1996 is abbreviated to *96*; an apostrophe should show the omission of the *19*.

9. B

The cat's name *is* UFO—it's not an abbreviation. The error in this sentence is *it's*, the contraction for *it is* (see chapter 13).

10. A

All three of these informal abbreviations should be written out.

11. C

None of these sentences are strong enough to warrant an exclamation point. The question mark at the end of the third sentence, a direct question, is correct.

12. A

Shaban and Beti own the house together, so add the apostrophe and *-s* to *Beti* only.

13. C

Do not use the apostrophe to make plurals of letters except to prevent confusion. Here, the best correction is to capitalize the letters or italicize them.

14. B

Use a slash to separate lines of poetry.

15. C

Avoid informal uses of the slash.

16. D

What follows the colon is a direct question and should end in a question mark.

17. D

Both of these informal abbreviations should be written out.

18. E

This sentence is correct.

19. B

Add an apostrophe to *We're* because it is a contraction.

20. A

Don't use *P.M.* except with a specific time. Don't abbreviate titles unless used with a name.

SECTION IV

Cumulative Test

Congratulations! You've completed all the lessons. Now challenge yourself to pull together everything you've learned. Work carefully and read the answers and explanations thoroughly. If you miss a question, review the chapters that deal with the relevant topics.

PART A

Questions 1–5 refer to the following sentence:

Love is what's left of a relationship after all the selfishness has been removed.
—*Cullen Hightower*

1. In this sentence, *is* is a/an
    (A) helping verb.
    (B) linking verb.
    (C) action verb.
    (D) infinitive.
    (E) adverb.

2. In this sentence, *love* is a/an
    (A) noun.
    (B) verb.
    (C) adjective.
    (D) adverb.
    (E) preposition.

3. Which of the following excerpts from the sentence is a prepositional phrase?
    (A) Love is
    (B) Of a relationship
    (C) All the selfishness
    (D) Has been removed
    (E) None of the above

4. Which of the following excerpts from the sentence is the subject complement?

   (A) What's left
   (B) Of a relationship
   (C) After all the selfishness has been removed
   (D) What's left of a relationship after all the selfishness has been removed
   (E) None of the above

5. Which of the following excerpts from the sentence is a subordinate clause?

   (A) Love is what's left
   (B) Of a relationship
   (C) After all the selfishness has been removed
   (D) Has been removed
   (E) None of the above

PART B

For questions 6–20, identify the best version of each sentence based on grammar, mechanics, and style. If the original is best, choose (A).

6. Esperanza, like many children, want to be a fireman when she grows up.

   (A) No change
   (B) Esperanza, like many children, wants to be a fireman when she grows up.
   (C) Like many children, Esperanza wants to be a fireman when she grows up.
   (D) Like many children, Esperanza wants to be a firefighter when she grows up.
   (E) Wanting to be a firefighter when she grows up, Esperanza is like many children.

7. The word fetus means offspring in latin.

   (A) No change
   (B) The word *fetus* means *offspring* in Latin.
   (C) The word "fetus" means "offspring" in latin.
   (D) The word Fetus means Offspring in Latin.
   (E) The word fetus has the meaning of offspring in the language of Latin.

8. Did you know that a flag flying upside-down is a signal of distress.

   (A) No change

   (B) Did you know that a flag, flying upside-down, is a signal of distress?

   (C) Did you know, that a flag flying upside-down is: a signal of distress.

   (D) Did you know that if a flag is flying upside-down, that flag is a signal of distress?

   (E) Did you know that a flag flying upside-down is a signal of distress?

9. Refusing to compromise her artistic freedom, Yelena decided to produce the CD on her own.

   (A) No change

   (B) Refusing to compromise her artistic freedom, it was decided by Yelena to produce the CD on her own.

   (C) Refusing to compromise her artistic freedom, on her own, Yelena decided to produce the CD.

   (D) Refusing to compromise her artistic freedom, Yelena did decided to produce the cd on her own.

   (E) In an effort to avoid the compromising of her artistic freedom, Yelena adjudged that it behooved her to produce the cd on her own.

10. Each new member must serve on two committees in there first year.

   (A) No change

   (B) Each new member must serve, on two committees, in their first year.

   (C) Each new member must serve on two committees in his or her first year.

   (D) All new members must serve on two committees in their first year.

   (E) All members who are new must serve on two committees in the first year of their membership.

11. Name tags and school uniforms should be worn by all children to insure that they are easily identified while in the museum.

    (A) No change
    (B) While in the museum, name tags and school uniforms should be worn by all children to insure that they are easily identified.
    (C) Name tags and school uniforms should be worn to ensure that all children are easily identified while in the museum.
    (D) The wearing of name tags and school uniforms is required for all children while they are in the museum for the purpose that they be easily identified.
    (E) To assure that they are easily identified, name tags and school uniforms should be worn by all children in the museum.

12. Between you and I, the whole thing totally stinks.

    (A) No change
    (B) Between you and me, the whole thing stinks like a rotten egg.
    (C) Between you and me, the proposed changes are appalling.
    (D) Between you and I; the whole thing has a very foul odor.
    (E) Between you and me, the whole thing with the proposed changes is very upsetting.

13. In Pieter Bruegels painting Landscape With The Fall Of Icarus no one notices as Icarus falls into the sea.

    (A) No change
    (B) In Pieter Bruegel's painting *Landscape with the Fall of Icarus*, no one notices as Icarus falls into the sea.
    (C) In Pieter Bruegels painting, "Landscape with the Fall of Icarus", no one notices, as Icarus falls into the sea.
    (D) In Pieter Bruegel's painting Landscape With The Fall Of Icarus. No one notices as Icarus falls into the sea.
    (E) In the painting by Pieter Bruegel called Landscape with the fall of Icarus, the Death of Icarus is not noticed by anyone.

14. On my vacation I will go snorkeling, visit the rain forest, and attending local festivals.

   (A) No change
   (B) Snorkeling, visiting the rain forest, and attending local festivals are all things that I plan to do while on vacation.
   (C) On my vacation, I will do many things, including: go snorkeling, visit the rain forest, and attend local festivals.
   (D) On my vacation I will go snorkeling and visit the rain forest, I will also attend local festivals.
   (E) On my vacation, I will go snorkeling, visit the rain forest, and attend local festivals.

15. I have to lay down because I have a really bad headache.

   (A) No change
   (B) I have to lay down because I have a nasty headache.
   (C) I have to lie down because I have a monstrous headache.
   (D) I have to lie down because my head hurts a lot.
   (E) Because I have a really awful headache. I have to lie down.

16. I ordered stationary a month ago, it still has not arrived!

   (A) No change
   (B) The stationary I ordered—a month ago—has still not arrived.
   (C) I ordered stationery a month ago, however it still hasn't arrived!
   (D) I ordered stationery a month ago—and it *still* hasn't arrived.
   (E) I ordered stationary a month ago; and it STILL hasn't arrived.

17. If I were as talented as Arvina, I'd be on Broadway by now.

   (A) No change
   (B) If I was as talented as Arvina, I'd be "on Broadway" by now.
   (C) If I was as talented as Arvina. I'd be on Broadway by now.
   (D) If I were as talented as Arvina, Broadway is where I'd be by now.
   (E) If I was as talented as Arvina, I would have been on Broadway by now.

18. In my judgement, the best profs. are those who teach you how to think, not just tell us the facts.

    (A) No change

    (B) In my judgement, the best Professors are those who teach you how to think, not just tell you the facts.

    (C) In my judgment, the best profs. teach you how to think not just tell you the facts.

    (D) In my judgment, the best professors teach us how to think, not just tell you the facts.

    (E) In my judgment, the best professors teach students how to think, not just tell them the facts.

19. I've always done really good in math but have lots of trouble with science.

    (A) No change

    (B) I've always done really well in Math but have lots of trouble with Science.

    (C) I've always done really well in math but struggled with science.

    (D) I've always done really good in math, but struggling with science.

    (E) I've always did really well in math, but with science I've always struggled.

20. After a bazaar series of coincidences, Sev and Lucinda decide they must be meant for each other and got married.

    (A) No change

    (B) After a bazaar series of coincidences Sev and Lucinda decided they must be meant for each other and got married.

    (C) After a bizarre series of coincidences; Sev and Lucinda decide they must be meant for each other and get married.

    (D) After a bizarre series of coincidences, Sev and Lucinda decided they must be meant for each other and got married.

    (E) After a series of coincidences that were bizarre—Sev and Lucinda decided they must be meant for each other—and got married.

PART C

The following paragraphs contain numerous errors in grammar, mechanics, and style. Identify and correct these errors.

The first living creature in Space was a small dog named, Laika, she was sent into orbit on the Sputnik II. In 1957. Laika completed seven orbits. Then the oxygen supply on the spacecraft ran out. Laika died. But not before she proved: that living creatures could survive in space.

Three and a half years later the first man went into orbit. That man was Yuri Gagarin. He was from the Soviet Union. He spent two-hours in space. Before he came back down. Less than a month later was the first American astronaut, Alan Shepard Jr.. It was the shortest space flight in history. His spacecraft didn't go into orbit. It simply rose to an altitude of 115 miles and then returned to earth. The american John Glenn Jr., was the first American to orbit earth a year later in 1962. He was also the oldest astronaut ever to go into space, thirty six years later when he was 77 he went back into orbit.

ANSWERS AND EXPLANATIONS

Part A

1. B

A linking verb connects a subject to its complement—the part of the predicate that renames or defines the subject.

2. A

A noun is a person, place, or thing. While *love* can function as a verb (an action), in this sentence, *love* is a thing being defined.

3. B

Of is a preposition, and *of a relationship* is a prepositional phrase.

4. D

The subject complement renames or defines the subject. Here, the entire predicate minus the linking verb is the subject complement.

5. C

A subordinate clause contains a subject and verb but cannot stand on its own. It often begins with a subordinating conjunction such as *after*.

Part B

6. D

There are two errors: the verb *want* does not agree with the singular subject *Esperanza*, and *fireman* is sexist. (D) corrects both. The modifying phrase *like many children* is still next to the word it modifies (*Esperanza*) and now does not interrupt the subject-verb pattern. (E) changes the meaning of the sentence.

7. B

When words are used in special ways, they should be italicized or placed in quotation marks. Therefore, the answer must be either (B) or (C). However, *Latin* should be capitalized, so (C) is incorrect.

8. E

The original asks a direct question; it needs a question mark. This is corrected in (E). (B) sets off the essential phrase *flying upside-down* in commas. (C) separates the essential clause *that…upside-down* from the verb *know* and misuses a colon. (D) is wordy.

9. A

The original is best. (B) changes from active to passive and, in the process, creates a vague antecedent problem: What does *it* refer to? (C) creates awkward word order and slightly changes the meaning. (D) mixes the past tense *did* with the past tense *decided*; if the helping verb *do* is in the past tense, the main verb should be in its simple form (*did decide*). It also does not capitalize *CD*. (E) is wordy and pretentious and neglects to capitalize *CD*.

10. D

The original has an error in pronoun agreement: *each new member* is singular, but *there* (or more correctly *their*) is plural. (B) incorrectly sets off *on two committees* with commas. (C) is correct—*his or her* agrees with the antecedent—but (D) is less bulky. (E) is wordy.

11. C

The original contains an ambiguous pronoun (*they* could refer to the tags and uniforms or to the children) and uses the incorrect homophone *insure*. (C) is the best revision. The passive voice is useful here. (B) misplaces the modifier *while in the museum*. (D) is wordy. (E) also misplaces a modifier and uses a different but still incorrect homophone.

12. C

The original uses the subjective *I* instead of the objective *me* for the object of the preposition *between*. In addition, the word choice is imprecise and slangy. (B) adds a cliché. (C) corrects the pronoun error and adds precise, appropriate language: *the proposed changes are appalling*. (D) incorrectly places a semicolon after the introductory prepositional phrase. (E) addresses the slang, replacing it with *is very upsetting*, but *appalling* is more powerful. (E) is also wordy.

13. B

The original is missing the possessive apostrophe in *Bruegel's,* the title of the painting should be italicized, and the introductory phrase should be followed by a comma after *Icarus*. Furthermore, the words *with, the,* and *of* in the title should not be capitalized. (B) corrects these errors. (C) sets the title of the painting off in commas, but the title is essential. It also places the second comma outside of the quotation marks and incorrectly places a comma after the verb *notices*. (D) does not italicize the title and creates a sentence fragment. (E) makes the second half of the sentence passive and is wordy.

14. E

The original lacks parallel structure; *attending* should be *attend*. (B) reverses word order, adding unnecessary words and creating an awkward structure. (C) incorrectly places a colon after *including*. (D) is a run-on sentence and unnecessarily repeats *I will*.

15. C

(A) incorrectly uses *lay* instead of *lie* and uses imprecise language (*really bad*). (B) does improve the language, changing *really bad* to *nasty,* but (C) is better, using *monstrous*. (D) is less precise and effective than (C). (E) creates an imprecise sentence fragment.

16. D

The original uses the incorrect homophone *stationary* instead of *stationery*. It is also a run-on sentence and would be better off without the exclamation point. (B) incorrectly uses dashes, which should set off words or ideas for emphasis. (C) retains the run-on error (*however* is a conjunctive adverb and should be used with a semicolon). (D) correctly uses a dash to set off the second clause and italicizes *still* (instead of using an exclamation point) to emphasize the speaker's frustration. (E) misuses a semicolon and incorrectly uses capitals for emphasis.

17. A

The original is the most clear and correct. The verb must be in the subjunctive (*were*) to express something contrary to fact. (B) incorrectly changes the verb to the simple past and incorrectly puts quotation marks around *on Broadway*. (C) creates a sentence fragment. (D) adds unnecessary words. (E) incorrectly changes the conditional *would* to the past progressive *would have been*.

18. E

The original has three errors: (1) it misspells *judgment* (which drops the *-e* in *judge*), (2) it abbreviates *professors*, and (3) its pronouns shift from the second-person to the third-person plural. (B) incorrectly capitalizes *professors* and retains the misspelling. Only (E) corrects all three original errors. It also eliminates the phrase *are those who* (not incorrect but unnecessary) and changes the pronouns to the third person to make a more inclusive statement.

19. C

(A) uses *good* when it needs the adverb *well* to modify the verb *done*. (B) incorrectly capitalizes the subject areas *math* and *science*. (D) uses the participle *struggling* instead of the simple past tense. (E) incorrectly uses the past tense *did*; the past participle *done* should be used with the helping verb *have*. (C) correctly uses *well* and streamlines the sentence by using a more precise verb, *struggled*, instead of *have lots of trouble*.

20. D

(A) uses *bazaar* instead of *bizarre* and is inconsistent in verb tense. (B) incorrectly removes the comma after the introductory phrase. (C) incorrectly puts a semicolon after the introductory phrase (semicolons belong only between independent clauses or in a list with internal commas). (E) incorrectly uses dashes to set off part of the main clause. The *second* dash alone might be fitting in this sentence, but the first should definitely be eliminated. Only (D) corrects the errors of the original without introducing another error.

Part C

The 20 errors in these paragraphs are marked with numbers in brackets; explanations follow. There are numerous errors in style, primarily in sentence structure. Thus, after the explanations, we offer a revision that includes variety in sentence structure and combines sentences as needed to reduce wordiness.

The first living creature in Space[1] was a small dog named,[2] Laika,[3] she was sent into orbit on the Sputnik II[4]. In 1957.[5] Laika completed seven orbits. Then the oxygen supply on the spacecraft ran out. Laika died. But not before she proved:[6] that living creatures could survive in space.

Three and a half years later[7] the first man[8] went into orbit. That man was Yuri Gagarin. He was from the Soviet Union. He spent two-hours[9] in space. Before he came back down.[10] Less than a month later[11] was the first American astronaut, Alan Shepard Jr..[12, 13] It was the shortest space flight in history. His spacecraft didn't go into orbit. It simply rose to an altitude of 115 miles and then returned to earth[14]. The american[15] John Glenn Jr.,[16] was the first American to orbit earth[17] a year later in 1962. He was also the oldest astronaut ever to go into space,[18] thirty six[19] years later[20] when he was 77[20] he went back into orbit.

1. *Space* should not be capitalized.

2. The name of the dog should not be set off by commas.

3. This comma creates a run-on sentence (comma splice) because it stands alone between two independent clauses.

4. The name of the spacecraft *Sputnik II* should be italicized.

5. The prepositional phrase *in 1957* is not a sentence (it is not even a clause) and therefore cannot stand alone; it is a fragment.

6. The colon is incorrect; it does not belong between a verb and its object (here, the clause explaining what Laika proved).

7. A comma should follow most introductory phrases.

8. A gender-free term (*human*) should be used to avoid sexist language (*man*).

9. *Two hours* should not be hyphenated; these two words do not work together as a compound noun or adjective.

10. *Before he came back down* is a subordinate clause and cannot stand alone; it is a sentence fragment.

11. Use a comma after a modifying phrase.

12. If a sentence ends in an abbreviation that uses a period, do not add another period.

13. The whole sentence (*Less than...Shepard Jr.*) is a fragment.

14. *Earth* should be capitalized when it refers to the planet.

15. *American* should also be capitalized.

16. The name of the American that the sentence refers to (*John Glenn Jr.*) is essential information and should not be set off by commas. In any case, a single comma separating the subject from the verb (*was*) is never correct.

17. Again, capitalize *Earth* when it refers to the planet.

18. The comma here creates another run-on sentence.

19. Compound numbers from 21 to 99 should be hyphenated (*thirty-six*). This could also be changed to a numeral, *36*.

20. This nonessential clause (*when he was 77*) should be set off by commas.

Revision: These paragraphs can be revised in many ways. Notice how the sentences have been combined in this version to create variety and reduce wordiness.

The first living creature in space was a small dog named Laika who was sent into orbit on the *Sputnik II* in 1957. Laika completed seven orbits before the oxygen supply on the spacecraft ran out. Laika died, but not before she proved that living creatures could survive in space.

Three and a half years later, the first human went into orbit. Yuri Gagarin of the Soviet Union spent two hours in space before he came back down. Less than a month later, the first American astronaut, Alan Shepard Jr., followed with the shortest space flight in history. His spacecraft didn't go into orbit; it simply rose to an altitude of 115 miles and then returned to Earth. John Glenn Jr. was the first American to orbit Earth a year later in 1962. He was also the oldest astronaut ever to go into space: 36 years later, when he was 77, he went back into orbit.